Vietnam's New Order

Vietnam's New Order

International Perspectives on the State and Reform in Vietnam

Edited by
Stéphanie Balme
and
Mark Sidel

First published in 2007 by
PALGRAVE MACMILLAN™
175 Fifth Avenue, New York, N.Y. 10010 and
Houndmills, Basingstoke, Hampshire, England RG21 6XS
Companies and representatives throughout the world.

PALGRAVE MACMILLAN is the global academic imprint of the Palgrave Macmillan division of St. Martin's Press, LLC and of Palgrave Macmillan Ltd. Macmillan® is a registered trademark in the United States, United Kingdom and other countries. Palgrave is a registered trademark in the European Union and other countries.

ISBN-13: 978–1–4039–7552–2
ISBN-10: 1–4039–7552–3

Library of Congress Cataloging-in-Publication Data

Vietnam's new order : international perspectives on the State and reform in Vietnam / edited by Stéphanie Balme and Mark Sidel.
p. cm.— (CERI series in international relations and political economy)
"This volume is primarily the product of two conferences on contemporary Vietnam convened by the Research Group on Contemporary Vietnam of the Centre d'Études et de Relations Internationales (CERI) at the Institut d'Études Politiques de Paris (Sciences Po) in the fall of 2003 and 2004"—Introd.
Includes bibliographical references and index.
ISBN 1–4039–7552–3
1. Vietnam—Foreign relations—Congresses. 2. Vietnam—Politics and government—1975—Congresses. 3. Vietnam—Economic conditions—1975—Congresses. 4. Law reform—Vietnam—Congresses. 5. Law—Vietnam—Congresses. I. Balme, Stéphanie. II. Sidel, Mark. III. Groupe d'études sur le Vietnam contemporain.

DS559.912.V548 2007
327.597—dc22   2006047445

A catalogue record for this book is available from the British Library.

Design by Newgen Imaging Systems (P) Ltd., Chennai, India.

First edition: January 2007

10 9 8 7 6 5 4 3 2 1

Printed in the United States of America.

Transferred to digital printing in 2007.

L I S T   O F   T A B L E S   A N D   F I G U R E S

Tables

Figures

ACKNOWLEDGEMENTS

This volume is primarily the product of two conferences on contemporary Vietnam convened by the Research Group on Contemporary Vietnam of the Centre d'Etudes et de Recherches Internationales (CERI) at Sciences Po in the fall of 2003 and 2004.

The editors are grateful to the French Ministry of Foreign Affairs and the Embassy of France in Hanoi for their continuing financial support of the Research Group since its founding by Benoît de Tréglodé in 2000. The Research Group on Contemporary Vietnam was originally a joint project between Sciences Po, la Maison des Sciences de l'Homme and the Centre National de la Recherche Scientifique (CNRS). The Group, which took shape under the aegis of Jean-Luc Domenach, seeks to give a new impetus to research on contemporary Vietnam in Europe with a focus on strengthening the rich French heritage of studies on Vietnam, encouraging interdisciplinary study and providing a meeting ground for the new generation of scholars of Vietnam. In addition to organizing annual international conferences, the group also provides financial assistance to scholars for translations of research and fieldwork in Vietnam.

This volume brings together the work and perspectives of sixteen scholars from Australia, Denmark, Finland, France, Russia, Singapore, Sweden, the United States, and Vietnam, and reflects the Research Group's commitment to advancing French and international research on Vietnam. We are also particularly grateful to Christopher Goscha, a prominent specialist on Vietnam, professor at the Université du Québec à Montréal (UQAM), and co-director of the Research Group.

At the 2003 conference, we were honored by the presence of Nguyen Van Binh, director of the Maison du droit Vietnamo-Française in Hanoi, Professor Monique Chemillier-Gendreau (Paris 7), and Professor Monique Sélim (IRD). We are thankful for their contributions.

At CERI, we are particularly grateful to its director, Christophe Jaffrelot, for his steady support; to Matthieu Salomon and Céline Marangé for their dedicated work in co-organizing the 2004 symposium, and to Cynthia Schoch for her superb work on the publishing process. At the Ecole des Hautes Etudes en Sciences Sociales (EHESS), Yves Chevrier, former director of the China Studies Center, has consistently agreed to take part in our conferences and has nourished the intellectual debates that flow from them. At the University of Iowa, we are grateful to Dean Carolyn Jones, Jay Semel, Gordon Tribbey, John Bergstrom, and Amanda Bibb.

We are pleased that this volume appears as part of the series of books from the Centre d'Etudes et de Recherches Internationales published by Palgrave Macmillan. At Palgrave, we are grateful to Toby Wahl, Heather VanDusen and Joanna Mericle for their fine efforts.

Introduction

Stéphanie Balme and Mark Sidel

This volume is primarily the product of two conferences on contemporary Vietnam convened by the Research Group on Contemporary Vietnam of the Centre d'Etudes et de Recherches Internationales (CERI) at the Institut d'Etudes Politiques de Paris (Sciences Po) in the fall of 2003 and 2004. The first conference brought together specialists for a discussion on Vietnam's energetic efforts to strengthen its legal system and its debates on the meaning of a rule of law. The second focused on Vietnam's emerging role in the region and international communities and the effects of rapid reform on Vietnamese sovereignty. The participants in the two symposia represent a wide array of international perspectives on Vietnam's reform process and development, and the diversity of that perspective is one of the core strengths of this volume. The two conferences included views from Australia, China, Denmark, Finland, France, Russia, Singapore, Sweden, the United States, and Vietnam.

The views on Vietnam's transition vary widely from country to country and, of course, particularly from scholar to scholar. We have been particularly fortunate to work with and to include in this volume the diverse, sometimes conflicting, perspectives from scholars in Vietnam as well as in countries that are often less well represented in discussions on the state and reform in Vietnam, such as Denmark, Finland, Russia, Singapore, and Sweden. We are grateful to all the contributors for their work.

Professor Leslie Holmes (chapter 1) (University of Melbourne) opens the volume with a review of five key areas in Vietnam's reforms and policy of opening to regional and international integration. He explores the reorientation of external and domestic policies that the collapse of the Soviet Union and its economic bloc wrought for Vietnam, including the need to "reorient themselves" to a world in which "the remaining superpower was their former enemy" and in which virtually all socialist models had disappeared or were rapidly adapting (i.e., China). In this new world "Vietnam has had to accept that it cannot avoid global capitalism," and that led the Vietnamese Party and state toward a major transition that Holmes sketches through a variety of important factors. Of these, legitimacy for the Vietnamese Party and state is particularly important, and Holmes asks whether Vietnam is experiencing a legitimacy crisis. Reviewing data on corruption, an important indicator of legitimacy problems, Holmes concludes that Vietnam is not primarily using China's post-1989 methods of coercion as a substitute for legitimacy, a policy that then transitioned to rapid economic reform as a direct route to legitimacy in the early 1990s. His conclusion is that "[f]or as long as it can maintain or improve on [its economic] performance, Vietnam's communist system should be reasonably legitimate and secure—assuming it is not accompanied by significant inflation or unemployment. But if the economy falters, it is unclear that the communist leadership has many alternative sources of legitimation. At that point, their options will be either to become more coercive, or else to concede defeat and accept that the time has come to move to full-blown post-communism."

In part 1, six essays explore Vietnam's changing role in the region and the international community. Carl Thayer (chapter 2) (University of New South Wales and the Australian Defence Force Academy) begins with a clear and detailed discussion of Vietnam's regional integration, raising the question of external and domestic challenges to Vietnam's state sovereignty in the integration process, particularly "to what extent the process of regional integration has weakened the vertical power and sovereignty of the Vietnamese state." He focuses on the history and details of Vietnam's engagement with Association of Southeast Asian Nations (ASEAN) and ASEAN Free Trade Area (AFTA) throughout the 1990s and into the twenty-first century, querying areas where the "obligations of regional integration intersect with state sovereignty and highly sensitive issues involving political power and political economy." Professor Thayer concludes that "Vietnamese state authorities have used both domestic reform and an open door foreign policy to strengthen the state," managing the processes of regional (and international) integration and domestic change resulting partially from it with relative fluency and effectiveness in a complex domestic and international environment.

Nguyen Vu Tung (chapter 3) (Institute for International Relations, Hanoi) takes Vietnam and ASEAN as a case study to explore the institutionalist approach to international relations, in which "a country's decision . . . to join an international organization may depend to a large extent on the policymakers' awareness of its functions and organizational and institutional frameworks, its principles, rules, and procedures, as well as the rights and responsibilities of members. In addition to this, national leaders have to take actual steps to harmonize state policies with those of the organization by adjusting domestic arrangements, establishing new bodies, and adopting new norms, principles, and rules upheld by the organization, thus facilitating the type of cooperation that the organization seeks to promote." He reviews the history of Vietnam's engagement with ASEAN in detail, focusing on the effects on Vietnamese foreign policy and economic institutions and the understanding that Vietnamese institutions had of ASEAN before and during these processes. This is one of the most detailed institutional studies of Vietnamese foreign policy yet published, drawing upon documentation and interviews with Vietnamese policymakers that perhaps only a Vietnamese scholar could effectively mine. Tung concludes that "joining ASEAN is one thing, but Hanoi must work hard to streamline its organizations and enhance its capacity to really benefit from economic cooperation and integration with ASEAN."

Ramses Amer (Umeå University, Sweden) and Nguyen Hong Thao (Hanoi National University Faculty of Law) (chapter 4) offer a review of Vietnam's efforts to resolve its myriad of border disputes—land and sea—with its many neighbors, a clear but hard-headed summing up of a complex and difficult set of relationships. They then go further, seeking to explore how Vietnam's intensive policy of resolving border problems contributes to its developing role in the region and to regional stability, what they call an "evident indication of Vietnam's commitment to and continued integration into the regional framework of collaboration and integration in Southeast Asia." Vietnam's stance on its border contributes to both strengthened sovereignty and strengthened integration and is a successful policy that Vietnam has pursued with clarity and vigor over a number of years.

Vladimir Mazyrin (Institute of Asian and African Studies at Moscow State University) (chapter 5) reviews and critiques Vietnam's policy toward international economic integration, particularly its accession to the WTO. Here, as on border issues, we see a focused and effective Vietnamese state at work—a state that must not only adapt to new, changing, and (in the WTO context) high international norms, but also conform and harmonize a wide range of domestic laws, policies, and practices in order to shift toward international economic integration as well. These are not easy tasks, nor are they without potential domestic political, economic, and social costs, but the Vietnamese Party and state have chosen to face them head on. From the perspective of another postsocialist state, Mazyrin explains both the stakes and the steps Vietnam has chosen. In recent years Western scholars have had relatively little contact with Russian scholarship on Vietnam, a lacuna that Professor Mazyrin helps to fill.

The world of foreign policy, international economic integration, and regional economic and political integration remains complex despite Vietnam's "policy of wanting to be friends with all countries of the international community," notes Hien Do (Sciences Po, Paris) (chapter 6). Eero Palmujoki (Tampere University, Finland) (chapter 7) turns to the power of words in the formulation and communication of Vietnam's foreign policy and strategies, an element of Vietnamese political culture, and a useful window into understanding the complex changes in Vietnam's view of the world and the problems of integration since the early 1980s. He discusses the shift in Vietnamese language to describe the nation's international engagements and the increasing adoption of language from ASEAN, the WTO, and other centers of regional and international integration that not only puts Vietnam on a communicative path with the world but also signals domestically that real shifts are underway. The Vietnamese Party and state continue, however, to wrestle with the "difficult task of reconciling international and domestic developments with Marxist–Leninist ideology" "to adapt to globalisation as well as to maintain older political structures," in Palmujoki's words. His chapter shows complex byplay at work as well in Vietnamese policy development and in the language that Vietnam's senior policymakers have used to discuss its transition for domestic and international audiences.

The chapters on these topics in this volume help to bring some order into what sometimes appears as a confusing and blurred picture. What emerges is a state with clear objectives, a certain flexibility in reaching those goals, recognizing the significant adaptations that international and regional integration are forcing on Vietnam, and not always, particularly in the foreign policy and international economic establishments in Hanoi, with sufficient human resource capacity to cope with the myriad of domestic, regional and international demands that integration has quickly brought to Vietnam.

In part 2 that covers the legal and political arena, the picture is somewhat different. The year 2006 coincides with the twentieth anniversary of Vietnam's *doi moi* policy and the Tenth Congress of the Vietnamese Communist Party. In the aftermath of the collapse of the Soviet Union, Vietnam, like China but unlike the former Eastern bloc or the persistent revolutionary regimes such as North Korea or Cuba, has declined either to embark on a democratic transition or to eradicate the leading economic role of the state. But Hanoi has converted to the international paradigms of the market economy and rule of law. In view of such political choices, the country has been classified as a postrevolutionary socialist regime, a "resisting while developing communist state" (Wu 2001). Embracing this new context, the chapters on law and legal reform in this volume raise a common and crucial question: What are the dynamics between law and political change under *doi moi*? Is the "power of law," as Pierre Bourdieu and others have put it, only a ritual formula? According to David Koh (Institute of Southeast Asian Studies, Singapore), in chapter 12 in this volume, "the arena of the rule of law seems to have witnessed the most far reaching and penetrating changes in state-society relations."

In methodological terms, we no longer rely on false official statistics or solely on the policy rhetoric that is typical of revolutionary regimes to address this issue. The chapters in this volume provide some field work and in-depth research and analysis, including of the sensitive questions raised about legal reform. But at the same time serious qualitative analysis based on research in Vietnam may not fully compensate for the scarcity of updated and detailed official data.

During the launching phase of the *doi moi* policy in the mid- and late 1980s, the purpose of the legal system was to implement Party guidelines as well as to compensate for the Party's declining authority due to institutionalized corruption or widespread clientelism. Elsewhere, Gillespie and Nicholson have shown that legal developments responded to a "dialogical exchange between the state and the society" and were a way of "proactively seeking access to international capital and markets" (Gillespie and Nicholson 2005, 4). In this volume, Gillespie (chapter 8) (Monash University, Australia) confirms that "the history of legality in Vietnam is inextricably bound up with the adaptation of foreign ideas." Beginning with the Seventh Party Congress in 1991, the notion of a law-based state (*nha nuoc phap quyen*) was understood as a key political reform of the *doi moi* era. Not only does it help consolidate the reforming state, but this new legality also challenges the overall Party-led political system. Indeed, the rule of law rhetoric tends to emphasize the conflicts between modern imported and traditional indigenous ideologies, that is, communism and modern scientific thought versus Confucian morality. Tensions also exist between the prevailing Leninist legacy and the paradigms of separation of powers and hierarchy of norms. Rousseau's absolute conception of people's sovereignty embodied in the theoretically overwhelming power of national legislatures in communist regimes and the elimination of law in democratic centralism conflict with the philosophy and processes of a rule of law.

Conflicts of legitimacy are sharper but the definition of law in Vietnam remains blurred and the transition in its legal system somewhat unbalanced. Deriving from a variety of indigenous sources and imported legacies (China, colonial France, the Soviet Union, and Western capitalist economies, as shown by Gillespie in this volume), the vagueness of what law is and what indigenous legal traditions are in Vietnam after all those layers have been assimilated means that law can be asserted in many ways. For example, if law has been defined as the highest source of the Party's own legality, and if the Communist Party is truly to be bound by the state Constitution, political control by the Party over society should now be exercised through law. Yet, this is obviously not always the case. While the socialist conception of law no longer prevails, class-based law has been renounced, and the equality of citizens before the law has been formally recognized, a socialist conception of law remains the core dogma of Vietnamese legal professionals. As Bui Thi Bich Lien explains, "the purpose of legal education is to train state officials to perpetuate socialist management practices and privilege state interests." Therefore, "law teachers have been forbidden from working in the legal profession and only 3 or 4% of students find work in the legal system" (Bui Thi Bich Lien 2005).

Conflicts of legitimacy are also determining issues in the independence of the judiciary, an area of intense interest from legal scholars and from foreign donors. As Nicholson (University of Melbourne) puts it in her chapter in this volume, "courts are required both to be subservient to Party leadership and independent." The material and educational conditions and backgrounds of legal professionals, and notably of the judiciary, are also important factors. The professionalization of legal actors will help deal with the issues of political dependency and popular disregard. And the fact that Party members dominate legal professions may be a more neutral variable as the Party becomes a significant institutional lobby of competent technocrats. "We see a trend away from morality being the basis of [judges'] appointment to a combination of Party approval and technical competency," writes Nicholson. Private lawyers and newly trained and appointed judges now hope that, with the consolidation of the legal reforms, the politicization of its content will gradually diminish toward the level accepted in developed rule of law states.

The general picture in Vietnam contrasts with its giant neighbor and a key economic partner, China, perhaps primarily in terms of the timing of the reform agenda. Contrasting leadership decisions, differences in governance challenges and in the legacies of history, as well as a diverse capacity to manage the pressures of international legal harmonization and convergence may account for some of these differences. Nonetheless, two main similarities can be observed between the two regimes: the process of legal reforms within a period of two decades, and faithfulness to socialist principles. Similarly to the development of Western nations since the eighteenth century, the recent evolution in Vietnam has involved urbanization and industrial transitions; a diversification of ownership rights if not capitalism, and a steady growth of wealth; globalization and its domestic effects; and the leadership's technocratic policies and reactions. These developments help a certain type of political and legal modernity emerge, by contributing to the spreading of certain processes peculiar to a modern state while not bringing democracy with them.

Although the overall reform programs have, in Vietnam, developed later than China's early 1978 open-door policy, Vietnam has been active in the professionalization of legal personnel, judicial reform, and the codification of law. Moves toward legal reform started in the 1980s. By 2005, according to Nguyen Hung Quang in this volume (chapter 9), 64 bar associations have been established across the country. In China, the All China Lawyers Association was founded in 1986 and the Laws on Judges and Lawyers were promulgated respectively in 1996 and 1997, though there was very substantial earlier development in the 1980s and early 1990s. Other legal reforms such as the rule of law and rule by law debates and the early discussion and adoption of administrative litigation reforms began considerably earlier in China than in Vietnam. The administrative litigation reforms began in China in the late 1980s, and with the passage of the Administrative Litigation Law in 1990. The Vietnamese 1992 Constitution affirmed citizens' right to sue state authorities and to request compensation for illegal state action, followed by the formation of administrative courts in the mid-1990s, as Karin Buhmann (Roskilde University, Denmark) (chapter 13) outlines in this volume. In China, the debate on constitutionalism goes back to dissident calls for legal and political reform at the end of the Cultural Revolution, to extensive discussions in the late 1970s and then during the period of liberal discussion in 1988 and 1989 and again in the discussion and aftermath of the recognition of private property rights (Balme 2005). Constitutionalist debate in Vietnam has its roots somewhat later, in the 2001 debate over the revision of the 1992 Constitution, and in the recent debates over appropriate mechanisms for constitutional enforcement (Sidel 2005).

Despite these reforms and many others, core socialist reference points and values remain deeply entrenched. Vietnam is not experiencing a transition in the sense it is usually understood in political science to describe the political process of emergence from communism to democratization; it is experiencing incremental but important transformations within its existing system. Neither China nor Vietnam are rule of law states or countries engaged in a top-down democratic transition process. Citizens are not yet, for the most part, individual legal subjects with the extensive individual rights of the older democracies. The state retains its strong economic management and ownership role, as well as a role in social control, though those are gradually becoming somewhat eroded. As Gillespie argues, "neo-liberal legality has not swept aside socialist legality." And the Vietnamese Communist Party continues to maintain the strongest political network, and a unique mobilizing lobby, the most powerful force for building the state.

In institutional terms, the *doi moi* policy has led to a growing differentiation of political functions that often seems contradictory in nature: some centralization of executive power, but also greater authority in the hands of provinces and localities, transition in the National Assembly, and a growing role for legal institutions such as the Ministry of Justice and the Supreme People's Court. The analysis by Matthieu Salomon (Sciences Po, Paris) (chapter 11) of the transformation of the National Assembly *(Quoc Hoi)* shows the Assembly to be an increasingly professionalized, even corporatist body, carrying out extensive and often important debates and lobbying activity, with a greater number of full-time delegates and an increasingly active Standing Committee. The exercise of Assembly power in supervising state officials, budgets, and related areas, along with the publicity given to its activities, have raised expectations from many Vietnamese that, according to Salomon, "the future and credibility of political *doi moi* [can] be found in the National Assembly." Are these expectations for the Vietnamese National

Assembly too high, reflecting expectations of political opportunity that is too optimistic?

If China is any guide, these reforms and the increasing role of its national legislature (the National People's Congress) are gradual phenomena that occur over decades. In today's China, the popular representation of the National People's Congress remains that of a weak and dependent institution. Reforming and strengthening the power of Leninist structures, perhaps particularly such institutions as legislatures and courts, is deeply challenging. French thinkers such as François Furet or Claude Lefort used to consider these transitions "impossible." Designed by non-democratic institutions, these reforms aim at controlling while also respecting popular sovereignty.

According to Nicholson (chapter 10), the Vietnamese Supreme People's Court "has become much more legislatively active" and plays a significant advisory and supervisory role in the work of the lower courts. The Supreme Court now enjoys "in conjunction with local people's councils, the responsibility for the management of local people's courts," even if judicial budgets are formally approved by the National Assembly. Nicholson's work shows that the management of the courts is shifting progressively "from direct political control to self-management if not yet autonomy." These are indeed changes, and they create new opportunities for further institutional reforms. In this way, they parallel the debates underway in China on the necessity of establishing a system of judicial review.

These evolutions, both formal and structural, reveal the emergence of an increasingly complex network of legal actors, including private lawyers, who also interact with local media and increasingly assertive public opinion, as described by Nguyen Hung Quang in his chapter with respect to the trial of the godfather Nam Cam. The rebirth of the legal professions seems to be producing an epistemic community that is made up of individuals who often seem more liberal than the political system in which they are living and working. This is probably crucial if a different sort of legality, some type of rule of law, is to replace the former socialist legitimacy. Socialism has long focused on the historic roles played by state and society. These days the Vietnamese polity and society is not engaged in a revolution to liberate itself, but the Party is committed, for its survival, to reform and rationalize the state and the legal system in order to reinforce the Party and state's position. While serving as a challenge to traditional Marxist theory, their policies provide more chances for the country to gradually build some sort of a rule of law.

References

Balme, Stéphanie. 2005. The judicialisation of politics and the politicisation of the judiciary in China (1978–2005). *Global Jurist Frontiers* 5: 1.

Bui Thi Bich Lien. 2005. Legal education in transitional Vietnam. In *Asian socialism and legal change: The dynamics of Vietnamese and Chinese reform*. Edited by John Gillespie and Pip Nicholson. Canberra: Asia Pacific Press, 135–58.

Gillespie, John and Pip Nicholson (eds). 2005. *Asian socialism and legal change: The dynamics of Vietnamese and Chinese reform*. Canberra: Asia Pacific Press.

Sidel, Mark. 2005. Principle and power: The emerging debate over Constitutional review and enforcement in Vietnam. In *Law and society in Vietnam*. Edited by Mark Sidel. Forthcoming, 2007.

Wu Yu-shan. 2001. Les voies du Communisme. In *Ce qui reste du communisme*. Edited by Stéphanie Balme. *Raisons Politiques* 3 (Fall).

Vietnam in a Comparative Communist and Postcommunist Perspective

LESLIE HOLMES

Introduction: Vietnam and the Collapse of the Soviet Bloc

The period 1989–91 was a traumatic one for Russians. In the space of just over two years, they experienced a quintuple loss. One of these—of the Inner Empire (the disintegration of the USSR)—need not detain us, since it was not directly relevant to Vietnam's situation in recent years. But four of the losses are of major significance. The first was the collapse of what is often called the Soviet Outer Empire. Vietnam had been a member of the Council for Mutual Economic Assistance (CMEA or Comecon) since 1978. This meant that it had access to preferential trade arrangements, and ready markets for its goods. Following a rather slow start, its high level of economic integration into the Soviet-dominated economic bloc by the mid-1980s can be readily seen in tables 1.1 and 1.2.

Even allowing for the rubberiness and incompleteness of the given data,[1] it appears that, by the mid-1980s, almost three quarters of Vietnam's imports were from Comecon partners, while some 60% of its exports was to those partners. At the same time, Vietnam's trade with most of its Asian neighbors—above all Japan—had significantly declined in the comparatively brief period from 1980 to 1985. While the relative proportions had begun to change direction again by the end of the 1980s, this was only marginal. Hence, the collapse of Comecon

12

Table 1.1 Vietnam's imports (in percentage) from selected partners 1980–2004[a]

	1980	1985	1989a	1989b	1995	2000	2002	2004
USSR	18.3							
CEE[b]					2.5			
Comecon		>73.2	67.0	79.3	N.A.[c]	N.A.	N.A.	N.A.
Singapore	6.9	7.0			16.7	17.2	12.8	10.5
Thailand					4.4	6.9		6.2
Japan	15.8	8.2		6.4	8.6	16.3	12.7	10.5
India	12.9							
Hong Kong	6.2	3.0			5.9	4.5		4.0
China					6.7	12.7	10.9	13.7
Taiwan					9.5		12.9	11.3
Korea (South)					12.6	13.9	11.6	10.8
United States		None		0.8	1.6	2.9		
EU[d]		3.0		2.8	8.1	>4.3		

Note: a. Sources for tables 1.1 and 1.2—either directly cited, or calculated by the author, from: 1980—Brittannica Book of the Year (BBY) 1985, 811; 1985—BBY 1990, 747; 1989a—Statisticheskii Yezhegodnik Stran Chlenov Soveta Ekonomicheskoi Vzaimopomoshchi 1990, 568; 1989b—BBY 1990, 845; 1995—Economist Intelligence Unit Country Profile—Vietnam, 2002, 58; 2002—BBY 2005, 733; 2004—CIA World Fact Handbook 2005, online version, updated January 10, 2006, visited February 2006.

b. Central and Eastern Europe *including* Russia.

c. In tables 1.1 and 1.2, N. A. means not applicable.

d. European Union; European Economic Community until the early 1990s.

Table 1.2 Vietnam's exports (in percentage) to selected partners 1980–2004

	1980	1985	1989a	1989b	1995	2000	2002	2004
USSR	11.6							
CEE[a]					2.5			
Comecon		>59.5	40.7	58.8	N.A.	N.A.	N.A.	N.A.
Singapore	11.4	8.6			7.1	4.7	5.8	4.8
Japan	31.0	9.1		13.5	27.3	15.0	14.6	13.6
Hong Kong	14.1	13.8			2.8			
China					5.3	5.3	9.0	9.0
United States[b]		None	None	None	3.3	4.9	14.5	20.2
EU[c]		3.1		3.8	>18.3	>14.7		>10.5
Australia						7.9	8.0	7.0

Note: a. Central and Eastern Europe *including* Russia.

b. The United States imposed a trade embargo on Vietnam until 1994.

c. European Union: European Economic Community until the early 1990s.

in mid-1991 had potentially very significant implications for Vietnam, and suggested it would have to reorient its trade once again.

The second loss for Russians was of their international recognition as the dominant nationality in one of only two superpowers. While Vietnam had never been a member of the Soviet-dominated military alliance commonly known as the Warsaw Pact (the Warsaw Treaty Organisation, or WTO), the fact that there existed a vast military machine to challenge the West, if need be, was reassuring to the Vietnamese leadership, their professions of independence notwithstanding. The Soviets had not assisted the Vietnamese communists as much as they might have done during the war with the United States (1964–73), but Moscow's renewed interest in and commitment to Asia could be seen in the Soviet invasion of Afghanistan in 1979. With the collapse of the Warsaw Pact in 1991, the Vietnamese were no longer allied to a super-power, and had to reorient themselves. Not only this, but the remaining superpower was their former enemy.

The third loss for Russians was intimately linked to the second; this was of the Cold War. Despite the overlap between this point and the previous one, there are important differences. Above all, there had been a major ideological difference between the two superpowers, which had ramifications for both the institutional arrangements and policies of member states of the two respective camps. With the emergence of post-communism from 1989, the majority of CEE states opted to move toward the liberal-democratic capitalist model and the West more generally. Even many former Soviet states began this move, albeit somewhat later (e.g., Georgia, Ukraine). While Fukuyama's triumphalist "end of history" thesis was in many ways naive, too wide-ranging and premature, much of the underlying argument did apply to many postcommunist states.

The Russians' final loss relates to the third. It was of their country's status as the home of socialism, and the major alternative model for countries anxious to reject Western-style capitalism and imperialism. Given Vietnam's long history of colonization—in the twentieth century, primarily by France—it was attracted to a model that encouraged independence from external forces. Although, strictly speaking, it had never been a colonizer, the United States' major (if failed) involvement in the attempt to prevent the spread of communism in Vietnam was one reason why the American model of development was not a viable option. Vietnam's relations with and attitudes toward the West, and the United States in particular, were fundamentally different from those of Poland, Hungary, or Estonia, for example. With the collapse of communist power throughout Europe and even much of Asia (Afghanistan,

Cambodia, Mongolia, South Yemen), Vietnam was left with the bare bones of the former communist world. It no longer had a suitable role-model if it needed ideas for future development. After all, two of the remaining five communist countries—North Korea and Cuba—were, from many perspectives, failed states, since they could barely feed their own people.

For many African and Latin American revolutionaries, there had been an alternative to the Soviet model, namely the Maoist. But the long history of hostility between China and Vietnam meant that this was not a realistic option for Hanoi either, at least in terms of open embrace (though, as we see, Vietnam has indeed embraced a range of policies first pioneered by China). In addition, China had by the early 1990s moved so far away from what many had believed were key and immutable aspects of the Maoist model of communism that it was in many respects already postcommunist itself. While it was still run by a communist party, and in this formal sense was communist, China's economic and social systems looked increasingly similar to the Western and postcommunist models. In the economic sphere, the clearest indication of this was private leasing of state enterprises, and then—from the late-1990s—outright privatization of the means of production. In the social sphere, growing acceptance and rising rates of unemployment, as well as greater tolerance of growing inequality (evidenced by rising Gini coefficients—see Meng et al., 2004, especially Table 2), were concrete markers of China's moves away from communism. In fact, China can by now be described as a postcommunist system led by an authoritarian state that happens, for historical reasons, to call itself communist.

Vietnam since the Collapse of the Soviet Bloc

Despite its wish to maintain a certain distance from China, Vietnam has found itself in a rather similar position in the past decade and a half. As Lockwood (2000) has convincingly argued, a major factor in the collapse of so much of the communist world was the fact that communist states could not remain outside the increasingly globalized market, their original claims to the contrary notwithstanding. China has embraced globalization with a vengeance; not only has its international trade grown almost exponentially in recent years, but it even beat postcommunist Russia to membership of the World Trade Organisation.[2] Similarly, Vietnam has had to accept that it cannot avoid global capitalism; countries that have ended such an attempt, such as North Korea and Myanmar, have ended up as authoritarian failed states.

This has been the context in which Vietnam's *doi moi* and "open door" policies have developed.[3] These emerged *before* the collapse of communist power in Europe, the USSR, and elsewhere. But their timing and nature coincided with the USSR's policies of *perestroika* and "new political thinking"; with the disappearance of these—and in line with our earlier argument about losing the Soviet role-model—the Hanoi leaders had to decide whether to make their model more radical or attempt to reverse it. The apparent policy vacillations since about 1990 testify to the dilemmas that have faced the communist leaders as they seek an optimal balance. If their policies are too radical, they might raise expectations that they cannot meet—and as theorists from Tocqueville on have argued, revolution is most likely to occur when leaders raise expectations but then fail to deliver (the collapse of the USSR is compatible with this "theory of rising expectations"). Conversely, putting the brakes on or attempting to reverse change, especially economic reform, can result in declining system and economic performance, which in turn can undermine eudaemonic legitimacy.[4] Since 2001, the leadership appears to have decided that the former option is less politically risky than the latter; but the history of *doi moi* suggests that there could still be policy reversals.

Vietnam as a Transition State

In a 1997 book (Holmes 1997, 15–21), I argued that the type of transition commonly known as postcommunism involves a total of 14 key features, which can be subdivided into groupings of seven. The first subgroup of factors related to the political cultural implications of a common heritage, and comprised:

- Assertion of independence and the rise of nationalism
- Near absence of a culture of compromise
- High expectations of leaders
- Cynicism toward and/or mistrust of political institutions
- Rejection of teleologism and grand theories
- An ideological vacuum
- Moral confusion

The first of these relates to sovereignty and national identity. In many ways, in the 1990s this became a salient feature of countries in which the communists had come to power primarily through having been installed by the Soviets in the aftermath of World War II, and over which the Soviets had continued to exert considerable influence. Vietnam was not in this situation, since it had become communist largely through its own efforts. Moreover, even after joining Comecon, Hanoi managed to retain a certain political distance from Moscow. In this sense, there is no need for Vietnam to recapture a largely lost identity and sovereignty as it transits into postcommunism. Conversely, it does have a long tradition of asserting its independence and being nationalistic; this renders it closer to full-blown postcommunist states than it might initially appear to be. Given space limitations here, we cannot consider the other six variables; but elements of many of them are to be found in contemporary Vietnam. The second group of seven features identified—the common-alities of early postcommunism—were as follows:

- Comprehensive revolution (economic, political, social, in terms of international allegiances, and so on)
- Temporality (postcommunism is an interim stage between commu-nism and the consolidation of a new system)
- Dynamism (this necessarily follows on from the previous point)
- Instability
- A widespread sense of insecurity
- Unfortunate timing
- Legitimation problems

Although considerations of space limit full discussion of these factors, key elements of the first feature can be found in Vietnam in recent years. This is most obvious in the economic sphere, in which the leadership has increasingly had to recognize the need to move away from the clas-sic communist model of state ownership of the means of production and central planning. These two pillars of the communist approach to eco-nomics may have been useful in the past to modernize an economy, but have proven to be dysfunctional in the later stages of modernization. The move to *doi moi* is a clear sign that the Communist Party understands this. Yet in implicitly recognizing this, the leaders may well be increasing the likelihood of an overt legitimacy crisis. The issue of legitimation problems is the final feature in our 14-point model of postcommunism, and constitutes the focus of the next section.

Is Vietnam Experiencing a Legitimacy Crisis?

When Jürgen Habermas (1973a) wrote of serious legitimation problems— or legitimacy crisis, as his thesis is better known in the English-speaking world (see Habermas 1973b)—in the early 1970s, his primary focus was on developed capitalist liberal democracies. Ironically, his argument is better suited to the communist world; after all, the capitalist states have survived and expanded in number, whereas it was communist states that collapsed and were thrown into the dustbin of history.

Legitimacy is a notoriously difficult phenomenon to measure. As Alfred Meyer (1972, 67) pointed out long ago, we can really be certain that a given state or society has been in a legitimacy crisis only when it collapses or appears to be in real danger of collapsing. In this sense, most communist states clearly were in a legitimacy crisis by the end of the 1980s, and many postcommunist states (including Albania, Bulgaria, Georgia, Kyrgyzstan, Serbia, and Ukraine) have been on various occasions since. But Vietnam was an exception. Whereas even China had experienced a major crisis—in the form of the Tian'anmen events of 1989—Vietnam remained relatively stable, and largely untouched by events elsewhere in the communist world. In that it has not subsequently experienced overt mass unrest, any signs of a legitimacy crisis must be looked for elsewhere.

In the absence of major public demonstrations, one of the indicators of severe legitimacy problems in a country is a high level of corruption. This indicates legitimacy problems for two reasons. First, surveys in many parts of the world suggest that citizens who perceive that there are high levels of corruption in their society have little trust in their state and its officials. But many theorists of legitimacy and delegitimation (e.g., Skocpol 1979, 32; Bialer 1980, 194–5; Rigby 1982) have argued that popular legitimacy—what the masses believe—is ultimately of secondary importance. For these theorists, it is the attitudes of state officials and top political elites—whether or not *they* believe in their own right to rule— that are crucial. Thus the second reason is that high levels of corruption indicate rottenness in the state, whereby its own officials, and possibly even its leaders, place their personal interests ahead of those of the system, endangering the system's very survival. In doing so, they are demonstrating a lack of commitment to and faith in the agency for which they have in one way or another claimed the right to rule.

Unfortunately, measuring corruption levels is almost as difficult as measuring the degree of legitimacy. But if several methods—each with drawbacks of its own—produce similar results, we can be reasonably confident that our relative (i.e., cross-polity) assessments are more or less accurate. In contemporary analyses of corruption, four principal methods are used. These are official (legal) statistics; perception-based methods; experience-based methods; and tracking methods.[5] Of these, the second is the most commonly used, and of all the indices, the Corruption Perceptions Index (CPI) produced by Berlin-based Transparency

International (TI) is the best known and most frequently cited, despite its many problems (see Sík 2002; Kaufmann et al., 2003, 32–9).

TI has been producing the CPI annually since 1995. The number of countries covered varies from year to year, since the compilers of the CPI will rate a country only if they have at least three surveys on which to base their assessment.[6] Vietnam was first assessed in 1997, when it was ranked forty-third out of fifty-two states, in which the fifty-second state was considered the most corrupt. However, the actual rank of a country is not particularly enlightening, in part because of the point just made, that the number of countries varies each year.[7] Of more value is a given country's actual score. The TI uses a 0–10 scale, in which the *lower* the number, the *more* corrupt the country is perceived to be. Vietnam's scores 1997–2005 can be seen in table 1.3.

It is clear from table 1.3 that Vietnam is perceived to be a highly corrupt country, and that it is not really improving (though it is not deteriorating either). Given our claim that corruption can be a sign of legitimacy problems, does this mean that Vietnam is likely to experience overt unrest, and possibly even the eventual collapse or replacement of communist power?

In order to answer this question, it is necessary to engage in a brief theoretical discussion. In the contemporary world, states can seek legitimacy via at least 10 different channels or legitimation modes (Holmes 1997, 42–5). Seven of these are essentially internal (domestic) to the country, whereas the other three are external. Building on Weber (1970, especially 78–9), Rigby (1982), and others, the following legitimation modes can be identified:

Internal (Domestic)

- Old traditional (e.g., divine right of monarchs, mandate of heaven)
- Charismatic (typically, during and immediately following a revolutionary change)
- Goal-rational or teleological (a common mode in communist systems, in which leaders claim the right to rule by knowing the most efficient and fastest way to reach the end-goal, or telos of communism)
- Nationalism (including defense of sovereignty)

Table 1.3 Vietnam's corruption score in the TI Corruption Perceptions Index

	1997	1998	1999	2000	2001	2002	2003	2004	2005
Score	2.8	2.5	2.6	2.5	2.6	2.4	2.4	2.6	2.6

- New traditional (e.g., a communist leader harks back to an earlier—typically charismatic—communist leader's approach to legitimize their own rule and policies)
- Eudaemonic (in essence, performance based—see note 4)
- Legal rational (rule of law)

External (International)

- Formal recognition (by other states and/or international organizations such as the United Nations)
- Informal support (other countries show support for the approach of a leadership, which encourages that leadership to retain confidence in its own project and right to rule, even if it knows it is losing popular support at home)
- External role-model (a country's leadership retains faith in its own project and direction because it is in essence following the approach of another country or set of countries that constitute a role-model; Vietnam originally basing its 1986 *doi moi* policy on the USSR's 1985 *perestroika* is a good example)

When a system is losing legitimacy, its leaders can attempt to reverse this by moving to another legitimation mode as the principal one. This is the so-called legitimating effect of legitimation shifts. A real crisis emerges when a leadership team loses its way, and, for whatever reason, seems incapable of moving to an alternative primary mode of legitimation. One clear example of this was the way in which many communist states attempted to move to legal-rational legitimation during the 1980s, only to find that this was fundamentally incompatible with the Leninist model, and that they had by then largely exhausted other modes (Holmes 1993, especially 274–91).

This basic incompatibility between some legitimation modes and the communist model is a fundamental way in which Vietnam can be seen to be experiencing major legitimation problems. In Habermas's analysis of legitimation problems in capitalist states, one of the key indicators is a fundamental mismatch or contradiction between the ideology and the system, particularly the economic system. For instance, if a leadership team in a capitalist system claims it is committed to the free market, but then, in response to a major economic turndown and high unemployment, adopts a Keynesian approach to kick-start an economy, it has undermined its own commitments. But this incompatibility is not as basic as that between the Leninist model and legal-rationality.

One of the ways in which communist states can attempt to avoid system collapse when it falls into a popular legitimacy crisis is to place far less emphasis on legitimation, and instead significantly increase the level of coercion. This helps to explain what happened in China for some time after June 1989; despite the obvious crisis of popular legitimacy, the leaders retained sufficient faith in their own project and position successfully to overcome this. But most communist leaders (including the Chinese) realise that high levels of coercion are not an optimal solution, and are likely to be effective only in the shorter term. The same is usually true of official (i.e., state-sponsored) nationalism, which in most countries sooner or later needs to be replaced or heavily supplemented by other modes of legitimation. Equally, some legitimation modes are more powerful than others; while some are basically free-standing, others operate most effectively if linked to other modes. An example of the latter is formal external recognition, which is often linked by leaders to official nationalism. One case from the former communist world that exemplifies this well is the GDR, which used its admission to the UN in 1973 as part of its 1970s focus on official nationalism.

Which legitimation modes would be suitable and feasible for today's Vietnam? The fundamental incompatibility between legal-rationality and communist power still pertains, so that this legitimation mode is not a viable option. In many ways, the most suitable approach nowadays would be a combination of eudaemonism and external role-model. If there were not so much historical "baggage," the most obvious external role-model would be China. But Vietnam can, in practice, emulate much of the Chinese approach, yet link this to an emphasis on the economic achievements of the Asian Tigers (Dragons). Such a package will not necessarily save the Vietnamese communist system in the longer term. If eudaemonism is not combined with a more solid basis of legitimacy, notably legal-rationality, it is fragile, and major economic problems could result in legitimacy crisis, mass unrest, and ultimately system collapse (as could also happen in China). Table 1.4 summarizes Vietnam's economic growth performance in recent years:

Table 1.4   Vietnam's average annual growth rate (in percentage) over four quinquennia

	1986–1990	*1991–1995*	*1996–2000*	*2001–2005*
GDP growth rate	4.6	8.2	6.7	6.8

Note: Calculated by the author on the basis of data in Tran Dinh Thien 1999; Pham Hoang Mai 2004, 20; CIA World Factbook, various years.

These data indicate healthy economic growth in Vietnam, though it is not quite as impressive as China's. For as long as it can maintain or improve on this performance, Vietnam's communist system should be reasonably legitimate and secure—assuming it is not accompanied by significant inflation or unemployment.[8] But if the economy falters, it is unclear whether the communist leadership has many alternative sources of legitimation. At that point, their options will be either to become more coercive, or else to concede defeat and accept that the time has come to move to full-blown postcommunism.

Vietnam and ASEAN

The need to ensure strong economic performance as a major part of system legitimation brings us back to the issue of Vietnam's trade reorientation since the collapse of Comecon. Given their overall situation, the Vietnamese leadership's decision to join ASEAN was a wise one. In doing so, they do not too obviously follow the Chinese model, nor do they appear to enter the Western camp. At the same time, they cooperate with other countries with—for the most part—impressive growth rates. Finally, several of the other ASEAN states themselves have authoritarian or quasi-authoritarian political systems, so that by linking up with them, the Vietnamese leaders are not taking major risks that their close partners will seek fundamental political change in their country. In the event of mass unrest in Vietnam, it is far from clear that other ASEAN states would seek to fan this; the opposite scenario—that fellow member states would lend direct or indirect support to the Hanoi leadership—is at least as likely.

Although it has been argued that Vietnam's membership of ASEAN does not in itself add to Hanoi's legitimacy problems, certain facts about that relationship cast Vietnam's position in a different light. Most obviously, the large and growing trade imbalance with its ASEAN partners means that Vietnam's economy may be more troubled than it appears from the growth statistics, and the sustainability of this situation can be questioned. But there is another potential longer-term issue, to which we now turn.

ASEAN and the European Union

In assessing Vietnam's future, and possible legitimacy problems, it is worth briefly considering the potential for ASEAN to become more like the EU. The relevance of this question here is that European states in the EU have had to renounce some of their sovereignty; as argued earlier, an essentially nationalist emphasis on sovereignty and independence has been a key component of Vietnamese communist legitimation.

Given the high levels of standardization of so many aspects of everyday life within the EU, the widespread use of a common currency, and the wishes of many leading figures within it to deepen the level of political integration, it is easy to forget that the EU started life as a relatively small organization of just six states, in which closer economic cooperation was the immediate objective. Admittedly, there was a broader political—indeed a security—consideration behind this; by rendering the French and German economies increasingly interdependent, it was hoped to avoid a repeat of the traumas that two World Wars had brought to Europe. Nevertheless, the early stages of the EU focused on economic integration and market liberalization—much as ASEAN has in recent times. Since the EU has subsequently not merely expanded, but also changed direction, it is worth considering the possibilities for similar change in ASEAN over the coming decades, and the implications of this for Vietnam.

It is often maintained that there is little in common between the European situation over the past half century or so and conditions pertaining in Southeast Asia in recent times. Some of the principal arguments for this position are that the cultures of Southeast Asia are far more diverse than they were in Europe; the levels of economic development span a wider range; and the politicoeconomic systems are also more varied in Asia. Each of these can now be briefly considered.

There is a certain level of cultural homogeneity even in the recently expanded EU; most notably, all countries have a primarily Christian tradition. In contrast, there is a wide range of religious and philosophical traditions in East and Southeast Asia, from Moslem Indonesia and Malaysia through Shinto Japan to Buddhist Vietnam and atheist but Confucian China. This does have certain implications even for economic integration; the concept of charging interest on capital loans is in theory anathema to most Moslems, for instance. But such differences are exaggerated; many Moslem countries have found ways to circumvent the ban on "usury," for example. Indeed, while an objective observer might question this assertion, some Asian leaders and Western academics endorse the notion that there exists a common and distinctive "Asian way." Some of the concrete indicators that could be cited in this context are the basically similar approaches to capital punishment and human rights more generally, and the common belief in most of the region—so different from the Anglo-Celtic world's—that one country should not interfere too directly in the affairs of another.

Moving beyond religious traditions to consider historical tensions as a cultural factor—while it cannot be denied that many Asians (especially in China and Korea) have a deep-seated dislike of the Japanese, somewhat similar—if much less intense and less widespread—feelings toward the Germans can be found in a few parts of Europe, such as the UK. The generally much more positive attitude in Europe toward Germany probably relates to the latter's acknowledgment of its serious mistakes during the twentieth century, which Japan appears unwilling to make. But it is not inconceivable that a Japanese leadership will one day recognize Japan's evil past, which could further reduce differences between Asian states. Moreover, despite their economic problems since the beginning of the 1990s, the overall postwar economic successes of both Japan and Germany, and their reputations for producing sophisticated high quality goods, are admired by many in both Asia and Europe; once again, there is a resonance between the European and Asian attitudes.

That there are serious differences between the levels of economic development of states within ASEAN cannot be denied. But there are also significant differences within the EU, for instance in GDP per capita. These differences increased with the May 2004 enlargement, and will grow further as the EU expands to the southeast. Thus the average GDP per capita (purchasing power parity) in Luxembourg—the wealthiest member-state of the EU—in 2005 was estimated to be almost five times higher than that in the poorest member-state, Latvia, and some seven and a half times higher than in would-be member state Romania. The ratio is larger within ASEAN, with Singapore's GDP per capita in 2005 being estimated as more than 16 times higher than Myanmar's, and almost 10 times higher than Vietnam's (all data from *CIA World Factbook 2005*, online). But the ratio (wealthiest to poorest states) of GDP per capita differences in the two blocs is quantitative rather than qualitative, and is high in both the EU and ASEAN. It is therefore a less distinguishing feature then might initially be assumed.

One of the criteria for joining the EU is that applicant states be democracies and have market economies. In this sense, there is a relatively high level of system homogeneity within the EU. At first glance, ASEAN appears to be fundamentally different from the EU on this variable, since there is no system uniformity. Vietnam is still a communist republic; Singapore is a relatively authoritarian but anticommunist republic; Myanmar is a military dictatorship; while Thailand is a monarchy with democratic forms.[9] But looking beyond ideology and the formal status of heads of state, the manner in which the systems actually function is not so dissimilar. Most of the states are either authoritarian or quasi-authoritarian. Economically, while dominant modes of ownership and attitudes toward the role of the state vary considerably, the commitment to economic modernization and rising living standards—and hence a focus on eudaemonic legitimation—is widespread. Moreover, there are many who advocate the formalization of different paces of integration within the EU; one concrete symbol of the partial realization of this notion is the fact that the Euro has not been introduced throughout the whole region. Thus, despite a major difference between the EU and ASEAN on this—states can join ASEAN before they become democracies or even market economies—the possibility that there will in the future be subgroupings within ASEAN, based on different approaches to politics and economics, should not be totally discounted. And when considering the dynamism of the EU, it is worth recalling that, as relatively recently as the mid-1970s, almost half the number of the present 25 member states of the EU were dictatorships, either right wing (Greece, Portugal, Spain) or communist (Czechia, Estonia, Hungary, Latvia, Lithuania, Poland, Slovakia, Slovenia).[10]

A Sting in the Tail?

It has been argued that communist Vietnam is experiencing legitimacy problems, but that it might be able to stave off outright crisis for some time if it can make eudaemonism function well as a legitimation mode. It has further been suggested that the move into ASEAN does not per se intensify the fundamental clash between the communist leadership's putative long-term goals and political style on the one hand, and the economic system on the other. But Vietnam is treading a fine line, and endeavours to join the WTO indicate that Hanoi is taking ever bigger risks. One of the ironies of international trade and relations is that while the United States is now the number one destination for Vietnamese exports, it has played the major role in blocking Vietnam's membership of the WTO. Contrary to widespread expectations, Vietnam was not admitted to the WTO in 2005, largely because conservative members of the U.S. Congress sought to link Vietnam's membership with Hanoi's policy on religious freedom. If Vietnam makes major concessions on religious rights in order to secure admission to the WTO, the discrepancy between its *telos* and everyday practices will grow, adding to its legitimacy problems. Moreover, while the Vietnamese leadership downplays this, the fact is that Vietnam receives approximately 5% of its GDP in aid from developed capitalist states and international capitalist organizations such as the IMF and the World Bank. This, together with its heavy trading relationship with the United States, renders Vietnam more susceptible to external pressure than its communist leaders would care to admit. If its economy encounters major problems, the legitimacy crisis—that fundamental tension between its stated political goals and its actual economic system—identified in this chapter will become very visible. At that point, the Vietnamese communist system could well go the way of its former Central and East European communist partners.

But were this to happen, the implications are difficult to predict, in part because the fully postcommunist states have fared very differently. For the Vietnamese people, a move to full-blooded postcommunism would almost certainly be a good thing, at least in the medium-to-long term; many CEE countries are now progressing well, after what must be recognized as a very bumpy entry into postcommunism. The postcommunist outlook for Vietnam's elites is less clear. They might attempt to emulate communist successors in several post-Soviet states, engaging in *nomenklatura* privatization and other shady practices—including unambiguous corruption—to retain their privileged positions. But even if they do, recent events in Georgia, Kyrgyzstan, and Ukraine have demonstrated that they might simply be delaying the inevitable.

Notes

1. Vietnam was for many years highly secretive about trade data; those cited in the Britannica Yearbooks, which in turn are mostly based on the UN's *Commodity Trade Statistics* and *International Trade Statistics Yearbook*, are mainly based on data from Vietnam's trading partners. Although the CMEA source (1989a) is in one sense "official," a number of government statisticians from the communist era have in recent years admitted falsifying many economic data. The data are further softened by the fact that some trade was conducted on a barter basis.
2. China was finally admitted to the WTO in December 2001, whereas Russia had still not been admitted as of early 2006. One must wonder if those who named the World Trade Organization when it succeeded the GATT were aware of the irony of their decision; the WTO used to be the acronym for the communist world's major military bloc, and there might appear to be an element of triumphalism in using the same acronym for one of the primary agencies of capitalist economic globalization.
3. A classic, if now dated, analysis of *doi moi* is the collection edited by Turley and Selden (1993).
4. Literally, eudaemonic means "conducive to happiness." In contemporary social science literature, eudaemonic legitimation refers to attempts by political elites to legitimise their rule and the system primarily in terms of the system's performance, especially in the economic sphere. For an analysis of this and other modes of legitimation, with particular reference to communist and postcommunist states, see Holmes 1997, 42–52, 337–43.
5. For a full analysis of these methods, plus examples, see Holmes 2006, 90–145.
6. Transparency International does not conduct surveys itself for the CPI. Rather, it describes its index as a "poll of polls," in which it averages over a number of surveys—mostly of the business community—conducted by other organizations.

7. If a country is ranked twenty-fifth out of fifty one year, and fortieth out of eighty the next, its relative position has not really changed—it remains in the middle of the pack. However, some observers overlook "details" such as the number of countries assessed, and might therefore (erroneously) assume, on the basis of the rank alone, that the country has markedly deteriorated from one year to the next.

8. Vietnam's averaged inflation rate in 2005 was estimated to be a higher than desirable 8 %, while its averaged unemployment rate was estimated at a low 2.4%. The comparable figures for China were much lower for inflation (estimated 1.9% in 2005), but considerably higher—at perhaps as much as 20%—for unemployment (2003 figure). All data from CIA World Factbook 2005 (online version, updated January 10, 2006, visited February 2006).

9. In its most recent democracy ranking, Freedom House assesses Thailand as the most democratic ASEAN state, and Myanmar the least (Vietnam is seen as the least democratic of the ASEAN states after Myanmar). But even Thailand does not rank well in comparison with the consolidated democracies of Europe, North America, and elsewhere.

10. The list here is of only 11 countries that were not democracies; in addition, there was East Germany, which no longer exists as a separate state, but did—as a communist dictatorship—until the end of the 1980s. If Bulgaria and Romania join the EU in 2007, the proportion of "recent nondemocracies" will rise further.

Bibliography

Bialer, Seweryn. 1980. *Stalin's successors*. Cambridge: Cambridge University Press.

Habermas, Jurgen. 1973a. *Legitimationsprobleme im Spätkapitalismus*. Frankfurt: Suhrkamp.

———. 1973b. What does a legitimation crisis mean today? Legitimation problems in late capitalism. Reproduced in *Legitimacy and the state*. Edited by W. Connolly. Oxford: Blackwell, 1984, 134–79.

Holmes, Leslie. 1993. *The end of communist power: Anti-corruption campaigns and legitimation crisis*. New York: Oxford University Press.

———. 1997. *Post-Communism*. Durham: Duke University Press.

———. 2006. *Rotten states? Corruption, post-communism and neoliberalism*. Durham: Duke University Press.

Kaufmann, Daniel, Aart Kraay, and Massimo Mastruzzi. 2003. *Governance Matters III: Governance Indicators for 1996–2002 (Draft)*. World Bank website, visited August 2004.

Lockwood, David. 2000. *The destruction of the Soviet Union: A study in globalization*. Basingstoke: Macmillan.

Meng Xin, Robert Gregory and Wang Youjuan. 2004. Poverty, inequality and growth in urban China, 1986–2000. Online at http://www.clmr.ecel.uwa.edu.au/ASLE/workshop%20papers/Meng-Gregory-Wangfinal.pdf, visited January 2006.

Meyer, Alfred. 1972. Legitimacy of power in East Central Europe. In *Eastern Europe in the 1970s*. Edited by Sylva Sinanian, Istvan Deak and Peter Ludz. New York: Praeger: 45–68.

Pham Hoang Mai. 2004. *FDI and development in Vietnam: Policy implications*. Singapore: Institute of Southeast Asian Studies.

Rigby, T. H. 1982. Introduction: Political legitimacy, Weber and communist mono-organisational systems. In *Political legitimation in communist states*. Edited by T. H. Rigby and Ferenc Fehér. Basingstoke: Macmillan, 1–26.

Sík, Endre. 2002. The bad, the worse and the worst: Guesstimating the level of corruption. In *Political corruption in transition: A skeptic's handbook*. Edited by Stephen Kotkin and Andras Sajó. Budapest: Central University Press, 91–113.

Skocpol, Theda. 1979. *States and social revolutions*. Cambridge: Cambridge University Press.

Thien, Tran Dinh Thien. 1999. Impact of the regional crisis on the Vietnamese economy. Online at http://www.ismea.org/asialist/Tran-Dinh-Thien.html, visited February 2006.

Turley, William and Mark Selden (eds.). 1993. *Reinventing Vietnamese socialism: Doi Moi in comparative perspective*. Boulder: Westview.

Weber, Max. 1970. Politics as a vocation. In *From Max Weber: Essays in sociology*. Edited by Hans H. Gerth and Charles Wright Mills. London: Routledge and Kegan Paul, 77–128.

PART I

International Relations and Regional Integration

CHAPTER TWO

Vietnam's Regional Integration

Domestic and External Challenges to State Sovereignty

CARLYLE A. THAYER

Introduction

This chapter explores the challenges to the sovereignty of the Vietnamese state as it pursues regional integration in Southeast Asia through the twin policies of domestic renewal (*doi moi*) and an open door foreign policy. In particular, this chapter discusses to what extent the process of regional integration has weakened the vertical power and sovereignty of the Vietnamese state. This proposition is examined in a case study focused on the process of Vietnam's regional integration through membership in the Association of South East Asian Nations (ASEAN).

This chapter is organized into four parts. Part one discusses several key conceptual and definitional issues. Part two reviews Vietnam's experience with regional integration as a member of ASEAN since 1995. Part three evaluates the challenges to state sovereignty arising from Vietnam's participation in the ASEAN Free Trade Area (AFTA) and the reform of state-owned enterprises (SOEs). Part four offers some conclusions arising from Vietnam's experience with regional integration and the challenges to state sovereignty.

Sovereignty, Multilateralism, and the State

The notion of state sovereignty is one of the central concepts that defines the contemporary international system. Sovereignty has both domestic and external dimensions. Sovereignty defines the holders of state authority and their prerogatives and grants them supreme authority within their territorial boundaries and in dealing with each other. The European or Westphalian notion of sovereignty precluded the existence of any higher authority beyond state borders.

Sovereignty, unlike other attributes of the modern state such as territory, population and government, is not tangible or a material given. States must use their resources to assert sovereignty. The concept of sovereignty is not a static one, its meaning has changed over time. There are different types of sovereignty (Krasner 1999, 2001). It is common to distinguish between juridical and empirical sovereignty. Empirical sovereignty refers to a state's ability to demonstrate its political and economic capacity for self-governance, while juridical sovereignty refers to sovereignty as a moral right. In contemporary usage, sovereignty has two distinct meanings—supreme power and autonomy. Southeast Asian's nationalist leaders and their successors adopted sovereignty as the cardinal principle of interstate relations in the postcolonial period. They stress the importance of autonomy or freedom from constraint or independence. Whatever the historical period, state sovereignty was never absolute.

In sum, state sovereignty today is based on norms and practices and shared understandings among states that evolved as a particular historical process. The European Union is held up as a model in which aspects of state sovereignty have been yielded to a higher or supra-national authority. The impact of globalization has sparked debate over whether globalization undercuts or reconfigures state sovereignty.

The international relations literature on multilateralism distinguishes between minimalist and maximalist positions, identified with the writings of Robert Keohane and John Ruggie, respectively. Keohane defines multilateralism as "the practice of coordinating national policies in groups of three or more states through ad hoc arrangements or by means of institutions" (1990, 731). This definition is termed the minimalist definition because of its quantitative nature (three or more states) and because multilateral institutions are defined as simply "multilateral arrangements with persistent sets of rules."

Ruggie asks what it is about international institutions that make them multilateral (1992, 566–8). He argues that it is not simply the number of actors involved but the qualitative dimension or character of their cooperation. According to Ruggie, multilateral relations involve three or more states coming together to tackle a specific issue or set of issues on the basis of generalized principles of conduct. In other words, multilateral institutions adopt appropriate conduct for a class of actions irrespective of particular interests or circumstances.

Ruggie identifies three generalized principles that are important: non-discrimination, indivisibility, and diffuse reciprocity. The first principle is virtually self-explanatory. States that engage in multilateral cooperation do so on an equal basis. The principle of indivisibility means that decisions made through a multilateral institution are mutually binding on state parties. This principle may be illustrated with reference to the General Agreement of Tariffs and Trade (GATT) or the most-favored-nation (MFN) principle. Under GATT and MFN the trade system is an indivisible whole and all parties agree to treat each other in a like fashion. The principle of diffuse reciprocity means that all members are expected to share equivalent benefits over a period of time. To take another example from the international trading regime, with respect to exports, for example, each party should receive roughly the same amount of benefit in aggregate over a period of time as all the other parties.

A final point on multilateralism needs to be made: the practice of multilateralism varies across regions. Multilateralism in Europe, as embodied in the European Union is heavily institutionalized, based on rules, regulations and laws, and involves some derogation of national sovereignty. In Asia, the process of multilateralism tends to focus more on process and is shaped by norms and principles. Vietnam's regional integration through membership in ASEAN is an example of the latter.

According to one Vietnamese writer, ASEAN is a "loose economic alliance" and "not really a coherent bloc" (Tran Phuong Lan 2004, 75–9). Clearly ASEAN is a different type of multilateral organization from the European Union, falling in between the minimal and maximalist positions. ASEAN has eschewed formal institutionalization. The powers of the ASEAN Secretary General are quite limited and the ASEAN Secretariat comprises no more than one hundred full-time staff. ASEAN puts a premium on consultation and consensus decision making based on the norms of noninterference in a member state's internal affairs. ASEAN's generalized principles are enshrined in the 1967 Bangkok Declaration, the 1976 Treaty of Amity and Cooperation (TAC or Bali Concord I), and the more recently adopted Bali Concord II (2003).

The norms and principles that guide ASEAN decision making are known collectively as the ASEAN Way. A detailed study of this question concluded that ASEAN's "shared meaning structures" were based on a "narrow foundation of regional norms of conduct and agreement on the benefits of power balancing in security affairs" (Nischalke 2002, 107). This study also found that ASEAN states quite often took unilateral foreign policy decisions without prior consultations with other members. ASEAN, therefore, was not an identity-based community but an emerging rules-based community in which the norms of the TAC were increasingly accepted.

ASEAN has no mechanisms to force compliance with its decisions. Its main dispute resolution mechanism, the ASEAN High Council, has never operated. The one possible exception is the AFTA and its implementing mechanism the Common Effective Preferential Tariffs (CEPT) arrangements discussed later. Increasingly, on other economic issues, ASEAN has adopted a decision-making formula that permits members that disagree on a certain policy proposal to opt out, while other states that are in agreement proceed. ASEAN also practices positive discrimination in economic matters in relation to its newest and less developed members—Vietnam, Laos, Myanmar, and Cambodia. In sum, ASEAN and the ASEAN Way operate as a process designed to prevent a clash between state sovereignty and institutional multilateralism.

If the concepts of sovereignty and multilateralism are problematic, so too is the nature of the Vietnamese state. Scholars have debated whether Vietnam is "weak" or "strong" (Migdal 1988 and Dauvergne 1998). Some argue that the Vietnamese state is strong in certain policy spheres while weak in others. Other academics see an erosion of party-state fusion with the state taking on a more powerful role via the National Assembly and other government institutions. Still other scholars question whether concepts of strong and weak are at all useful in characterizing contemporary relations between Vietnamese party-state authorities and society (Painter 2003, 22). This issue is discussed later in the context of an official program to equitize SOEs.

Vietnam in ASEAN

This section reviews the factors that influenced Vietnam's decision to join ASEAN, and how Vietnamese officials and scholars evaluated Vietnam's experience of regional integration before and after the Asian financial crisis of 1997–8.

Political and Strategic Motivations

Vietnam pursued regional integration primarily for a mix of political, strategic, and economic motivations (Amer 2001, 89–93; Nguyen Dy Nien 1996). According to Nguyen Phuong Binh and Luan Thuy Duong (2001, 186–9), there were three driving forces behind Vietnam's desire to join ASEAN: a favorable external environment with peaceful and friendly relations with neighboring countries; enhanced standing in the wider Asia-Pacific region and the world, and economic cooperation.

Vietnam's decision to join ASEAN signaled a fundamental change in its foreign policy orientation. Vietnam now sought security with rather than security against Southeast Asia. For the first time since independence, Vietnam faced no imminent military threats to its borders. This resulted in a massive peace dividend as Vietnam slashed defense spending and demobilized over two-thirds of its main forces (Thayer 2000a, 199–219).

As part of Vietnam's new open-door foreign policy Hanoi moved quickly to overcome the historical legacy of suspicion and mistrust with its ASEAN neighbors arising from the Vietnam War and conflict in Cambodia. Vietnam resolved such problem areas as displaced Vietnamese persons, demarcation of continental shelves, overlapping territorial claims involving Malaysia, the Philippines and Thailand, and fishing disputes (Amer 1999; Truong Giang Long 1997). These legacies of history were seen as irritants that could impede the development of close ASEAN-Vietnam relations.

Vietnam's membership in ASEAN was expected to lead to enhanced standing and prestige in the Asia-Pacific and the world. Vietnam hoped this would provide an enhanced bargaining position in external affairs and provide leverage in its dealing with major powers, China and the United States. Chinese assertiveness in the South China Sea in 1992 was undoubtedly a consideration in Vietnamese decision making regarding ASEAN membership, but was not the prime motivating factor. Vietnam did not join ASEAN to balance against China (Thayer 2002). As noted by Hoang Anh Tuan, "Vietnamese history shows that one-sided relations have led to political isolation and economic difficulties. . . . Therefore, Vietnam's ASEAN membership should be achieved in a way that would strengthen instead of harm Vietnam's relations with China" (1993, 288–9). In Hanoi's view, ASEAN membership transformed what was a bilateral issue between Beijing and Hanoi into a multilateral one involving China and ASEAN as a group.

Vietnam sought membership in ASEAN as a means to improve its relations with the United States. In Hanoi's view, Vietnam would be strategically more important to Washington as a member of ASEAN. In 1994, before Vietnam was a member, it was still subject to a U.S.-imposed trade and aid embargo. In July 1995, on the eve of Vietnam's membership in ASEAN, the United States unconditionally lifted its embargo. Vietnam also expected that ASEAN membership would provide it some political insulation in its dealings with the United States and Europe on such issues as human rights and democratization. According to one Vietnamese analyst, Vietnam would be "quite happy to hide behind Malaysia and Singapore on those issues" (quoted in Schwartz 1995).

Vietnamese scholar Nguyen Vu Tung (2002) has argued that an additional factor explaining Vietnam's motivations for seeking regional integration is the importance of state identity. Tung wrote:

> The tentative argument is that there is a strong linkage between the search for a new state identity in the aftermath of the Cold War and the making of foreign policy in Hanoi. The search for a new state identity—which is compatible to that of the ASEAN states—suggests that Vietnam would forge a closer co-operative relationship with the ASEAN states, and that membership in ASEAN would inform Vietnam's present and future foreign policy.

While this argument has some merit, it should also be born in mind that ideological considerations continued to shape Vietnamese foreign policy perceptions (Bui Tin 1995, 191; Thayer 1999b, 1–14, and Phan Doan Nam 2003, 52–8). When Vietnam joined ASEAN it was required to subscribe to the principles of the Treaty of Amity and Cooperation. Yet one Vietnamese writer, Pham Cao Phong (1996, 3) has revealed that Hanoi retained reservations: "despite announcing its commitment to the Treaty of Amity and Cooperation . . . Hanoi is not so certain whether it accepts the rules of the game, that is, accepts all the written and unwritten norms of the relationship among ASEAN countries without any exceptions."

Economic Considerations

According to Hoang Anh Tuan, "[p]olitically, due to ASEAN's high international prestige, ASEAN membership would enhance Vietnam's diplomatic standing and integrate Vietnam's security with the security of the whole of Southeast Asia, thus creating an external environment favorable for economic development" (1993, 283). This was a view put forward by a government official who asserted that Vietnam expected ASEAN membership to provide enhanced national security, external support for economic development, and as a catalyst for its domestic reform process (Doan Manh Giao 1995). In other words, in addition to political and strategic considerations, there was an economic motivation for Vietnam to join ASEAN.

There are several dimensions to this. First, Vietnam as a developing country expected to learn from the developmental experience of ASEAN's original members and receive their support in addressing Vietnam economic concerns. In other words, membership in ASEAN would act as a catalyst for and further accelerate domestic reforms in Vietnam. Second, Vietnam expected to benefit from increased trade and investment from ASEAN states (Ramasamy 1996, 29–47). And third, Vietnam wanted to secure integration with the regional and global economies as a long-term goal.

In 1996, after the first anniversary of Vietnam's membership in ASEAN, Vietnamese officials were generally upbeat in their assessments. The Vietnamese foreign minister stated that Vietnam made the right decision to join ASEAN despite the difficulties it now faced in liberalizing its economy in an effort to catch up with the other six members (Nguyen Manh Cam 1995, 223–30). Cam also mentioned difficulties caused by differences in the political systems, noting in particular Vietnam's socialist government, planned economy, inexperience with the free market, and the lack of English-speaking officials. Nonetheless, Cam stated, Vietnam would meet its obligations to open its economy under AFTA by 2006. Among the Vietnamese foreign policy elite there too was a general consensus that the decision to join ASEAN was correct and had been a success (Vu Khoan 1998, 17–23).

By May 1997, three ASEAN countries—Singapore, Malaysia, and Thailand—ranked among the 10 largest foreign investors in Vietnam. Indonesia ranked eighteenth, and the Philippines twenty-first. Singaporean investment was concentrated in the fields of hotel construction and tourism. Malaysia and Indonesia invested in Vietnam's oil sector, while Thailand concentrated on mineral exploitation and processing. ASEAN investment was expected to rise as investors sought to exploit Vietnam's lower labor costs in resource and labor intensive industries (Nguyen Xuan Thang 1998, 190–204).

What was the situation with trade? By 1997, Vietnam developed a trade imbalance and growing deficit with other ASEAN members. As intra-ASEAN trade expanded, Vietnam reoriented its exports to take advantage of this large market. About 30% of Vietnam's exports went to ASEAN states. Imports from ASEAN accounted for nearly one-half of Vietnam's total imports. The volume of trade with ASEAN countries rose markedly in dollar value terms and resulted in a situation in which more than half of Vietnam's trade deficit of US$3.5 billion (1996 figures) was with other ASEAN countries.

The Triple Crises of 1997

In 1997, ASEAN was affected by a series of crises that severely tested its unity and cohesion. These included the Indonesian haze problem, the violent breakdown of coalition government in Cambodia, and the impact of the Asian financial crisis (Phan Thanh Ha 2001). The later provoked serious political instability and unexpected leadership change in Indonesia. These triple crises overlapped with ASEAN's expansion in membership to include Myanmar and Laos. According to Binh and Duong, ASEAN members became preoccupied at this time with internal stability and sought to recover by emphasizing policies of self-help over regional cooperation. The Asian financial crisis also undermined both regional and national resilience as well as ASEAN's collective self-confidence (Nguyen Phuong Binh and Luan Thuy Duong 2001). ASEAN's disarray in dealing with these issues also served to reinforce those voices in Vietnam that urged a go-slow approach to economic integration and political reform.

Vietnamese officials became alarmed by three developments in particular. The first concerned the impact of these multiple regional crises on Vietnam's economic and political stability. In late 1997, Vietnam was wracked by a series of peasant disturbances in Thai Binh province that may have contributed to a change in leadership at this time (Thayer 2001, 22). The second development concerned the economic impact of the Asian financial crisis and ASEAN disarray on Vietnam (Pham Quoc Tru 2003, 59–62). This took multiple forms. Several ASEAN members reduced their expected contributions to Vietnam's economic development at intergovernmental and private sector levels. Monetary devaluations in the region resulted in stiff competition in some sectors as ASEAN goods entered the Vietnamese market place in greater amounts (Nguyen Phuong Binh and Luan Thuy Duong 2001). In other words, economic transactions between ASEAN and Vietnam became less effective as the structure of trade worked against Vietnam's economic interests. As ASEAN's cohesion came under challenge, Vietnamese leaders worried that the development gap within ASEAN between old and new members would widen and create a two-tiered organization. Vietnamese concerns were fueled by statements attributed to officials from the original ASEAN Five that alleged enlargement had led to a slow-down in ASEAN decision making and consensus building and new members were an economic and political burden.

The third development concerned a move by Thailand, supported by the Philippines and the Deputy Prime Minister of Malaysia, Anwar Ibrahim, to modify ASEAN's long-cherished principle of noninterference in the internal affairs of other member states (Thayer 1999a). Thailand's proposal was aimed at Myanmar whose domestic policies, it was alleged, spilled over and threatened regional stability. Malaysia's Deputy Prime Minister wanted to include Cambodia in this discussion on constructive intervention. Vietnam supported the status quo.

In the aftermath of the triple crises in the late 1990s, ASEAN experienced a number of difficulties in managing differences among its members. These differences included: democratization and human rights, security threats, and relations toward international institutions and the great powers (Thayer 2004, 177–82). Disarray meant that ASEAN became less effective as an organization in dealing with external powers. Singapore, for example, pursued a policy of self-help in negotiating a number of free trade agreements with external powers (Mahani 2002, 1263–77). Vietnam has been extremely wary about over-riding ASEAN's principle of nonintervention, a key component of the ASEAN Way.

The Asian financial crisis and its aftermath shook Vietnam's expectations of mutual support from fellow ASEAN members and raised serious concerns in Hanoi about the benefits and advantages of ASEAN membership. As a result, Vietnam adopted a three-pronged approach in its external relations: advocacy of positive discrimination in the case of ASEAN's new members; developing a caucus of less developed politically closed states within ASEAN (Thayer 2000b, 26–7); and increased emphasis on bilateral relations with China and the United States.

Vietnam used its status as the host for ASEAN's sixth summit meeting in 1998 to successfully obtain endorsement from other ASEAN members for special treatment for the four newer members: Cambodia, Laos, Myanmar, and Vietnam. In order to overcome the development gap between ASEAN's more developed and less developed economies, the ASEAN Six (the five original members plus Brunei) agreed to assist and grant special treatment to the latter in their development efforts. This positive discrimination was embedded in the Hanoi Plan of Action and other documents adopted by the sixth summit. The theme of reducing the development gap between the ASEAN Six and ASEAN's newer members has become of central feature of ASEAN economic programs, such as the ASEAN Investment Initiative.

Vietnam has had close and long-standing historical ties with the regimes in Cambodia, Laos, and Myanmar (CLM) that predated their membership in ASEAN. After the CLM countries were admitted into ASEAN, and particularly after the 1997–8 debate over constructive intervention, Vietnam moved to ensure that bilateral relations remained as firm as ever. In addition, Vietnam also encouraged multilateral cooperation through a subregional grouping of Mekong states. These economic and political linkages were designed to create a nascent caucus of politically closed states to mirror the influence of the ASEAN Five/Six within the Association (Thayer 2000b, 26–7).

Finally, it is notable that in the aftermath of the Asian financial crisis, Vietnam moved to improve its bilateral relations with the major powers. In 1999, Vietnam was one of the first ASEAN members to sign a long-term cooperative framework agreement with China that sets the context for bilateral relations into the first decade of the twenty-first century (Thayer 2003). Bilateral relations with the United States took on a decidedly new dimension in 2000 when Vietnam finally agreed to a long-term Bilateral Trade Agreement (BTA) with the United States. Under the BTA, Vietnam was obligated to undertake a comprehensive set of commitments on tariffs and non-tariff barriers for industrial and agricultural goods, services, intellectual property rights, investment, transparency, and other matters. This has required Vietnam to amend legislation and bring new laws and regulations into effect in order to meet its BTA commitments. In addition to gaining access to the American market, the BTA also acts as a stimulus to further domestic economic and legal reforms and serve as an essential foundation for membership in the World Trade Organization.

The improvement of Vietnam's bilateral relations with China and the United States should be seen as complementary actions. As a neighbor, Vietnam must adjust to the rise of the Chinese economy. At the same time, Vietnam needs access to the world's largest market if it is to become fully integrated with the global economy, a goal long advocated by its leaders. In sum, Vietnam too has pursued self-help measures to advantage itself in light of ASEAN's disarray.

Regional Integration Through AFTA

During their decades-long struggle against foreign intervention, Vietnam's leaders were widely known for their nationalism and independence in defense of state sovereignty. When Vietnam joined ASEAN it had to become a team player and adjust its external policies to fit in with the ASEAN consensus. The ASEAN process is a weak form of multilateralism, ASEAN has no formal compliance mechanisms to compel its members, and institutionalization is at a nascent stage.

Vietnam's decision to join AFTA marks the first time Vietnam has taken part in regional economic cooperation. AFTA is one of the least restrictive regional trading agreements (Lao-Araya 2003, 62). Timetables for the implementation of CEPT commitments vary among individual states (Vo Thi Thanh Loc 2001, 3). An AFTA Council set up to supervise AFTA's implementation has no powers to force members to comply. This section explores Vietnam's experience in regional integration through AFTA.

AFTA came into being in January 1992 with the objective of eliminating tariff barriers among ASEAN members and thus integrating the ASEAN economies into a single production base and regional market by 2010 (Bowles 1997, 219–33). This target date was later brought forward and separate deadlines were set for newer members. The key integrating mechanism was the Common Effective Preferential Tariff (CEPT) scheme. Signatories were required to classify all manufactured goods into four categories: Inclusion List, Temporary Exclusion List, Sensitive List and General Exclusion List. AFTA members agreed on a schedule to reduce tariffs on goods in the first two lists to 0–5% according to an agreed schedule. AFTA members were also required to remove quantitative restrictions and other non-tariff barriers (Lao-Araya 2003, 61).

When Vietnam initially sought admission to ASEAN it requested not to participate in the AFTA process (Flatters 1997, 1). ASEAN members, however, made this a requirement for entry. ASEAN foreign affairs and economic ministers, however, were split on the modalities of Vietnam's admission. Hanoi took advantage of this to obtain a three-year extension in meeting AFTA's tariff reduction goals (Guina 1997, 13, 24). On December 15, 1995, Vietnam signed the protocol acceding to the agreement on the CEPT as a first step in joining the ASEAN Free Trade Area (Setboonsarng 1996, 36–8). As required, Vietnam phased in tariff reductions on its temporary exclusion lines in five equal installments between 1999 and 2003, at which time 92% of all tariff lines used by Vietnam came under the CEPT scheme. Most of Vietnam's sensitive list includes unprocessed agricultural products.

The deadlines for CEPT tariff reductions have been repeatedly brought forward so Vietnam was required to reach the last stage of tariff reductions in 2006. The deadline for the ASEAN Six states came into force in 2004. ASEAN has also had to back track in the situation in which members first announced tariff reductions on items on their Temporary Exclusion List (TEL) only to rescind these reductions in the face of protectionist pressures. ASEAN has agreed only to permit this for goods on the last schedule of the TEL.

ASEAN's experience with the implementation of the CEPT scheme has generally been quite good. The ASEAN Six are basically CEPT-compliant although "certain long-standing member countries have not fully complied with requirements of the CEPT scheme in spite of written deadlines" (Lao-Araya 2003, 62). ASEAN has not moved to force compliance when its members experience genuine difficulties. In May 1997, for example, Vietnam instituted a ban on imported fans to save foreign exchange and to protect local industry. This ban violated AFTA provisions. It was quietly revoked later.

Despite Vietnam's initial reservations, there are a number of advantages to its participation in AFTA and the CEPT scheme. First, Vietnam's participation in AFTA has resulted in trade creation and trade diversion benefits to Vietnam. Trade between Vietnam and the other ASEAN members has risen. Vietnam imports quality materials from ASEAN that it uses in both domestic production and export. This has benefited its textile, garment, leather, and electronic assembly industries in particular. Vietnam has also benefited from increased ASEAN foreign direct investment (although this declined following the Asian financial crisis). Vietnam has also benefited from modest technology transfers.

Vietnam's participation in AFTA has provided it with familiarity with the norms and practices of international trade. This experience has facilitated Vietnam participation in the Asia Pacific Economic Cooperation (APEC) forum that Vietnam joined in 1998. This experience is invaluable for Vietnam as it negotiates membership in the World Trade Organization. And finally, Vietnam's participation in AFTA provides it with a modest buffer against China's economic rise and an off-set to goods smuggled from China (Vo Thi Thanh Loc 2001, 7).

It should be noted that the increase in Vietnam's trade with ASEAN is marked by a simultaneous improvement of trade volume with China and the United States is increasing at an even faster rate. One economic study argues that it is "too soon to conclude that ASEAN is the dominant market for Vietnamese products" due to Singapore's role in reexporting Vietnamese goods (Vo Thi Thanh Loc 2001, 6). It further states: "AFTA does not have direct impact on import-export relations of Vietnam. And AFTA will not create any extremely quick momentum or fundamental changes for Vietnam's trade unless there are improvements in the structure of domestic production" (Vo Thi Thanh Loc 2001, 7).

Vietnam has been reliant on tariff revenues for a major portion of state revenues as well as a protective device for inefficient industries (Vo Thi Thanh Loc 2001, 9; Lao-Araya 2003, 59). These revenues will be lost as tariff reductions kick in. Vietnam has had to adopt a Value Added Tax (VAT) in compensation and this requires development of a greater capacity in the administration of tax collection. Vietnam has also protected sensitive economic sectors by including them on the General Exclusion List (GEL). This is in contravention of the purpose for which the GEL was established. Finally, a definite assessment of the costs and benefits of AFTA to Vietnam can be made only when the effects of the last stage of CEPT-mandated tariff reductions in 2006 are analyzed.

Since joining AFTA, Vietnam has been under constant pressure to reduce tariff barriers to meet ever-advancing deadlines. The International Monetary Fund (IMF), World Bank, and donor countries have also applied their own pressures (Clarke 2001, 22; Painter 2003, 32–4). A lowering of tariffs and other barriers to trade under AFTA means that Vietnamese enterprises will be forced to compete with their ASEAN counterparts. The positive side of this process for Vietnam will lie in its ability to import material used in export production at cheaper prices than before. Vietnam will also be able to participate in an ASEAN-wide labor chain of production utilizing its comparative advantage of cheap skilled labor.

While Vietnam's export sector has demonstrated robust growth in the years preceding the Asian financial crisis, as indicated by the increasing share of exports as part of Vietnam's GDP, one economic study has concluded "there is no firm econometric evidence to suggest that exports are an engine of economic growth and development in Vietnam as they have been in other East Asian economies" (Phan Minh Ngoc et al. 2003, 229). There are a number of factors that account for this including the static nature of Vietnamese exports (low value-added unprocessed agricultural products and minerals), the lack of an efficient service industry to support exports and excessive concentration on too few export partners.

Vietnam is presently facing crunch time as the obligations of regional integration intersect with state sovereignty and highly sensitive issues involving political power and political economy. These issues are highlighted with respect to the state sector that has come under domestic and external pressure to restructure and reform. According to one study, "[a]s Vietnam completes its AFTA commitments in 2006, intra-ASEAN traded goods will flood the domestic market and hamper the development of domestic sectors unless Vietnam's economy is sufficiently strong. At present, competitiveness of the Vietnamese enterprises has not yet been well established" (Vo Thi Thanh Loc 2001, 14).

At the time Vietnam joined ASEAN, there were approximately 6,400 SOEs operating in Vietnam (Dang Duc Dam 1997, 124–5). Over the past decade, Vietnam has attempted to reform this sector through restructuring and a program known as equitization. This program has proceeded slowly and by 2001 the total number of SOEs had been reduced to roughly 5,600. The purpose of SOE reform was to make them more efficient in the market place and curb the drain on state finances. One study found that the reform process led to an increase in total factor productivity (Vu Quoc Ngu 2003b, 168–9).

The ninth national congress of the Vietnam Communist Party, which met in April 2001, endorsed a five-year program of SOE reform (World Bank 2002, 26). This program has moved in fits and starts; by the end of this period, 3,349 SOEs were restructured of which 2,188 were equitized (Viet Nam News, January 20, 2006). Although Vietnam is developing a market economy, party ideology maintains that the state sector should remain dominant. The state retains full ownership of 1,800 SOEs (McCarty 2006, 13), including newly formed large-scale conglomerates in posts and telecommunications, coal, oil and gas, electricity, shipbuilding, cement, and textile and garments (Vietnam Economy, January 4, 2006).

Despite nearly two decades of reform efforts, Vietnam has not succeeded in leveling the playing field. The state sector is privileged over the private sector in terms of preferential bank credit, tax breaks, state contracts, access to land, and government services (Quan Xuan Dinh 2000, 363; Vu Quoc Ngu 2003a, 330). The SOE sector is also heavily indebted (World Bank 2002, 23). State commercial banks continue to pour credit into industries that are most at risk from ASEAN competitors (Nguyen Manh Hung 2004, 301).

Detailed studies of Vietnamese SOEs and the SOE reform process reveal a complex picture of the state in Vietnam (Quan Xuan Dinh 2000; Clarke 2001; Painter 2003; Fforde 2004a, 2004b). SOEs are owned/controlled at national, provincial, or district level by line ministries and various local government departments. As a result of equitization, one analyst has argued that SOEs have become virtual stockholding companies in which the lines of ownership and control are overlapping and blurred between state and party (Fforde 2004b). Before equitization, the line ministries or people's committees owned entire firms while the

Ministry of Finance was charged with the responsibility of controlling financial matters.

This discussion of SOE reform raises serious questions about what constitutes "the state" in Vietnam. It is clear that the Prime Minister and other office holders at central level and their advisers in state-run institutes support SOE reform and equitization as essential to Vietnam's larger process of economic renovation. Outside agencies such as the IMF, World Bank, and donor countries play an important role in strengthening the position of those pushing for further SOE reforms. The reformist component of the state is opposed by conservative party officials at national and local level, as well as managers and owners of SOEs, who wish to maintain control over the capital funds and other assets of their enterprises (Quan Xuan Dinh 2000, 365–75). Managers and workers also oppose equitization out of the fear that they will lose guaranteed wages and retirement benefits. This later group still clings to protectionism to ward off external competitive pressures and domestic resistance to transform. Indeed, it is the resistance by insiders including directors and workers of large SOEs that partly accounts for the slow pace of transformation at present (World Bank 2002, 25–6; Vu Quoc Ngu 2003a, 230).

Conclusion

This overview of Vietnam's regional integration through membership in ASEAN has demonstrated how state sovereignty in Vietnam has come under challenge as a consequence of Vietnam's policies of domestic renovation (*doi moi*) and the open-door foreign policy. These policies have led, perhaps paradoxically, to the strengthening of the Party-state in unexpected ways rather than undermining its vertical control. It should be recalled that no state has ever exercised absolute sovereignty. Krasner (1999) argues that Westphalian sovereignty is a form of organized hypocrisy because states have always experienced some form of external intervention in their internal affairs.

ASEAN's weak form of multilateralism has led to particular foreign policy challenges to Vietnamese sovereignty. Vietnam joined ASEAN in the expectation that the norms included in the ASEAN Way—noninterference in particular—would strengthen state sovereignty. Yet the debate within ASEAN over this very norm, particularly with respect to Myanmar, has served to undermine this expectation. Vietnam responded by developing a set of regional policies that privileged the newer ASEAN members, as I discuss in detail later.

Vietnam joined ASEAN, inter alia, to be able to deal more effectively with a rising China and to insulate itself from Western pressures on its domestic political arrangements. ASEAN has proved a weak institutional reed in dealing with China on territorial disputes in the South China Sea. Instead of a binding code of conduct, the best ASEAN could negotiate was a general statement on the "conduct of parties" in the South China Sea (Nguyen Hong Thao 2000, 2003). Although China, Vietnam, and the Philippines agreed in 2005 to trilateral exploration activities, individual claimants have continued to pursue activities designed to advance their individual territorial claims.

Vietnam's participation in AFTA has brought repeated pressures on state authorities to advance the deadlines for tariff reductions and restructure state revenue from import taxes to the collection of VAT. It remains to be seen if Vietnam will be able to meet its final tariff reduction commitments or whether special circumstances will be invoked for delays in specified areas. State authority will be weakened to the extent that Vietnam will be compelled to remove goods wrongly placed on its GEL. These goods were initially placed on the GEL in order to afford domestic industry some measure of protection against competition. AFTA and the CEPT scheme provide only a limited test of the extent to which external pressures challenge state authority in Vietnam. The impact of external pressures on Vietnam from the IMF and World Bank are probably more decisive at this stage. A better test case will arise when Vietnam becomes a member of the World Trade Organization.

ASEAN represents a weak form of multilateralism, one found at the minimal end of the minimal-maximalist spectrum. ASEAN does not have any mechanism to force its members to comply with agreed economic and political policies. The ASEAN process of multilateralism positively discriminates in favor of the newer less developed members rather than uphold strict non-discrimination. This is not only the case with AFTA and the CEPT scheme, but also with the proposed Free Trade Agreement between ASEAN and China (Wattanapruttipaisan 2003). ASEAN has been flexible in its application of the criterion of indivisibility particularly with respect to CEPT commitments. However, ASEAN does pursue diffuse reciprocity as part of the long-term objectives of AFTA.

Multilateralism tends to work well when the external environment is stable. Economic setbacks and other strains, such as were experienced in Southeast Asia in the late 1990s, have taught Vietnam that the principles of non-discrimination, indivisibility, and reciprocity can be manipulated to shore up state sovereignty. It is only to a limited extent that Vietnam's external commitments have required it to accept norms and principles of behavior that are not of its making. Vietnamese state authorities have proved particularly adept at maneuvering around these constraints when it suits their purpose.

Vietnam continues to emphasize the importance of relations with individual Southeast Asian states as well as ASEAN as an organization. Vietnam has been at the forefront ensuring that ASEAN adopts socioeconomic policies designed to reduce the development gap between new and old members. Vietnam has adopted a more realistic view of the ASEAN Way and the benefits of multilateralism in a weak institutional setting. Vietnam is now more adept at pursuing multilateral and bilateral foreign policies in tandem.

The case study of SOE reform has thrown light on internal contestation within Vietnam on the very structure of the political economy of the party-state and state power. The SOE story exposes the nexus between domestic and external pressures on the Vietnamese state to alter policy in conformity with international norms and practices in economic affairs. State authorities have used Vietnam's membership in ASEAN to strengthen their position by binding Vietnam to economic policy changes and thus constrain any attempt at backtracking or foot dragging. Vietnam's membership in ASEAN can be viewed as a mechanism that puts pressure on Hanoi's policymakers to push through further reforms (Guina 1997, 11).

Vietnam has been able to prevent the erosion of state authority with respect to its dealings with the major powers. Vietnam has shored up its bilateral relations with China and the United States. Vietnam has not only worked to develop bilateral ties with the CLM states, but also has initiated cooperation among the three Indochinese states. Vietnam has played a blocking role in trying to prevent any modification of the principle of nonintervention. These efforts have resulted in an informal caucus of politically closed states within ASEAN designed to uphold juridical sovereignty in sensitive political matters. In sum, Vietnamese state authorities have used both domestic reform and an open-door foreign policy to strengthen the state.

References

Amer, Ramses. 1999. Conflict management and constructive engagement in ASEAN's expansion. *Third World Quarterly* 20(5): 1031–49.

———. 2001. Vietnam's integration into the Southeast Asian region. In *Vietnam, regional integration and the Asian financial crisis: Vietnamese and European perspectives*. Edited by Martin Großheim and

J. H. Vincent Houben. Passau: Department of Southeast Asian Studies, University of Passau, 73–98.

Bowles, Paul. 1997. ASEAN, AFTA and the "new regionalism." *Pacific Affairs* 70(2): 219–33.

Bui Tin. 1995. *Following Ho Chi Minh: Memoirs of a North Vietnamese colonel*. London: Hurst & Company.

Clarke, Gerard. 2001. The social challenges of reform: Restructuring state-owned enterprises in Vietnam. Paper presented at the Third European Conference on South-East Asian Studies (EUROSEAS), September 6–8 (London).

Dang Duc Dam. 1997. *Vietnam's macro-economy and types of enterprises: The current position and future prospects*. Hanoi: The Gioi Publishers.

Dauvergne, Peter. (ed.). 1998. *Weak and strong states in Asia-Pacific societies*. St. Leonards: Allen & Unwin.

Doan Manh Giao. 1995. Why Vietnam joins ASEAN. Paper presented at the international seminar on Vietnam and ASEAN: Business Prospects and Policy Directions (Kuala Lumpur).

Fforde, Adam. 2004a. *State owned enterprises, law and a decade of market-oriented socialist development in Vietnam*. Hong Kong: City University of Hong Kong, Southeast Asia Research Centre, Working Papers Series No. 70.

———. 2004b. *Vietnamese state owned enterprises: "Real property," commercial performance and political economy*. Hong Kong: City University of Hong Kong, Southeast Asia Research Centre, Working Papers Series No. 69.

Flatters, Frank. 1997. Vietnam and AFTA: By choice or obligation? United Nations Development Program, Promoting Vietnam's Integration with ASEAN Project VIE/95/015. Hanoi: Bureau of the National Committee for ASEAN, Office of the Government of Vietnam.

Guina, Carolina S. 1997. Vietnam's integration into ASEAN: The challenges of institutional processes and transformations. United Nations Development Program, Promoting Vietnam's Integration with ASEAN Project VIE/95/015. Hanoi: Bureau of the National Committee for ASEAN, Office of the Government of Vietnam.

Hoang Anh Tuan. 1993. Why hasn't Vietnam gained ASEAN membership. *Contemporary Southeast Asia* 15(3): 280–92.

Keohane, Robert O. 1990. Multilateralism: An agenda for research. *International Journal* 45: 731–64.

Krasner, Stephen, D. 1999. *Sovereignty: Organized hypocrisy*. Princeton: Princeton University Press.

———. (ed.). 2001. *Problematic sovereignty: Contested rules and political possibilities*. New York: Columbia University Press.

Lao-Araya, Kanokpan. 2003. How can Cambodia, Laos, Myanmar and Vietnam cope with revenue lost due to AFTA tariff reductions? *Asia-Pacific Tax Bulletin* 58–73.

Mahani, Zainal-Abidin. 2002. ASEAN integration: At risk of going in different directions. *The World Economy* 25(9): 1263–77.

McCarty, Adam. 2006. Vietnam: Economic update 2006 and prospects to 2010. Paper presented at the Institute of Southeast Asian Studies Regional Outlook Forum 2006 (Singapore).

Migdal, Joel. 1988. *Strong societies and weak states: State-society relations and state capabilities in the Third World*. Princeton: Princeton University Press.

Nguyen Dy Nien. 1996. Tiep tuc doi moi va mo cua vi su nghiep cong nghiep hoa, hien dai hoa dat nuoc. *Tap chi Cong san (Communist Review)* 12: 46–9.

Nguyen Hong Thao. 2000. Vietnam and the Code of Conduct for the South China Sea. *Ocean Development & International Law* 32: 105–30.

———. 2003. The 2002 Declaration of the Conduct of Parties in the South China Sea: A note. *Ocean Development & International Law* 34: 279–85.

Nguyen Manh Cam. 1995. Gia tri lau ben va dinh huong nhat quan. In *Hoi nhap quoc te va giu vung ban sac*. Edited by Ministry of Foreign Affairs (Bo Ngoai Giao). Hanoi: Nha xuat ban chinh tri quoc tgiae, 223–30.

Nguyen Manh Hung. 2004. Vietnam: Facing the challenge of integration. In *Southeast Asian Affairs 2004*. Edited by Daljit Singh and Chin Kin Wah. Singapore: Institute of Southeast Asian Studies, 297–311.

Nguyen Phuong Binh and Luan Thuy Duong. 2001. Expectations and experiences of the new members: A Vietnamese perspective. In *Reinventing ASEAN*. Edited by Simon S. C. Tay, Jesus P. Estanislao and Hadi Soesastro. Singapore: Institute of Southeast Asian Studies, 185–205.

Nguyen Vu Tung. 2002. Vietnam-ASEAN co-operation after the Cold War and the continued search for a theoretical framework. *Contemporary Southeast Asia* 24(1): 106–21.

Nguyen Xuan Thang. 1998. AFTA and ASEAN foreign direct investment in Vietnam. In *ASEAN today and tomorrow*. Edited by Institute of Southeast Asian Studies, National Centre for Social Sciences and Humanities. Hanoi: National Political Publishing House, 190–204.

Nischalke, Tobias. 2002. Does ASEAN measure up? Post-Cold War diplomacy and the idea of regional community. *The Pacific Review* 15(1): 89–117.

Painter, Martin. 2003. The politics of economic restructuring in Vietnam: The case of state-owned enterprise "reform." *Contemporary Southeast Asia* 25(1): 20–43.

Pham Cao Phong. 1996. Trends. *Business Times*, June 29–30, 1996.

Pham Quoc Tru. 2003. Thuc tran va trien vong cua trinh lien ket kinh te ASEAN. *Tap chi Cong san (Communist Review)* 34: 59–62.

Phan Doan Nam. 2003. Mau thuan va phuong thuc giai quyet mau thuan trong quan he quoc ten gay nay. *Tap chi Cong san (Communist Review)* 30: 52–8.

Phan Minh Ngoc, Nguyen Thi Phuong Anh and Phan Thuy Nga. 2003. Exports and long-run growth in Vietnam, 1975–2001. *ASEAN Economic Bulletin* 20(3): 211–32.

Phan Thanh Ha. 2001. The Vietnamese economy and the Asian financial crisis—Problems and perspectives. In *Vietnam, regional integration and the Asian financial crisis: Vietnamese and European perspectives*. Edited by Martin Großheim and J. H. Vincent Houben. Passau: Department of Southeast Asian Studies, University of Passau, 111–30.

Quan Xuan Dinh, 2000. The Political economy of Vietnam's transformation process. *Contemporary Southeast Asia* 22(2): 360–88.

Ramasamy, Bala. 1996. The second enlargement of ASEAN: The inclusion of Vietnam. *ASEAN Economies* 25(2): 29–47.

Ruggie, John. 1992. Multilateralism: The anatomy of an institution. *International Organization* 46(3): 566–68.

Schwartz, Adam. 1995. Joining the fold. *Far Eastern Economic Review*, March 16, 1995.

Setboonsarng, Suthad. 1996. Vietnam in AFTA: Towards cooperation for mutual benefits. *AFTA Reader (vol. 4), The Fifth ASEAN Summit*. Edited by the ASEAN Secretariat. Jakarta: ASEAN Secretariat, 36–8.

Thayer, Carlyle A. 1999a. Reinventing ASEAN: From constructive engagement to flexible intervention. *Harvard Asia Pacific Review* 3(2): 67–70.

———. 1999b. Vietnamese foreign policy: Multilateralism and the threat of peaceful evolution. In *Vietnamese foreign policy in transition*. Edited by Carlyle A. Thayer and Ramses Amer. Singapore: Institute of Southeast Asian Studies, 1–24.

———. 2000a. Demobilization but not disarmament—Personnel reduction and force modernization in Vietnam. In *War force to work force: Global perspectives on demobilization and reintegration*. Edited by Natalie Pauwels. Baden-Baden: Nomos Verlagsgesellshaft, 199–219.

Thayer, Carlyle A. 2000b. New fault lines in ASEAN? *Asia-Pacific Defence Reporter* 26(9): 26–7.

Thayer, Carlyle A. 2001. Vietnam's integration into the region and the Asian financial crisis. In *Vietnam, regional integration and the Asian financial crisis: Vietnamese and European perspectives*. Edited by Martin Großheim and J. H. Vincent Houben. Passau: Department of Southeast Asian Studies, University of Passau, 17–53.

———. 2002. Vietnamese perspectives of the "China threat." In *The China threat: Perceptions, myths and reality*. Edited by Herbert Yee and Ian James Storey. London: RoutledgeCurzon, 265–87.

———. 2003. China's "new security concept" and Southeast Asia. In *Asia-Pacific security: Policy challenges*. Edited by David W. Lovell. Singapore: Institute of Southeast Asian Studies, 89–107.

———. 2004. Southeast Asia's marred miracle. *Current History* 103(672): 177–82.

Tran Phuong Lan. 2004. Viet Nam voi "Y tuong Cong dong kinh te ASEAN" cua ASEAN. *Tap chi Cong san (Communist Review)* 16: 75–9.

Truong Giang Long. 1997. Mot so van de trong qua trinh ho nhap Viet Nam–ASEAN. *Tap chi Cong san (Communist Review)* 3: 57–9.

Vo Thi Thanh Loc. 2001. *The AFTA impact on Vietnam's economy*. Antwerp: Centre for ASEAN Studies, Centre for International Management and Development, Discussion Paper No. 35.

Vu Khoan. 1998. Vietnam two years after joining ASEAN: Opportunities and challenges, In *ASEAN today and tomorrow*. Edited by Institute of Southeast Asian Studies, National Centre for Social Sciences and Humanities. Hanoi: National Political Publishing House, 17–23.

Vu Quoc Ngu. 2003a. SOE equitization in Vietnam: Experiences, achievements, and challenges. In *Southeast Asian affairs 2003*. Edited by Daljit Singh and Chin Kin Wah. Singapore: Institute of Southeast Asian Studies, 327–38.

———. 2003b. Total factor productivity growth of industrial state-owned enterprises in Vietnam, 1976–98. *ASEAN Economic Bulletin* 20(2): 158–73.

Wattanapruttipaisan, Thitapha. 2003. ASEAN-China Free Trade Area: Advantages, challenges, and implications for the newer ASEAN member countries. *ASEAN Economic Bulletin* 20(1): 31–48.

World Bank. 2002. Strong fundamentals to the fore: Regional overview. East Asia Update, East Asia and the Pacific Region. Washington, DC: The World Bank.

CHAPTER THREE

Testing the Institutionalist Approach
Cooperation between Vietnam and ASEAN

NGUYEN VU TUNG

In essence, liberal institutionalists posit that international institutions and organizations help promote international cooperation, especially in economic fields, because they have the institutional staying power to influence states' decisions and behaviors as well as the functional capability to facilitate cooperation (Krasner 1983; Keohane 1984). In terms of policymaking, a country's decision to join an international organization may depend, to a large extent, on the policymakers' awareness of its functions and organizational and institutional frameworks, its principles, rules, and procedures, as well as the rights and responsibilities of members. In addition, national leaders have to take actual steps to harmonize state policies with those of the organization by adjusting domestic arrangements, establishing new bodies, and adopting new norms, principles, and rules upheld by the organization, thus facilitating the type of cooperation that the organization seeks to promote.

A liberal institutionalist explanation for the Vietnam-ASEAN relationship, therefore, might look like this: when Hanoi officially started the reform process in 1986, it recognized the close linkage between the ASEAN membership and economic developments in the individual member countries, as well as the organization's significant prestige in the international arena and its "viability and vitality" (IIR 1995a, 49). Hanoi thought that by joining ASEAN, it would take advantage of the organization's existing institutional arrangements, which have been seen as one of the "most successful experiments in regionalism in the developing world," (Acharya 1993, 3) to ensure peace and development in Vietnam.

But from the mainstream (i.e., Western) liberal institutionalist point of view, ASEAN is not an exemplary model of an international organization that has strong institutional frameworks. Among other things, ASEAN is a loose organization and its decisions, which are made by consensus, are not legally binding (Johnston 1999; Kahler 2000; Weatherbee 2005).[1] In addition, as others have pointed out, ASEAN cooperation is not a type of collective defense or collective security (Job 1992; Collins 2000; Morrison and Seosatro 2001). Moreover, ASEAN has not been instrumental in supporting economic development in Vietnam, and as the 1997 financial crisis unfolded, ASEAN and its member countries had serious economic problems. This leads to a key question: What had Hanoi known about the organizational structures and institutional arrangements of ASEAN, about its principles and norms, its cooperative projects, and especially its limitations before it decided to join the organization?

The answer to this question may clarify several points. For example, if it had believed that ASEAN had serious economic and security limitations, Hanoi might have been more unwilling to consider membership; or if ASEAN were of supranational nature, Hanoi might have been more reluctant to join; and if it was not easy to understand the organizational structure of ASEAN and its working procedures, as well as that membership entailed some major political and economic changes, the decision to join ASEAN, the process of joining, and adjusting to the new cooperative environment might have been longer. In short, this chapter examines if Hanoi had understood ASEAN well before it decided to join, and to what extent this understanding of ASEAN contributed to the decision in favor of, the subsequent preparations for, Vietnam's membership in ASEAN, and their implications to Vietnam-ASEAN relations today. In other words, by understanding the process of decision making and institutional arrangements related to Vietnam-ASEAN cooperation, this chapter attempts to analyze and test the logic of the liberal institutionalist position, with Vietnam and ASEAN as a case study (Nguyen Vu Tung 2002, 82–105).

Joining ASEAN: The Chronology

By mid-June 1991, certain of ASEAN's positive stance, Hanoi decided and made public statements that it was ready to accede to the Treaty of Amity and Cooperation in Southeast Asia (TAC, or the Bali Treaty). On September 16, 1991, Foreign Minister Nguyen Manh Cam sent the official letter to his ASEAN counterparts expressing Vietnam's readiness to accede to the Bali Treaty and confirming that this was one of the first steps toward the eventual membership in ASEAN. On October 15, in an interview with the Thai daily *The Nation*, Nguyen Manh Cam said, "If invited, Vietnam is ready to take part in the AMM [ASEAN Ministerial Meetings]." On October 21, Prime Minister Vo Van Kiet told the *Bangkok Post*, "Vietnam wants to join ASEAN." On October 31, Deputy Foreign Minister Vu Khoan said in Singapore, "Vietnam wishes to be an ASEAN member" (IIR 1995b, 17; Thayer 2004, 2–5).

As a senior Vietnamese diplomat recalled in an interview with the author in 2003, following the fourth ASEAN Summit in January 1992 that officially welcomed Vietnam's accession to the Bali Treaty, the Political Bureau of the Communist Party of Vietnam (CPV) sent a note to the Ministry of Foreign Affairs (MOFA) on February 25, 1992, giving a formal green light to the accession, and the Ministry's work immediately focused on preparations to join the organization. On May 20, 1992, Foreign Minister Nguyen Manh Cam sent a letter to ASEAN counterparts expressing the hope that Vietnam could become an ASEAN observer following its accession to the Bali Treaty. In June, MOFA had to coordinate with other ministries to work out plans for further cooperation with ASEAN in the capacity of an ASEAN observer. In the second week of July, before the AMM, MOFA finalized the documents for the Vietnamese delegation to the meeting. On July 22, 1992, at the twenty-fifth AMM in Manila, Vietnam, and Laos became parties to the Bali Treaty and observers to ASEAN. It was clear that Vietnam and ASEAN did not want the observer status to last indefinitely: observer status was the first step to eventual full membership in ASEAN. Therefore, the most important question of membership was not "whether," but "when and how."

To become an ASEAN member, however, was not an immediate step. There was a common understanding in Hanoi that it would take time before Vietnam could become a full-fledged member. On October 18, 1991, Prime Minister Vo Van Kiet told the *Bangkok Post* that Vietnam should improve bilateral relations with individual ASEAN members while Hanoi studied the "suitable forms and scope of relations with ASEAN." On October 31, Deputy Foreign Minister Vu Khoan said in Singapore that "Vietnam wishes to become an ASEAN member. Following the accession to the Bali Treaty, Vietnam hopes to take part in the annual ASEAN AMM. It, however, will take a long time before Vietnam would become an official member of ASEAN" (IIR 1995b, 17). In June 1992, the CPV Third Central Committee Plenum adopted a resolution that said in part, "For the time being, we accede to the Bali Treaty, [and] take part in dialogues with ASEAN. We should at the same time actively seek ways to further expand relations with ASEAN in the future" (Vu Duong Huan, et al. 2002, 138). And according to a MOFA Asia-2 Department official interviewed in 2003, by the end of October 1992, when MOFA sought the Political Bureau's opinion on the membership issue, the Political Bureau instructed that the Ministry should "continue to do more research."

In 1993, work continued on the question of ASEAN membership. On February 19, 1993 the Political Bureau instructed MOFA, "As an observer, we should select some cooperative projects in ASEAN and actively take part in them to gain knowledge and experience national construction and development and for full participation in ASEAN in the future. When ASEAN reaches a consensus on Vietnam's membership, we should be ready to join ASEAN as a full-fledged member" (Vu Duong Ninh 2003, 20).

In an article carried in the Central Committee's main theoretical journal, *Tap chi Cong san* (*Communist Review*) in April 1993 to explain the new direction of Vietnamese foreign policy outlined by the CPV's June 1992 Third Central Committee Plenum, Foreign Minister Nguyen Manh Cam wrote: "Vietnam should push the relationship with regional countries by integrating itself into the region," and stressed that "with Vietnam having acceded to the TAC and becoming an ASEAN observer, Vietnam's relations with ASEAN countries and ASEAN as an organization have achieved an important step." Yet he did not mention Vietnam's membership in ASEAN (Nguyen Manh Cam 1995, 161–3). During Party General Secretary Do Muoi's October 1993 visit to Malaysia, Singapore, and Thailand, he restated Vietnam's four-point ASEAN policy and officially said that "Vietnam plans to improve multi-sided relations with all individual ASEAN member states and with ASEAN as a regional organization. Vietnam is ready to join ASEAN at the appropriate time" (Do Muoi 1993).

These statements indicated that Hanoi was still uncertain as to whether ASEAN was ready to accept it as a member. They also showed a general understanding in Hanoi that it would take between five and ten years for Vietnam to learn the ASEAN principles, rules, and decision-making procedures as well as to be better aware of the members' rights and obligations before joining ASEAN. The general idea was that more research on ASEAN should be conducted before making the final decision on membership, and that Hanoi should consider observer status as "an active apprenticeship" to get well acquainted with the ASEAN processes before becoming a regular member (IIR 1991; Nguyen Vu Tung 1994a).

Thus, at that time, the general mood in Hanoi was that Hanoi should adopt a gradual approach with regard to the membership issue. Many believed that the ASEAN Way was new, and Hanoi had little experience with it. Nguyen Vu Tung (1994b) wrote,

> It took 30 years for ASEAN to develop the habit of building consensus among its members, thus forming "an ASEAN spirit" or "a state of mind" which helped turn ASEAN into a forum for enhanced cooperation and confidence building. Yet, consensus building is time-consuming and involves compromises. Therefore, the ASEAN spirit requires, among other things, sophistication, diplomatic skills, and great patience to handle difficulties and disputes and promote cooperation. (35–6)

Another researcher even went further with the argument that the ASEAN Way was in fact a challenge for Hanoi. According to him, Hanoi was more familiar with the "quick fix approach" to problems and therefore tended to resort to force in solving disputes. This approach to regional issues ran counter to the ASEAN Way that emphasizes gradualism, and the ASEAN principle that upholds nonuse of force in international relations. Therefore, it would be a long time before Hanoi could learn and act in accordance with the ASEAN principles and norms. He then suggested that Vietnam membership in ASEAN should not be immediate and would greatly depend on the learning process Hanoi was embarking upon (Hoang Anh Tuan 1996).

But by 1994, it turned out that Hanoi wanted early admission to ASEAN. In April 1994, during an official visit to Indonesia, Vietnamese President Le Duc Anh said that "Vietnam is taking concrete steps to gain . . . early membership in ASEAN" (IIR 1995b). Hanoi was now trying to find out whether ASEAN had reached a consensus on the exact timing of its membership. At the twenty-seventh AMM held in Bangkok in July 1994, ASEAN countries stated that ASEAN would welcome Vietnam to be the seventh member and the timing would be ideally before the ASEAN Summit to be held by the end of 1995. Upon receiving this information, on July 22, 1994, the Political Bureau held a meeting and concluded that Vietnam should join ASEAN in 1995 (Vu Duong Ninh 2003, 22; Vu Thi Mai 2004, 49). Giving an interview to *Nhan Dan* on July 29, Foreign Minister Nguyen Manh Cam said, "the common understanding reached during the AMM meeting was that Vietnam will be a full member of ASEAN in 1995" (Nguyen Manh Cam 1994). On October 17, 1994, Foreign Minister Nguyen Manh Cam sent a letter to his Brunei counterpart, who was then serving as Chairman of the ASEAN Standing Committee to officially request that ASEAN admit Vietnam as a member at the twenty-eighth AMM to be held in Brunei in July 1995. Vietnam became a new member of ASEAN on July 22, 1995, three years after it gained observer status and one year after the Political Bureau decided to join ASEAN.

Hasty Preparations

A MOFA official told the author in 2003 that in July 1994 "there [was] a high consensus among ASEAN countries on Vietnam's membership in ASEAN. Yet, they [had] not reached an agreement on the timing. For our part, we [were] not totally ready." When Hanoi actually started the preparations for becoming an ASEAN member after the July 1994 decision, the admission ceremony was just one year away. And as a result little could be done. In institutional terms, the ASEAN Department of the Ministry of Foreign Affairs was established in September 1994. Its initial staff included only 10 persons. Other ministries also set up ASEAN units or divisions. Nguyen Van Dam, a senior official in the Cabinet Office, told the author that by the end of 1994, the Prime Minister ordered the formation of an ASEAN Unit in the Cabinet Office to keep him informed about ASEAN-related issues and assist him in directing these activities (Nguyen Van Dam 2003). In terms of capacity building, one of the most important activities was to provide Vietnamese officials with English language and other skills to work in the multilateral context. About 300 government officials were taking short intensive English courses, out of which 100 were trained abroad. According to Dam, the most important criterion for selecting the staff of the ASEAN Unit was fluency in English.

In addition, the MOFA ASEAN Department published the first ASEAN guidebook to introduce ASEAN to the public at large. Only several months before the admission, the national television and radio networks started to publicize ASEAN among the public. Although Hanoi stated that under time constraints it could set up a "basic and important infrastructure" for taking part in ASEAN cooperation, one must say that the institutional preparations were made in a "hectic and hasty" manner and the results were modest (Do Ngoc Son 2000). And according to "talking points" prepared by MOFA for Vietnam's national leaders, after admission Hanoi still faced the personnel problem as it stressed that "for the sake of effective cooperation in ASEAN, Vietnam needs a contingent of officials who are fluent in English and possess a profound knowledge to work within ASEAN institutions. To train such a contingent is an urgent task for us" (Nguyen Van Dam 2003).

Nguyen Van Dam also told the author that other institutions, including the ASEAN Unit in the Cabinet Office, were dependent on MOFA's knowledge about ASEAN. It seemed, however, that even MOFA was not ready to provide sufficient knowledge on ASEAN. As a MOFA official recalled, in February 1992, the Political Bureau instructed MOFA to conduct further research and prepare policy suggestions for the Political Bureau on the question of membership. It insisted in October 1992 that more research should be done before the membership question could be addressed. By that time, however, MOFA had not produced any comprehensive study on ASEAN. More importantly, serious efforts to conduct such studies were made only after the question of membership became salient. For example, in February 1993, Hanoi stated that it would join ASEAN at an appropriate time; but it was not until March that Deputy Foreign Minister Tran Quang Co signed the MOFA 1993 Research Program that instructed departments and units concerned to identify issues related to ASEAN cooperation, such as modes of association with ASEAN including the associate-member and full-member forms of status. This Program listed the following specific objectives:

- to find out about the organizational and institutional structures of ASEAN, the modes of ASEAN operation, and the interests and obligations connected with the full-fledged membership;
- to clarify the advantages and disadvantages in the Vietnam–ASEAN relations with a view to identify potentialities and limitations in Vietnam–ASEAN interaction;
- to list the ASEAN existing cooperative projects and those that Vietnam would be able to participate as observer; and
- to list the advantages and disadvantages for Vietnam to cooperate in ASEAN as an associate member and as a full member (IIR 1993, 2).

MOFA Research Program revealed that even the Foreign Ministry, Hanoi's primary ASEAN watcher, was not quite clear about the basic facts of ASEAN and the suitable modes of association with it. In other words, research on ASEAN seemed to have lagged behind political decisions. As a result, ASEAN remained something "very new" to many policymakers when the ASEAN Department was established in October 1994, according to the Department's first Director (Vu Khoan 1998, 16; Do Ngoc Son 2000, 33).

At the national level, efforts to establish the Vietnam's Association for Southeast Asian Studies (ASEAS) were launched in July 1994. The Association's tasks—laid out in the Draft Charter—included "coordinating . . . studies on political, economic, and cultural development in Southeast Asia, [and] modes of Vietnam-ASEAN relations . . . thus providing State and Party offices with professional and academic consultation, reviews and appraisals on all matters related toward the region and Vietnam's policies toward the region." On July 7, 1994, Nguyen Duy Quy, director of the National Center for Social Sciences and Humanities, signed the official document sponsoring the association. On November 20, 1994, the proposal for ASEAS was sent to the Government Office to get the Prime Minister's approval. ASEAS was officially established in 1996.

As early as January 1992, there were suggestions that Hanoi should form fact-finding missions to ASEAN countries to have a better understanding of modes and mechanisms for intra-ASEAN cooperation, and possibilities for Vietnam to take part in ASEAN. The first high-ranking delegation, consisting departmental-level officials of the Cabinet Office, MOFA, Ministry of Trade (MOT), Ministry of Finance (MOF), and the State Planning Commission and headed by Deputy Foreign Minister Vu Khoan, visited all ASEAN countries and the ASEAN Secretariat from October 3 to 14, 1994. A MOT official told the author in 2003 that "[t]he study tour is of practical significance while we are preparing for joining ASEAN. With what we have learnt, we do now better understand the nature of ASEAN cooperation, and this provides us with a clearer idea about the next steps [proceeding toward full-fledged membership of ASEAN]."

Just two weeks before Vietnam was officially admitted to ASEAN, institutional efforts to study ASEAN seemed to move into higher gear. On July 8, 1995 two study groups were set up. The first group, consisting of officials from MOFA, MOT, Cabinet Office, General Department of Customs, and State Planning Commission, was to conduct studies on AFTA and Vietnam's participation in AFTA schemes.

The second group, consisting of officials from MOFA, Ministry of Public Security (MPS), and the Cabinet Office, was to conduct studies on visa-related issues for citizens of ASEAN countries. The tasks assigned to these two groups included organization of in-depth study and research with a view to showing the advantages and disadvantages for Vietnam as a member of ASEAN, and submitting policy suggestions. In addition, in January 1996, the ASEAN National Committee (ANC) Office placed a request with the National Center for Social Sciences and Humanities to conduct research on ASEAN and AFTA with a view to providing the ANC with more information, analyses, and policy suggestions regarding a host of issues the ANC had to deal with (ANC 1996, 4).

Thus, Hanoi began to study about ASEAN, its institutions, and working procedures and to set up institutions in Vietnam to manage Vietnam-ASEAN cooperation largely *after* a decision had been taken by the leadership to join the organization. In other words, Hanoi's understanding of ASEAN institutions and operating systems may have facilitated the steps taken to join ASEAN cooperation, but was not instrumental in bringing about Hanoi's decision to join ASEAN. And how detailed Hanoi's understanding of ASEAN was prior to the eventual accession is still open to doubt.

Post-Admission Awareness and Adjustments
of Domestic Institutions

Developments that led to membership in July 1995 indicated that the decision to join ASEAN was made in the absence of a detailed understanding of ASEAN mechanisms and processes, especially those related to economic cooperation. The postadmission period also showed that the adjustments of existing domestic institutional arrangements, the establishment of new institutions in Vietnam to promote cooperation with ASEAN, and Vietnam's actual participation in cooperative undertakings were of a somewhat reactive and ad hoc nature.

Personnel

Hanoi continued to know little about ASEAN systems and procedures even after it joined the organization. A report of the ASEAN National Committee's (ANC) second meeting on January 20, 1996 said: "Ministries and other institutions in Vietnam do not have sufficient information on the way ASEAN system works and performs its activities, both in general and in specific fields." Even the ANC Office "lacks information," according to the report (ANC 1996, 10–14). After joining ASEAN, Hanoi sent two departmental-rank officials to work in the ASEAN Secretariat in Jakarta to "further study the ASEAN systems and report to the ANC and MOFA" (ANC 1995, 5). But one of the two officials complained to the author in 2002 that they were assigned by the ASEAN Secretariat to work on "issues of low politics, including drug trafficking and prostitution." Hanoi was informed of only about one-fourth of the approximately 300 ASEAN meetings held in 1996. Due to short notice and financial constraints, in 1996, Hanoi could only attend about 30 meetings (ANC 1996, 2). The opportunities to learn firsthand what the ASEAN systems and procedures were, therefore, quite limited. Although having started earlier, the learning process through Vietnam's participation in ASEAN functional cooperation did not go well either. Starting from 1994 Hanoi participated in six ASEAN functional cooperation projects. In a two-year review of the participation in ASEAN functional cooperation, the ASEAN National Secretariat said,

> Our participation in this type of cooperation remained passive and reactive. When attending ASEAN conferences and meetings, our officials for most of the time sat quietly and failed to participate in the discussions. We failed to put forth new ideas, initiatives, and projects for the promotion of cooperation. The reasons for this include our limited knowledge and understanding of ASEAN and its cooperation, our officials' lack of knowledge and skills to work in multilateral settings, as well as institutional and financial constraints. In addition, we sometimes failed to assign the proper officials to attend ASEAN meetings and did not have a specialized staff to supervise the implementation of projects. Above all, however, fluency in English still remains a major problem. (ANC 1997, 7)

In a November 1999 report, MOFA suggested that "[r]egular courses should be conducted to improve the knowledge and skills of the officials who work on ASEAN-related issues. Knowledge about ASEAN decision-making procedures, capacity to propose and implement cooperative projects, and English skills are most needed in order to ensure our effective and beneficial participation in ASEAN" (MOFA 1999a, 14). In short, it seemed that at least in terms of personnel, Hanoi was not prepared to take a more active and greater part in ASEAN cooperation.

Institutional Arrangements

Virtually all the institutional arrangements to coordinate ASEAN-related activities in Vietnam were made after Hanoi had decided to join ASEAN. And the process of institutional adjustment was also reactive. On October 6, 1995, the Vietnamese Prime Minister issued a directive *On the Effective Participation in ASEAN Cooperation* that instructed units of the government

(1) to set up within ministries and ministerial-level government agencies ASEAN Units and/or Departments, which consist of skilled and English-fluent officials, to implement ASEAN-related activities in the specific fields, (2) to set up the ASEAN National Committee (ANC) within the Cabinet Office to coordinate Vietnam's cooperation in ASEAN at the national level, (3) to assign to the MOFA ASEAN Department the task to serve as the ASEAN National Secretariat (ANS) to report on the ASEAN-related activities in Vietnam and to give adequate information about ASEAN activities, programs, and projects to the ANC through the ANC Office. (*Cong Bao* 1995a)

On October 10, 1995, the Vietnamese Prime Minister signed a decision to establish the ANC, to be led by a Deputy Prime Minister and with the principal functions of "assisting the Prime Minister to direct Vietnam-ASEAN relations on security, political, economic, cultural, and scientific-technological fields and to coordinate ASEAN-related activities at the national level" (*Cong Bao* 1995b). The ANC was headed by the then Deputy Prime Minister Tran Duc Luong.

Snags soon developed in the division of labor among the newly established institutions. For example, the second ANC report dated January 20, 1996 revealed that MOT, MOF, and to a lesser extent, the General Department of Customs had disagreements concerning responsibilities over AFTA-related activities (ANC 1996, 11–12), due to the ambiguity in a November 1995 decision by the Prime Minister that put finance in charge of AFTA and trade in charge of economic and trade relations with ASEAN (*Cong Bao* 1995c). As a result, the ANC report suggested, "[i]ndividual ministries and ministerial-level agencies should be allowed to take the initiative in working out plans of action with regard to specific ASEAN-related activities. At the same time, more coordinating work should be done to avoid overlapping responsibilities between and among government agencies and to encourage officials to take a proactive approach in their work" (ANC 1996, 15).

These disputes reflect a greater confusion that pervaded the institutional arrangements and bureaucratic mechanisms in Vietnam, and in this case the principal victim, ironically, was the ANC. Nguyen Van Dam explained why the ANC was established: Prime Minister Vo Van Kiet, among others, was aware that ASEAN cooperation, especially in trade and investment, did not involve empty promises but concrete commitments and strict implementation, and this required a well-coordinated performance of the bureaucracy. He was also aware of the state of compartmentalization among government units. Therefore, the formation of the ANC (headed by a Deputy Prime Minister and staffed by members of the Cabinet Office) would be ideal to overcome poor coordination and institutional inertia (Nguyen Van Dam 2003). The initial outcomes, according to Dam, were encouraging. For example, the ANC could "force" the General Department for Customs and the General Department of Statistics to complete the work of converting the 6-digit coding system for taxation into the 8-digit one in accordance with the ASEAN system. Between 1993 and 1995, the two agencies worked on this project and completed only half the job. But the ANC, invoking Vietnam's AFTA commitments and making use of the Deputy Prime Minister's power, exerted influence on them and the rest of the job was completed within four months (ANC 1995, 3).

Yet after three years of existence, the ANC "died without a death certificate," according to Dam. On February 10, 1998, the new Prime Minister Phan Van Khai issued Decision No. 31/1998/QD-TTg to establish the National Committee for International Economic Cooperation (NCIEC), whose principal tasks were to assist the Prime Minister in coordinating and directing activities by ministries, ministerial-level agencies, and provincial authorities with regard to ASEAN, ASEM, APEC, WTO, and other international and regional economic and trade organizations (MOFA 1999b, 256). According to Dam, "the ANC turf" now overlapped with that of the NCIEC, which had greater power. Therefore, following the birth of the NCIEC, "the ANC gradually became powerless, and just existed on paper" (Nguyen Van Dam 2003).

There have been several explanations for this institutional confusion. According to Dam, the establishment of the NCIEC was due to the need to streamline the Cabinet Office. As a result, the actual division of labor with regard to ASEAN-related activities was redefined. Because the Ministry of Trade's Multilateral Trade Department now became the supporting staff for the NCIEC, issues related to economic relations with ASEAN were within the responsibility of the Ministry of Trade. The Foreign Ministry, and the Ministry of Public Security to a lesser extent, could maintain their responsibilities with respect to political and security cooperation with ASEAN and directly report to the CPV Political Bureau and the CPV Standing Committee. In addition, as Hanoi intensified its negotiations with the WTO, its activities in APEC, ASEAN, and AFTA became a lesser focus even in the NCIEC. Dam concluded that the compartmentalization of ASEAN-related activities became even greater.

In an interview with the author in 2003, an official of the MOFA ASEAN Department seemed to agree with Dam's compartmentalization thesis. According to that official, the MOFA ASEAN Department also de facto ceased to serve as the ASEAN National Secretariat (ANS), because other ministries and government agencies stopped reporting to the ANS "after they had established direct contacts with their ASEAN counterparts and thus felt that they did not need instructions." Reacting in part to this, an ANC report said that "the Government should make it clear that cooperation with ASEAN is the undertaking of the whole society, not just those of specific ministries or units within ministries" (ANC 1996, 13). Dam, however, insisted that "the ANC's death" and the growing compartmentalization of the bureaucracy harmed Vietnam-ASEAN cooperation in the absence of the lack of a coordinating body at the national level that could ensure the provision of "public goods" for ASEAN-related activities (Nguyen Van Dam 2003).

By the end of 1999, concerns over the lack of efficient personnel and institutional arrangements for ASEAN-related activities remained as they were before July 1995. A MOFA report in November said "[w]e are still in need of skilled officials, funds, and coordinating institutions for the promotion of cooperation in ASEAN" (MOFA 1999a, 12). By the end of 2002, the Government also acknowledged "the state of unprepared-ness in terms of personnel, legal and institutional frame-works, and coordination at both central and provincial levels has obstructed the promotion of Vietnam's international relations in general and with ASEAN in particular" (Report of the Government 2002, 9–10). In short, it became clear that Hanoi was not fully aware of the ASEAN structures as well as its procedures before joining it. The knowledge was not improved much thereafter. Vietnam's actual performance in ASEAN, including the initiation, appraisal, and implementation of cooperative projects, was further hindered by the lack of efficient personnel, funds, and the confusion in institutional arrangements.

Vietnam and AFTA

Vietnam's participation in the AFTA scheme clearly illustrated the above-mentioned state of unpreparedness. By January 2003, when AFTA began to take effect partially in Vietnam, Hanoi was not fully aware of its opportunities and challenges for the economy in general and for businesses in particular. Joining ASEAN, Vietnam had to participate in AFTA, which basically required that by 2003 ASEAN member countries should apply Common Effective Preferences Tariffs (CEPT) by reducing the tariffs to between 0% and 5% for intra-ASEAN trade. Due to Vietnam's low level of economic development, the twenty-seventh ASEAN Economic Ministers' Meeting (AEM) agreed that Vietnam would begin to implement CEPT by 2006. These timetables were adjusted during the sixth ASEAN Summit in 1998 in Hanoi in which ASEAN original members began to fully apply CEPT in 2003. Hanoi also decided to partially implement CEPT in the same year. The reduction of tariffs requires reforms of tax regimes, enhancement of competitiveness, and shifts in investment priorities. Hanoi seemed to be aware of the challenges posed by AFTA. An official position made it clear that "[f]rom now on we have to do our best to enhance the efficiency, productivity, and products' quality with a view to improve the competitiveness of the economy, thus being able to take advantage of economic integration into the region" (MOFA 1999b, 367).

Such slogan-like wording, however, is not sufficient to move the system away from its inertia. Hanoi has been slow on both research and implementation of AFTA. For example, AFTA-related research activities were not conducted even after Vietnam had joined ASEAN. According to a report by the ANC, the Ministry of Finance established a Research Unit on AFTA (RUA) with 12 members representing all the ministries concerned. Yet, by January 1996, when the second ANC meeting was convened, the RUA was still inactive (ANC 1996, 4). In addition, the Ministry of Finance failed to meet the deadline of January 2003 for introducing a new tax regime for 755 types of goods whose import taxes would be cut, along the CEPT line, from 40% to 50% to less than 20%. The new deadline now was July 2003. This delay, according to Le Thi Bang Tam, deputy minister of finance, was due to the fact that finance had failed to prepare the legal and institutional frameworks for the tax cut and the conversion of existing tax regimes applied to about 10,800 tax lines to meet the ASEAN standards (Le Thi Bang Tam 2003).

At the same time, the government has not done enough to raise enterprises' awareness about AFTA. Nguyen Minh Vu, an official of the

Foreign Ministry's Multilateral Economic Cooperation Department, cited a recent survey that indicated that only 25% of Vietnamese enterprises knew about AFTA and the understanding of AFTA by these enterprises were still very poor (Nguyen Minh Vu 2002). Pham Chi Lan, then deputy secretary general of the Vietnam Chamber of Commerce and Industries (VCCI) observed, "I have traveled widely to talk about the pressures of AFTA on Vietnam's economy. Yet, what I found is startling: enterprises still remain idle, blaming the government for the hasty process of joining AFTA and requesting government support" (Pham Chi Lan 2002; Minh Quang 2004). Assessing the level of preparedness on the part of government, Nguyen Hoai Son—an official in the Ministry of Trade's Multilateral Trade Policy Department—said that the plans of actions worked out by the government "were too general and failed to hold departments and ministries concerned accountable for the implementation of AFTA." As a result, when the "moment of truth" arrives, no specific entity has been accounted for the tasks that have been pledged but left undone (Nguyen Hoai Son 2003). Partly due to this low level of preparedness, Vietnam's economy will face great difficulties when AFTA is implemented. According to a Ministry of Finance report, with the reduction of tariffs to less than 20%, 62.5% of Vietnamese enterprises will become uncompetitive in the region. Moreover, if import taxes were reduced to 15% by 2004 and 5% in 2006, many Vietnamese glass, automobile, steel, and electronics producers would have to close down due to their failure to compete on a region-wide basis (Hanh Phuong 2003). In short, bureaucratic inertia and protectionist pressures from state enterprises have prevented preparation for and implementation of AFTA in Vietnam, hampering the progress of the country's economy.

Hanoi alone, however, cannot be blamed for being slow in AFTA-related matters. Justifying the postponement of AFTA implementation for six months, Trade Minister Truong Dinh Tuyen noted, "For AFTA, meeting deadlines in many cases is an act of willingness by individual member states" (Nguyen Hoai Son 2003). In a broader context, what has been lacking in ASEAN is the institutional and legal power that could force member states to adhere to their commitments to the organization's cooperative projects. Even ASEAN scholars have acknowledged that ASEAN lacks viable institutional mechanisms and the force of legality to foster regional cooperation, ironically at a time when proposing cooperative projects in various fields increasingly becomes the habits of ASEAN leaders at their meetings in which initiatives mainly serve the purpose of gaining political scores.[2] A February 2003 draft

Concept Paper on the ASEAN Economic Community prepared by a group of scholars in the Institute of Southeast Asian Studies (ISEAS, Singapore) commented,

> ASEAN still maintains a very loose institutional structure although there has been a strengthening of its institutions in recent years. ASEAN does not presently operate on the overriding principle of using a formal, detailed, and binding institutional structure to prepare, enact, and execute policies for economic integration. The "ASEAN Way" of dialogue is still very much entrenched with *Musyawarah* (discussion and consultation), *Mufakat* (unanimous decision) and Consensus being the *modus operandi* of the organization. (Singapore ISEAS 2003, 9)

The case of Vietnam's membership in ASEAN seems to suggest that the decision to join ASEAN was made in the absence of a detailed understanding of ASEAN's institutional arrangements, and the lack of preparedness in terms of personnel and institutions in Vietnam for this new type of regional cooperation. In fact, when Hanoi became more aware of the loose structures and the accommodating approach of ASEAN, it became more committed to go ahead with the membership issue. That explained why preparations for membership and for Vietnam-ASEAN cooperation could be minimal, (Nguyen Van Dam 2003). Bureaucratic inertia was part of the problem. Yet the ASEAN Way also contributed to this.

The weakness of Vietnamese institutions is no surprise, in view of its state of development. The point, however, is that after a decade of ASEAN membership, little institutional improvements have been achieved and few obstacles to economic cooperation have been removed. And provincial and lower level authorities, agencies, and enterprises are even less prepared for economic integration with ASEAN (*IAW* 2004; *Lao Dong Daily* 2004).

This indicates the weakness of institutionalist arguments: some in Hanoi reasoned that membership in ASEAN and adherence to ASEAN working procedures would force and help Vietnam to further reform domestic institutions and make them more efficient. They optimistically maintained that "although membership in ASEAN has brought about more challenges for Vietnam, it has offered us a valuable opportunity to do our best to reform and to become more mature as we integrate ourselves into the region." This report also stressed that "[m]embership of ASEAN will help us to readjust bureaucratic procedures and working styles so as to be more compatible with international and regional standards" (MOFA 1999a, 11). Others, however, had reservations about joining ASEAN at an early date. They argued that the decision to join ASEAN was not based on a careful study of AFTA and other economic cooperation projects and the implementation of these projects in Vietnam had not been based on institutional and personnel preparedness. As a result, economic integration and association with ASEAN became more problematic as the legal, administrative, and institutional frameworks are still "incomplete and incompatible with regional standards and practices," while businesses are still inactive (MOFA 1999a, 13). Partly reflecting the "revisionist" argument, a government report in late 1997 noted that "[r]egrettably, our knowledge and awareness of the principles, fields of cooperation, and working procedures of the regional organizations that we have to integrate ourselves in are still at the primitive level; in addition to this, interest and efforts by agencies and officials concerned have not been up to the mark" (Report of the Government 1997, 16).

The Ninth Congress of the Communist Party in 2001 also stressed in its resolution that the party should focus its efforts, among other things, on conducting research on foreign affairs, training a competent contingent of officials to work on international affairs, and completing the establishment of mechanisms and frameworks for managing foreign affairs (CPV 2001, 14). According to one analyst, this is an acknowledgment of the weak capacity of the Vietnamese foreign service and the other institutional arrangements that support the country's international relations. These weaknesses are major obstacles to Hanoi's efforts to enhance international and regional cooperation (Nguyen The Luc and Nguyen Hoang Giap 2004, 5–14).

In 2005, the Party acknowledged that the lack of knowledge and consensus on the contents, steps, and stages of economic integration, poor understanding of international market rules and practices, poor management skills, incompatible law and banking systems, red tape, poor infrastructure, out-dated mechanisms, shortage of officials capable for work related to economic integration, and the lack of coordination among state institutions and with local agencies were among the root causes of poor economic performance in Vietnam (CPV 2002, 4–5; 2005, 109–14). At the same time, ASEAN institutional power has not been sufficient in creating external pressures on Vietnam to carry out more radical, legal, and institutional reforms aimed at better economic performance in the domestic and regional contexts. In other words, little institutional gains could be achieved thus far from ASEAN membership.

Conclusion

Liberal institutionalism tends to be more plausible in explaining economic cooperation, positing that international organizations are capable of helping to foster economic cooperation among the members with their organizational structures and institutional properties that are encouraging cooperation, while forcing member states to adjust their national institutional arrangements and make them compatible to those of the organizations. This chapter has shown that standardized institutionalist arguments may find it difficult to explain Vietnam–ASEAN economic cooperation. Because ASEAN still has a loose institutional framework, and moreover, its member states are still reluctant to institutionalize ASEAN to make it an EU-type organization, it was relatively easier for Vietnam to decide to join ASEAN. For the same reason, Hanoi faces little pressure from ASEAN to readjust its domestic institutional arrangements and make them more compatible to those of other ASEAN members. It is also more difficult for Hanoi to participate and reap benefits from ASEAN economic cooperation, with bigger trade deficits with ASEAN as a case in point.

It should be noted here that the loose institutional arrangements of ASEAN organization did not prevent the five founding members from benefiting from the cooperation. The reason may be found in the weakness of the Vietnamese state: Vietnam is yet to have a modern state, with a modern bureaucracy that has well-trained officials, capable of studying various issues to predict the situation and work out effective policies, and ensures smooth and effective coordination among various agencies of the state and that between the state and business, among others. Therefore, joining ASEAN is one thing, but that Hanoi must work hard to streamline its organizations and enhance its capacity to really benefit from economic cooperation and integration with ASEAN is another, and one for the future.

Notes

1. The document that gave birth to AFTA is only nine pages long and an annex of the Joint Declaration of the 6th ASEAN Summit held in Singapore (January 1992), while the Treaty on the North American Free Trade Area (NAFTA) contains 22,000 pages and is a legal document.
2. The Indonesian economist Hadi Suestro at the Indonesian Center for Strategic and International Studies (CSIS) stressed this point in a conference the author attended in Yangon, Myanmar (February 7 and 8, 2003).

References

Acharya, Amitav. 1993. A new regional order in Southeast Asia: ASEAN in the post-Cold War era. Adelphi Paper No. 279.

ASEAN National Committee (ANC). 1995. Conclusions of the First ANC Meeting (Hanoi, November 20, 1995).

———. 1996. Report by the ANC Secretary-General at the ANC Second Meeting (Hanoi, January 20, 1996).

———. 1997. Review of two years of Vietnam's participation in ASEAN functional cooperation (Hanoi, October 2, 1997).

Collins, Alan. 2000. *The security dilemma of Southeast Asia*. New York: St. Martin's Press.

Communist Party of Vietnam. 2001. *Major documents of the IXth National Congress*. Hanoi: National Politics Publishing House.

Communist Party of Vietnam, Political Bureau. 2002. Resolution NQTW/07 on International Economic Integration (November 27, 2001). Hanoi: National Politics Publishing House.

Communist Party of Vietnam, Theoretical Council. 2005. *Final report on certain theoretical and practical issues over 20 years of reform (1986–2006)*. Hanoi: National Politics Publishing House.

Cong Bao (Official Gazette). Decision No. 637 of the Prime Minister. 1995a. October 6, 1995.

———. Decision No. 651 of the Prime Minister. 1995b. October 10, 1995.

———. 1995c. The Government. Decision of the Government No. 6358/VPUB. November 6, 1995.

Do Muoi. 1993. The new four-point position toward ASEAN. *People's Army Newspaper*, October 17, 1993.

Do Ngoc Son. 2000. Those unforgettable days. *Foreign Affairs Weekly* (Special issue for the fifth anniversary of Vietnam's joining ASEAN) (July 2000).

Hanh Phuong. 2003. The AFTA roadmap: Challenges to the Vietnamese economy. *Lao Dong*, January 4, 2003.

Hoang Anh Tuan. 1996. ASEAN dispute management: Implications for Vietnam and an expanded ASEAN. *Contemporary Southeast Asia* 18(1): 61–80.

Institute of International Relations (IIR). 1991. ASEAN: Formation, developments, and prospects. Hanoi: Institute for International Relations.

———. 1993. Research program for 1993. Hanoi: Institute for International Relations.

———. 1995a. ASEAN, Vietnam-ASEAN relations and prospects. Hanoi: Institute for International Relations.

———. 1995b. Chronology of Vietnam-ASEAN relations. Hanoi: Institute for International Relations.

International Affairs Weekly (IAW) and *Lao Dong Daily*. 2004. Coverage of the 13th National Conference of Provincial International Cooperation Departments. Hanoi, February 5–6.

Job, Brian. 1992. *The insecurity dilemma: National security of Third World states*. Boulder: Lynne Rienner.

Johnston, Alastair Iain. 1999. The myth of the ASEAN Way? Explaining the evolution of the ASEAN regional forum. In *Imperfect unions: Security institutions over time and space*. Edited by Helga Haftendorn, Robert Keohane, and Celeste Wallader. London: Oxford University Press, 287–324.

Kahler, Miles. 2000. Legalization as strategy: The Asia-Pacific case. *International Organization* 54(3): 549–71.

Keohane, Robert. 1984. *After hegemony*. Princeton: Princeton University Press.

Krasner, Stephen. 1983. *International regimes*. Ithaca: Cornell University Press.

Le Thi Bang Tam. 2003. *Trade Newspaper,* January 14, 2003.

Minh Quang. 2004. Vietnamese enterprises and AFTA commitments. *Hanoi Moi Daily,* January 30, 2004 and February 6, 2004.

Ministry of Foreign Affairs (MOFA). 1999a. ASEAN Department Report, On Vietnam–ASEAN Relations.

Ministry of Foreign Affairs (MOFA), General Economic Affairs Department. 1999b. *Globalization and Vietnam's economic integration.* Hanoi: National Politics Publishing House.

Morrison, Charles and Hadi Seosatro. 2001. Rethinking the ASEAN formula: The way forward for Southeast Asia. In *East Asia and the international system: Report of a special study group.* Edited by Charles Morrison. New York: The Trilateral Commission, 15–44.

Nguyen Hoai Son, Official in the MOT Multilateral Trade Policy Department. Interview with the author, May 2003.

Nguyen Manh Cam. 1994. Interview given to *Nhan Dan,* July 29, 1994.

———. 1995. Implementing a new foreign policy. Reprinted in MOFA, *International integration and preserving national characteristics.* Hanoi: National Politics Publishing House.

Nguyen Minh Vu. 2002. *Lao Dong,* August 7, 2002.

Nguyen The Luc and Nguyen Hoang Giap. 2004. Vietnam's international economic integration: The process and outcomes. *International Studies* (Hanoi) 5: 5–14.

Nguyen Van Dam, Senior official in the Cabinet Office, and one of the secretaries for Prime Minister Vo Van Kiet, in charge of ASEAN-related issues in the period from 1994–1996, interview with the author, January 15, 2003.

Nguyen Vu Tung. 1994a. Vietnam–ASEAN relations. *Security Dialogue* (March 1994): 85–92.

———. 1994b. On ASEAN activities since the establishment. *International Studies* (Hanoi) 3: 15–27.

———. 2002. Vietnam-ASEAN co-operation after the Cold War and the continued search for a theoretical framework. *Contemporary Southeast Asia* 24(1): 106–20.

Pham Chi Lan. 2002. *Trade Newspaper,* December 17, 2002.

Report of the Government. 1997. On the world situation and Vietnam's foreign affairs in 1997. Submitted to the National Assembly (November 1997).

———. 2002. On the world situation and Vietnam's foreign affairs in 2002. Submitted to the National Assembly (November 2002).

Singapore Institute of Southeast Asian Studies (ISEAS). 2003. Draft "Concept Paper on the ASEAN Economic Community." Submitted for the ASEAN-ISIS review (February 2003).

Thayer, Carlyle. 2004. Vietnam in ASEAN: Multilateralism and relations with the great powers. Paper presented at the Second Vietnam Studies Conference, June 15–17, 2004, Ho Chi Minh City.

Vu Duong Huan, et al. 2002. *Vietnam's contemporary diplomacy for the cause of renovation: 1975–2002.* Hanoi: Institute for International Relations.

Vu Duong Ninh. 2003. Vietnam and the adaptation to ASEAN. *Southeast Asian Studies Journal* (Hanoi) (March) 1: 19–31.

Vu Khoan. 1998. Introductory notes. In *An introduction to ASEAN.* Edited by MOFA ASEAN Department. Hanoi: National Politics Publishing House, 3–8.

Vu Thi Mai. 2004. The ASEAN mode of conflict resolution and lessons for Vietnam. MA thesis, Institute for International Relations (August 2004).

Weatherbee, Donald E. 2005. *International relations in Southeast Asia: The struggle for autonomy.* New York: Rowman & Littlefield.

CHAPTER FOUR

Vietnam's Border Disputes—Assessing the Impact on Its Regional Integration

RAMSES AMER AND NGUYEN HONG THAO

The main purpose of this chapter is to study Vietnam's border disputes, the way they have been and are managed and the challenges of resolving the remaining disputes. The second aim is to assess their impact on Vietnam's regional integration. We focus on developments since the early 1990s, emphasizing the progress the country has made in managing and resolving its border disputes and discussing its unresolved disputes and the challenges they pose. We explore Vietnam's degree of success in managing its border disputes through negotiations with its neighbors. Finally, we analyze the dimension of its regional integration primarily from the perspective of its contribution to the enhancement of conflict management in the Association of South-East Asian Nations (ASEAN).[1]

Settled and Unsettled Disputes

Vietnam's border disputes can be studied from various perspectives. We focus here on the current status of the disputes, looking first at settled issues and then at unresolved disputes.

Agreements Relating to Border Disputes

On July 18, 1977 Laos and Vietnam signed a treaty delimiting the land boundary between the countries. Following the completion of the demarcation process, a treaty was signed on January 24, 1986. On March 1, 1990 an additional protocol was signed and on the same day an agreement on border regulation was signed (Gay 1995; BBC/FE 2975 B/6–7).

On July 7, 1982 Vietnam and the then People's Republic of Kampuchea (PRK) signed an agreement on "historic waters" located between the coast of Kien Giang Province, Phu Quoc Island, and the Tho Chu islands on the Vietnamese side and the coast of Kampot Province and the Poulo Wai islands on the Cambodian side. The agreement stipulated that the two countries would hold, "at a suitable time," negotiations to determine the maritime frontier in the "historic waters." Pending such a settlement the two sides would continue to regard the Brévié Line drawn in 1939 as the dividing line for the islands within the "historic waters" and the exploitation of the zone would be decided by "common agreement" (BBC/FE 7074 A3/7–8; Kittichaisaree 1987, 180–1). On July 20, 1983 the two countries signed a treaty on the principles for the settlement of border problems and an agreement on border regulations (BBC/FE 7393 A3/1; Quang 1986, 8–9). On December 27, 1985 they signed the Treaty on the Delimitation of the Vietnam-Kampuchea Frontier (BBC/FE 8143 A3/1–3; Quang 1986, 8–9). On October 10, 2005 they signed a Supplementary Treaty to the 1985 Treaty (Vietnam MFA, 2005c).

On June 5, 1992 an agreement was reached between Malaysia and Vietnam to engage in joint development in areas of overlapping claims to continental shelf areas to the south-west of Vietnam and to the east-north-east off the east coast of Peninsular Malaysia in the Gulf of Thailand (Amer 1995, 306; Nguyen Hong Thao 1999, 79–88; 2002a, 53–6).

On August 9, 1997 Thailand and Vietnam reached an agreement delimiting their continental shelf and Exclusive Economic Zones (EEZ) boundaries in a disputed area in the Gulf of Thailand to the southwest of Vietnam and to the northeast of Thailand (BBC/FE 2996 B/4–5, Nguyen Hong Thao 1997, 74–9; 1998, 7–10; 2002a, 51–3).

On December 30, 1999 China and Vietnam signed a Land Border Treaty settling the land border dispute between the two countries (VNA 1999; AVI 1999; *News Bulletin* 1999).

On December 25, 2000 China and Vietnam signed the *Agreement on the Delimitation of the Territorial Seas, Exclusive Economic Zones and Continental Shelves in the Gulf of Tonkin* settling their maritime boundary disputes in the Gulf (Vietnam MFA 2000b; *Beijing Review* 2001, 9–10). On the same day the two countries signed an agreement on fishery cooperation in the Gulf of Tonkin (Zou 2002, 127–48; Nguyen Hong Thao 2005, 35–41).

On June 11, 2003 Vietnam and Indonesia signed an agreement on the delimitation of their continental shelf boundary in and to the north of the Natuna Islands (*News Bulletin* 2003).

Unsettled Border Disputes

The agreements between Vietnam and Cambodia reached in the 1980s were not recognized by all parties within Cambodia for most of the 1990s. New bilateral talks on the status of the borders between the countries were initiated to address the remaining disputed issues. This eventually led to the signing of a supplementary treaty to the Treaty of 1985 settling the land border dispute: However, the maritime disputes are still not settled, and therefore in the context of this study they cannot be considered resolved. The disputes relate to overlapping claims to maritime areas in the Gulf of Thailand (Amer 1995, 299–301; 1997, 80–91; Nguyen Hong Thao 2002a, 59–63).

Between Malaysia, Thailand, and Vietnam there is a multilateral dispute relating to an area of overlapping claims in the Gulf of Thailand (Prescott 1998).[2] Between Malaysia and Vietnam the major unresolved dispute relates to Vietnam's sovereignty claim to the whole Spratly archipelago that overlaps the Malaysian claim to the southern part of the archipelago (Prescott 1985, 218–22; Valencia 1991, 54–66; Amer 1995, 305–6). These parts are also claimed by China and Taiwan and partly claimed by the Philippines.

Between the Philippines and Vietnam there is a dispute in the South China Sea where Vietnam's sovereignty claim to the whole Spratly archipelago overlaps the Filipino claim to the major part (Amer 1995, 306–8; Prescott 1985, 218–22). These parts of the Archipelago are also claimed by China and Taiwan as well as partly claimed by Malaysia.

Between China and Vietnam the overlapping sovereignty claims to the Paracel and Spratly archipelagos are still unresolved. The same applies to China's claims to historical waters within the so-called dotted line to the east of the Vietnamese coast in the South China Sea. Vietnam's claims to the Paracel and Spratly archipelagos also overlap with Taiwan's claims to the two archipelagos.

Between Brunei Darussalam and Vietnam potential overlapping claims to a 200-mile EEZ could emerge if the two countries begin to assert such claims from islands and reefs that they claim in the South China Sea (Valencia 1991).

Between Conflict Management and Tension

Developments since the end of the Vietnam war in 1975 show that during the second half the 1970s, Vietnam and Laos reached agreements relating to their land border, with the demarcation being finalized in 1990. Although officially the two countries did not refer to any border dispute between them, the outcome of the demarcation process indicated that areas of overlapping claims did exist and that such differences were resolved in the negotiation and demarcation processes. During the 1980s there were agreements between Vietnam and the then PRK in 1982, 1983, and 1985. But there was no progress in negotiating border disputes with ASEAN member states and with China. The Cambodian conflict prevented progress to the extent that, apart from Indonesia and Cambodia, no talks on border issues took place between Vietnam and its other neighbors for the duration of the Cambodian conflict from 1979 to 1991.

The 1990s saw considerable progress in border negotiations. A joint development agreement (JDA) in an area of bilateral dispute in the Gulf of Thailand was reached with Malaysia in 1992. In 1995 Vietnam and the Philippines agreed on a "code of conduct" to be observed by the two countries in the South China Sea. The negotiations between Vietnam and Thailand eventually resulted in the agreement on maritime boundaries of 1997 in areas of bilateral dispute in the Gulf of Thailand. In the late 1990s Vietnam, Malaysia, and Thailand initiated trilateral talks on an area of the Gulf of Thailand where the claims of the three countries overlap; these talks were made possible by the maritime boundary agreement between Vietnam and Thailand in 1997.

The claims of Taiwan and Vietnam, respectively, to the Spratly and Paracel archipelagos overlap, and Vietnam has made official statements criticizing Taiwanese activities in the Spratly in recent years. However, Vietnam does not recognize Taiwan as a sovereign country. Adhering to a "one China policy," it recognizes only the People's Republic of China and not Taiwan and thus it cannot enter into official talks with Taiwan over the overlapping claims by the two parties.

Given the extent of the border disputes between China and Vietnam along the land border, in the Gulf of Tonkin, and in the South China Sea, these disputes deserve more extensive analysis. Even during the process leading up to the full normalization of relations between the two countries in November 1991, these issues were not resolved (Amer 1994, 365–6, 376–82; 1999a, 73–4, 105–8; 2002, 7–8; 2004b, 320–8).

Following the normalization of relations between Vietnam and China, most of the 1990s was characterized by a fluctuating level of tension relating to their border disputes. Sharp differences relating to all the border disputes, that is, overlapping claims to the Paracel and Spratly archipelagos, to water and continental shelf areas in the South China Sea and in the Gulf of Tonkin, and to areas along the land border existed from May to November of 1992. Differences relating to oil exploration in the South China Sea and the signing of contracts with foreign companies for exploration peaked in April–June 1994, April–May 1996, and March–April 1997. In 1998 there were shorter periods of tension along the land border and also in the South China Sea (Amer 2002, 8–26).

To cope with these fluctuating levels of tension, Vietnam and China developed a system of talks at the expert, government, and senior levels to deal with border issues. The talks at the government level began in August 1993 and the 12th round of those discussions was held in December 2005. The first achievement of these talks was the signing of an agreement on October 19, 1993 on the principles for handling the land border and Gulf of Tonkin disputes. The two sides further agreed to set up two joint working groups at the expert level. The first one on the land border issues held sixteen rounds of talks from February 1994 up to the signing of the *Land Border Treaty* in December 1999. The second on the Gulf of Tonkin met 17 times from March 1994 to the signing of the *Agreement on the Delimitation of the Territorial Seas, Exclusive Economic Zones and Continental Shelves in the Gulf of Tonkin* in December 2000. Talks at the expert level on the disputes in the South China Sea proper, the so-called sea issues, were initiated in November 1995; the tenth round of talks was held in June 2005 (Amer 2002, 9–41, 50–8; 2004a, 329–31; Amer and Nguyen Hong Thao 2005, 433–4; Vietnam MFA 2005d).

The agreements of 1999 and 2000 relating to the land border and the Gulf of Tonkin, respectively are ample evidence of the progress in dispute resolution. In 2000, both countries ratified the *Land Border Treaty* that officially took effect on July 6 (Amer 2002, 27–35; 2004b, 334–5). The maritime boundary agreement relating to the Gulf of Tonkin came into force on June 30, 2004 when the two countries exchanged documents relating to the ratification of the agreement in Hanoi (Nhan Dan 2004; *People's Daily* 2004). The ratification process and the coming into effect of the agreement were made possible by the completion of the talks on an additional protocol to the agreement of fishery cooperation. This agreement also came into force on June 30 (Nguyen Hong Thao 2004, 9–15 and 19; 2005, 25–44; *People's Daily* 2004; Vietnam Law 2004, 8–10; Zou 2005, 13–24).

A shooting incident that led to the death of at least eight Vietnamese in the Gulf of Tonkin in January 2005 highlighted the need to enhance the collaboration between the countries in managing the situation in the Common Fishery Zone. This process is well under way, as indicated in the Joint Communiqué issued in connection with President Tran Duc Luong's visit to China in July 2005. The Communiqué states that Vietnam and China will "exert joint efforts to ensure marine security and order in fishery development" in the Gulf and they agree to "conduct joint patrol between the two countries' naval forces" (Vietnam MFA 2005b).

The expert-level talks on the so-called sea issues (in the South China Sea—referred to as East Sea by Vietnam) have not made much progress, partly due to disagreements on what issues should be on the agenda. While Vietnam has pushed for the inclusion of the issue of the Paracels, China is against its inclusion on the agenda. Nevertheless, the tension relating to the disputes in the South China Sea was considerably reduced by 1999, a trend that has continued to prevail during the first half of this decade (Amer 2002, 27–35; 2004b, 334–5). Despite the lack of progress in the expert-level talks, the high-level talks have resulted in agreements on increasingly sophisticated principles for the behavior of the two countries in the South China Sea to avoid actions that can provoke tension and minimize tension if a dispute does arises.[3]

In the multilateral dispute relating to the Spratly archipelago and the broader issue of the situation in the South China Sea, Vietnam is actively involved in the ASEAN-China dialogue on these issues. Its most tangible outcome was the signing of the *ASEAN-China Declaration on the Conduct of Parties in the South China Sea* on November 4, 2002, during the Eighth ASEAN Summit in Phnom Penh. The Declaration is regarded as an important step toward establishing and agreeing on a "code of conduct" in the South China Sea. The parties have undertaken to resolve their border and jurisdictional disputes by peaceful means, without resorting to the threat or use of force, but through friendly consultations and negotiations by sovereign states directly concerned in accordance with universally recognized principles of international law, including the 1982 United Nations Convention on the Law of the Sea (Nguyen Hong Thao 2001, 105–30; 2002b, 19–21).

With respect to the situation in the South China Sea, an agreement on seismic surveys in the South China Sea between the Chinese National Offshore Oil Company (CNOOC) and the Philippines National Oil Company (PNOC) was signed on September 1, 2004 (DAF 2004). The area of seismic survey covers some parts of the Spratly archipelago.

Vietnam officially stated that the agreement had been concluded without consulting other parties. It "requested" that China and the Philippines inform Vietnam about the content of the agreement. Vietnam also reiterated its sovereignty claims to both the Spratly and Paracel archipelagos and called on all other signatories to join it in "strictly implementing the DOC [2002 Declaration on the Conduct of the Parties]" (Vietnam MFA 2004a).

In March 2005, the Department of Foreign Affairs of the Philippines announced that the Department's Maritime and Ocean Affairs Center would host the Third Philippines-Vietnam Joint Oceanographic Marine Scientific Expedition in the South China Sea (JOMSRE-SCS III) in April 2005 (DFA 2005a). On March 11, the spokesman of China's Ministry of Foreign Affairs expressed China's "concern" about the joint marine research and China's position that China and the "relevant parties" would follow the "principles enshrined in the Declaration on Conduct of Parties in the South China Sea" in their marine research (China MFA 2005a).

Second, on March 14, 2005 a Tripartite Agreement for Joint Marine Seismic Undertaking in the Agreement Area in the South China Sea was signed between China National Offshore Oil Corporation (CNOOC), Vietnam Oil and Gas Corporation (Petro Vietnam), and the Philippine National Oil Company (PNOC). One of the provisions of the agreement was that its signing "would not undermine the basic position held by the Government of each party on the South China Sea issue." But the parties also expressed their "resolve to transform the South China Sea into an area of peace, stability, cooperation and development" (China MFA 2005b; Vietnam MFA 2005a).[4]

There was no breakthrough in negotiations with Indonesia on border disputes during the 1990s, as the two countries failed to capitalize on their traditionally good bilateral relations. Furthermore, the impact of the Asian financial crisis on Indonesia brought other and more pressing needs onto the agenda of the Indonesian leaders. Thus, while no progress was made in negotiating border disputes, stability was maintained. This state of affairs continued to prevail into the early 2000s (Nguyen Hong Thao 2002a, 56–8) until a breakthrough was made in 2003 leading to the agreement of June 2003 settling the maritime boundary disputes between Vietnam and Indonesia.

On a less positive note, the 1990s also saw the reemergence of border issues in Vietnam's relations with Cambodia. In particular the land border issue and events along the border have caused periods of tension in bilateral relations. Leading Cambodian politicians have openly accused Vietnam of border violations, but Vietnam has repeatedly rejected such accusations. The initiation of renewed talks on the border issue in the late 1990s did not lead to any agreement by the end of the decade. The status of the 1982, 1983, and 1985 agreements was first put in doubt by the Cambodian side, but by the late 1990s those agreements seemed to have become acceptable again to both sides as a basis for further talks (Amer 1995, 299–301; 1997, 80–91; 2000, 40–2). Bilateral talks did progress into the year 2000, and a Vietnam official stated that an agreement would be reached by the end of that year (*News Bulletin* 2000a; Vietnam MFA 2000a). However, this did not materialize and for a few years talks were more sporadic. Eventually the two countries managed to make progress in the talks on the land border disputes, resulting in the agreement on a Supplementary Treaty on October 10, 2005. Following the completion of the ratification process in both countries, the exchange of ratification documents for the Supplementary Treaty took place on December 6, 2005 when it came into force (*Nhan Dan* 2005a).

Patterns of Conflict Management

From the observations above it can be noted that the resolution of the Cambodian conflict in October 1991 was a watershed moment in the management of Vietnamese border disputes with other Southeast Asian countries. Prior to October 1991, Vietnam had settled its border dispute only with Laos. Agreements reached with Cambodia in the 1980s did not resolve the border disputes, as indicated by continued differences and renewed attempts at negotiations in the late 1990s and the early years of this decade, though the land border dispute was settled at long last in late 2005.

Since the settlement of the Cambodian conflict, Vietnam agreed in 1992 on a joint development agreement with Malaysia in areas of overlapping claims, such as the area of the Gulf of Thailand. Then in 1997 Vietnam and Thailand agreed on maritime boundaries between the two countries in the Gulf of Thailand. This agreement also paved the way for talks between Vietnam, Thailand, and Malaysia on the area of the Gulf of Thailand where the claims of the three countries overlap. The 1995 agreement with the Philippines on a "code of conduct" to be observed in the South China Sea is another notable sign of progress that occurred after the resolution of the Cambodian conflict.

The full normalization of bilateral relations between China and Vietnam in late 1991 certainly facilitated management of their border issues. But the most interesting aspect here is that the full normalization took place without the resolution of the border issues. This can best be understood in light of the major efforts that both countries have invested in managing and resolving the border issues since full normalization. In fact, full normalization of relations between China and Vietnam would not have been possible in 1991 if resolving the border issues had been a precondition for normalization.

Overall, Vietnam has made considerable progress in managing and resolving its border disputes. Some bilateral disputes have not been formally settled but managed through various measures such as joint development agreements, codes of conduct, and continuing talks of various kinds. The multilateral dispute over the Spratlys is more difficult to resolve due to its complicated nature; however, Vietnam has made the most progress in its bilateral talks with the Philippines and China in dispute management in the area. Vietnam also contributes to ASEAN policy on the South China Sea situation and the Association's attempts at promoting peace and stability in the area. Differences such as those between Vietnam and China relating to the Paracels, and also with regard to areas to the east of the Vietnamese coast and the west of the Spratlys are likely to persist. But both sides have made considerable headway in containing tension in recent years and have agreed on a number of measures to avoid and contain possible sources of tension in the future (Amer 2002, 45–6).

Achievements

Since the early 1990s, Vietnam has emerged as an active actor in settling border disputes by peaceful means in the region. The years between 1992 and 2005, a period spanning less than fifteen years, saw Vietnam completing talks on land border disputes with China and Cambodia and on maritime disputes with Malaysia, Thailand, China, and Indonesia. In the Southeast Asian context, this is an impressive record. Through these agreements, Vietnam has contributed to the development of international law in areas such as the application of the *uti possidetis* principle, the equitable principle, the application of the single line for maritime delimitation, and the effect of islands in the maritime delimitation.

Of course, the credit for this progress in managing border disputes cannot go only to Vietnam, but credit must certainly be given to Vietnam for its work in peacefully managing its border disputes with neighboring countries. Vietnam has also persisted in pursuing similar policies for resolving unsettled disputes. Of course the agreements with Cambodia, China, Indonesia, Laos, Malaysia, the Philippines, and Thailand have been reached because these countries also opted to pursue policies to promote negotiations on their border disputes with Vietnam. Thus, the peaceful management of Vietnam's border disputes is a result of the common interests of Vietnam and its neighboring countries in pursuing such policies. It also reflects the vast improvement in the overall relationship between Vietnam and China as well as between Vietnam and the ASEAN member states during the 1990s, after the formal resolution of the Cambodian conflict and the full normalization of relations between China and Vietnam in late 1991.

Vietnam's Border Disputes and Regional Integration

How does Vietnam contribute to the enhancement of ASEAN's conflict management approach, regional integration, and peace and security through the resolution of border disputes? In order to address these complex issues it is important to understand the context in and process by which Vietnam gradually became integrated into the framework for regional collaboration in Southeast Asia. ASEAN-Vietnam relations were characterized by deep tension following Vietnam's military intervention in Cambodia in late 1978 and during the first half of the 1980s. The gradual rapprochement between ASEAN and Vietnam went hand in hand with regional initiatives to resolve the Cambodian conflict in the second half of the 1980s, and with the major breakthrough in improved relations following the formal resolution of the Cambodian conflict through the Paris Agreements on Cambodia of October 1991. Once the Cambodian conflict was removed from the agenda, relations between Vietnam and ASEAN improved and Vietnam gradually became integrated into the existing regional framework in Southeast Asia. Vietnam acceded to the Bali Treaty in 1992, became an ASEAN Observer the same year, and was granted full membership in ASEAN in 1995 (Hoang 1993, 280–91; 1994, 259–73; Nguyen Vu Tung 1993, 85–92; 2002, 106–20; Amer 2004a, 9–22).

The process of rapprochement between ASEAN and Vietnam can be seen as part of a broader ASEAN scheme to bring the Southeast Asian region in line with a common framework for conflict management and a code of conduct for governing interstate relations in the region, aimed at creating a situation conducive to the peaceful management of the existing inter-state disputes and of potential future disputes throughout the region. Expanding membership in ASEAN and expanding the acceptance of the ASEAN framework for conflict management within the region can be viewed as a process of conflict management brought about by various means that formed part of a broader policy of constructive engagement toward not only Vietnam but also Cambodia, Laos, and Myanmar.[5]

Since its entry into ASEAN has Vietnam adhered to the existing conflict management norms and what role has the management of border disputes played? In the earlier sections of this study, the agreements reached with other member-states relating to border disputes have been outlined, as have the remaining disputes. The progress achieved since the early 1990s is notable, with the JDA agreement with Malaysia in 1992 on the Gulf of Thailand, the 1997 agreement on maritime boundaries with Thailand in the Gulf of Thailand; the 2003 agreement between Vietnam and Indonesia relating to the delimitation of their continental shelf boundary in and area to the North of the Natuna Islands; and the 2005 Supplementary Treaty relating to the land border with Cambodia. Another positive development was the 1995 agreement between Vietnam and the Philippines on a de-facto "code of conduct" to be observed by the two sides in the South China Sea. The fact that Vietnam and Laos have not only agreed but completed the demarcation of their common land border should be noted. In addition Vietnam, Thailand, and Malaysia have initiated talks on an area in the then Gulf of Thailand in which the claims of the three countries overlap. All this points to an overall positive development relating to the management of Vietnam's border disputes with other ASEAN member-states.

Vietnam has made considerable progress in the management of its border disputes since it became a member of ASEAN in 1995. This has certainly been facilitated by Vietnam's membership because overall relations have been strengthened with other ASEAN members. This can help explain why the disputes have become more manageable, but not why a number of them have been resolved either through joint development schemes or through formal delimitation agreements. After all, other ASEAN members still have unresolved border disputes with fellow members some 38 years after the creation of the Association. Vietnam has also made considerable progress in managing border disputes with China. Thus it can be argued that the active and committed policy of peaceful management of border disputes implemented by the Vietnamese government is paying dividends. The overall progress achieved in the region indicates that several of Vietnam's neighbors are pursuing similar policies.

The progress made in managing and in some notable cases formally resolving border disputes between Vietnam and other member-states of ASEAN show that the process of peaceful management of disputes is being implemented by Vietnam in the relations with its ASEAN neighbors. This is another indication of Vietnam's commitment to and continued integration into the regional framework of collaboration and integration in Southeast Asia.

This overall positive trend in the management of Vietnam's border disputes contributes to the ASEAN goal to promote peace and security in Southeast Asia. It is also helping to improve interstate relations between the member-states of ASEAN, as Vietnam's policies on peaceful negotiations of its border disputes are in line with the ASEAN framework for dispute resolution between its members-states. It can even be argued that the positive developments relating to the management of Vietnam's border disputes in the decade following its entry into the Association have contributed to strengthen ASEAN's approach to conflict management.

Conclusion

This chapter has sought to indicate and analyze some of the positive developments relating to Vietnam's border disputes from two main perspectives—the outcome of formal negotiations resulting in dispute settlement or diffusion of tension, and their impact on Vietnam's regional integration. Our primary conclusion is that Vietnam's track record in settling border disputes has been impressive from the perspective of the Southeast Asian region. The reduction in tension relating to the remaining border disputes is also a positive development. On the whole, Vietnam has been very successful in managing its border disputes in the 1990s and well into this decade. This conclusion does not imply that all disputes have been settled, or that all agreements have been fully implemented. Therefore continued efforts are needed to resolve the remaining bilateral disputes, such as the maritime disputes with Cambodia, and to prevent tension from reemerging, as in the South China Sea. The full implementation of the agreements reached so far is essential. A case, in point is the agreement on the land borders with China and Cambodia, where the demarcation processes of the respective borders are yet to be completed. (The ongoing demarcation process between China and Vietnam is expected to be finalized in 2008 "at the latest" [Vietnam MFA 2005c, 2005d], and Cambodia and Vietnam expect their demarcation to be completed in December 2008 [Nhan Dan 2005a, 2005b]). Further work also remains to be done in the Gulf of Tonkin, where China and Vietnam must continue to fully implement their agreements on maritime boundaries and on fishing cooperation. The maritime agreement between Vietnam and Indonesia, still needs to complete the ratification process to make it effective.

Vietnam's integration into ASEAN can be further enhanced and strengthened if the trilateral dispute involving Thailand and Malaysia in the Gulf of Thailand can be formally managed through a joint scheme that could well serve as a model for handling other multilateral dispute in the region. The settlement of the maritime disputes with Cambodia would also be a positive contribution. In addition, continued and renewed efforts between Vietnam, but also China to manage their disputes in the South China Sea are also of importance not only to Vietnam, but also to the rest of the region. The importance placed on minimizing tension by the two sides can be seen in the agreements on mechanisms to reduce tension and the actual reduction in tension since the late 1990s.[6] As for the broader South China Sea situation, the adoption of the *ASEAN-China Declaration on the Conduct of Parties in the South China Sea* is certainly a positive step toward conflict management. Vietnam and other parties concerned can play active and constructive roles in implementing and abiding by the Declaration. The tripartite agreement between the national oil companies of China, the Philippines, and Vietnam also could possibly have an important impact on the South China Sea situation.

Notes

1. This empirical part and the analysis of the management of border disputes is a revised and updated version of the corresponding parts in Amer and Nguyen Hong Thao 2005. This study focuses on the regional integration dimension, while Amer and Nguyen Hong Thao 2005 also includes an analysis of the sovereignty dimension. The views expressed in this study represent only the private views of the two authors.
2. This area is currently included in the JDA between Malaysia and Thailand but is recognized by the two countries as claimed by Vietnam (Amer's discussions with officials in Bangkok December 1998, in April 1999 in November 2000).
3. Notable provisions relating to behavior in the South China Sea can be found in the Joint Declaration of February 27, 1999, issued in the connection with the visit to China by the then Secretary General of the Communist Party, Le Kha Phieu (Vietnam Law 1999, 13); the Joint Statement for comprehensive cooperation signed on December 25, 2000 by the foreign ministers of the two countries (AVI 2000; News Bulletin 2000b; VNA 2000; Vietnam MFA, 2006); and the Joint Communiqué of October 8, 2004, issued in connection with the visit of China's prime minister, Wen Jiabao, to Vietnam (China MFA 2004).

4. The official report of the Philippines concurs with China and Vietnam on the content of the agreement, but refers to a statement by the Secretary of Foreign Affairs of the Philippines Alberto G. Romulo in which no reference is made to the nonimpact on the "basic position" held by each of the three countries, that is, their claims in the South China Sea, that is spelled out in both the Vietnamese and Chinese reports, respectively. For the report of the Philippines see DFA 2005b.
5. For a more detailed analysis of the expansion of ASEAN with specific reference to the conflict management aspect see Amer 1999b, 1031–1048. For analyses of the broader issues relating to regional collaboration in Southeast Asia in the period leading up to ASEAN's expansion see among others: Chin 1997, 1–19; and, Paribatra 1994, 243–58.
6. Despite the sharp reduction in tension a few incidents have occurred since 1999 (Amer 2004b, 334–5; 2002, 27–35). The most recent was caused by activities carried out by China in areas of the South China Sea that Vietnam considers to be part of its continental shelf in November 2004 (Vietnam MFA 2004d).

References

Online Sources

Department of Foreign Affairs, Republic of the Philippines (Web Site)

RP-China Agreement on Joint Marine Seismic Undertaking in the Sea Constitutional—Rumulo / DFA hails PGMA's Successful State Visit to China; Signed Agreements to boost Trade and Investment between RP and China, SAF-AGR-524–04, September 2004, Press Release, Department of Foreign Affairs, Pasay City. Online at www.dfagov.ph/news/pr/pr2004/sep/pr524.htm (DFA 2004), accessed September 29, 2004, 108.

DFA-MOAC to host Third Joint Scientific Research Expedition in the South China Sea, SAF-AGR-133–05 (March 07, 2005), Press Release, Department for Foreign Affairs. Online at www.dfa.gov.ph/news/pr/pr2005/mar/pr133.htm (DFA 2005a), accessed March 17, 2005.

Secretary Romulo heralds RP-China-Vietnam Agreement on Joint Seismic Survey of the South China Sea, Press Release, SFA-AGR-149–05 (2005), Department of Foreign Affairs, Pasay City. Online at www.daf.gov.ph/news/pr/pr2005/mar/pr149.htm (DFA 2005b), accessed March 17, 2005.

Ministry of Foreign Affairs, People's Republic of China (Web Site)

China and Vietnam Issue a Joint Communiqué, October 8, 2004. Online at www.fmprc.gov.cn/eng/ wjb/zzjg/yzs/gjlb/2792/2793/t163759.htm (China MFA 2004), accessed March 22, 2005.

Foreign Ministry Spokesman Kong Quan's Comment on Philippines-Vietnamese Joint Marine Research in the South China Sea, 2005/03/11. Online at www.fmprc.gov.cn/eng/xwfw/s2510/t186844.htm (China MFA 2005a), accessed March 11, 2005.

Oil Companies of China, the Philippines and Vietnam signed Agreement on South China Sea Cooperation. (by Chinese Embassy in the Philippines), 2005/03/15. Online at www.fmprc.gov.cn/eng/wjb/zwjg/t187333.htm (China MFA 2005b), accessed March 22, 2005.

Ministry of Foreign Affairs of the Socialist Republic of Vietnam (Web Site)

Viet Nam, Cambodia to solve border issue this year, affirms Vietnamese Deputy Prime Minister (November 3, 2000). Online at www.mofa.gov.vn/ (Vietnam MFA 2000a), accessed December 28, 2000.

Joint Viet Nam-China Statement for Comprehensive Cooperation (December 25, 2000). Online at www.mofa.gov.vn/ (Vietnam MFA 2000b), accessed December 28, 2000.

Answer to Correspondent by Mr. Le Dzung, the Spokesman of the Vietnamese Ministry of Foreign Affairs on September 9, 2004. Online at www.mofa.gov.vn/en/tt_baochi/pbnfn/ns041028222202 (Vietnam MFA 2004a), accessed September 29, 2004.

Nanhai 215 Vessel has hauled oil drilling platform KANTAN 3 of China to the continental shelf of Vietnam. Online at www.mofa.gov.vn/tt_baochi/pbnfn/ns041119160109 (Vietnam MFA 2004b), accessed March 22, 2005.

Tripartite Agreement for Joint Marine Seismic Undertaking in the Agreement Area in the South China Sea. Answer to Correspondent by Mr. Le Dzung, the Spokesman of the Vietnamese Ministry of Foreign Affairs on March 14, 2005. Online at www.mofa.gov.vn/tt_baochi/pbnfn/ns050314164241 (Vietnam MFA 2005a), March 22, 2005.

Vietnam and China issue joint statement. Online at www.mofa.gov.vn/en/nr040807104143/nr040807105001/ns050726144049 (Vietnam MFA 2005b), accessed July 25, 2005.

PM Khai holds talks with Cambodian counterpart. Online at www.mofa.gov.vn/en/nr040807104143/nr040807105001/ns05101140825 (Vietnam MFA 2005c), accessed October 23, 2005.

Viet Nam, China to complete landmark demarcation in 2008. Online at www.mofa.gov.vn/en/nr040807104143/nr040807105001/ns051212154021 (Vietnam MFA 2005d), accessed January 9, 2006.

Vietnamese, Chinese experts on land boundary demarcation meet. Online at www.mofa.gov.vn/en/nr040807104143/nr040807105001/ns051228104311 (Vietnam MFA 2005e), accessed January 9, 2006.

Nhan Dan (Vietnamese Communist Party Newspaper Web Site)

Vietnam, China sign Land Border Treaty, News Bulletin, No. 146 (December 31, 1999) (English language bulletin). Online at www.nhandan.org.vn/ (News Bulletin 1999), accessed January 27, 2000.

Vietnam, Cambodia meet on border issues, News Bulletin, No. 344 (November 1, 2000) (English language bulletin) (www.nhandan.org.vn/) (News Bulletin 2000a), accessed December 15, 2000.

Vietnam, China sign joint statement, News Bulletin, No. 399 (December 26, 2000) (English language bulletin). Online at www.nhandan.org.vn/ (News Bulletin 2000b), accessed December 28, 2000.

Vietnam-Indonesia boundary agreement benefits regional stability, in News Bulletin, No. 1306 (June 27, 2003) (English language bulletin). Online at www.nhandan.org.vn/ (News Bulletin 2003), accessed December 22, 2003.

Vietnam, China exchange documents ratifying Tonkin Gulf demarcation agreement. Online at www.nhandan.org.vn/english/news/010704/domestic_vietnamchina.htm (Nhan Dan 2004), accessed July 19, 2004.

New achievement in Vietnam-Cambodia relations. Online at www.nhandan.org.vn/english/news/081205/domestic_new.htm (Nhan Dan 2005a), accessed January 9, 2006.

Vietnam and Cambodia discuss master plan on border demarcation. Online at www.nhandan.org.vn/english/news/231205/domestic_vn.htm (Nhan Dan 2005b), accessed January 9, 2006.

People's Daily (Beijing)(Web Site English Version)

Two China-Vietnam Beibu Gulf agreements take effect. Online at english.people.com.cn/200407/01/eng20040701_148157.html (People's Daily 2004), accessed October 3, 2004.

Vietnam News Agency (Web Site)

Signature du traité sur la frontière terrestre Vietnam-Chine, Agence vietnamienne de l'information (AVI) (décembre 30, 1999) (www.vnagency.com.vn/) (AVI 1999), December 31, 1999.

Déclaration Vietnam-Chine sur la coopération au nouveau siècle, Agence vietnamienne de l'information (AVI) (décembre 25, 2000) (www.vnagency.com.vn/) (AVI 2000), accessed December 27, 2000.

Viet Nam, China sign Land Border Treaty, Vietnam News Agency (VNA) (December 30, 1999) (www.vnagency.com.vn/) (VNA 1999), accessed December 31, 1999.

Joint Viet Nam-China Statement for Comprehensive Cooperation (take two), Vietnam News Agency (VNA) (December 26, 2000) (www.vnagency.com.vn/) (VNA 2000), accessed December 27, 2000.

Other Sources

Amer, Ramses. 1994. Sino-Vietnamese normalization in the light of the crisis of the late 1970s. *Pacific Affairs* 67(3): 357–83.

———. 1995. Vietnam and its neighbours: The border dispute dimension. *Contemporary Southeast Asia* 17(3): 298–318.

———. 1997. The border conflicts between Cambodia and Vietnam. *Boundary and Security Bulletin* 5(2): 80–91.

———. 1999a. Sino-Vietnamese relations: Past, present and future. In *Vietnamese foreign policy in transition*. Edited by Carlyle A. Thayer and Ramses Amer. Singapore: Institute of Southeast Asian Studies and St. Martin's Press, 68–130.

———. 1999b. Conflict management and constructive engagement in ASEAN's expansion. *Third World Quarterly* (Special Issue on New Regionalisms) 20(5): 1031–48.

———. 2000. Managing border disputes in Southeast Asia. *Kajian Malaysia, Journal of Malaysian Studies* (Special Issue on Conflict and Conflict Management in Southeast Asia) XVIII(1–2): 30–60.

———. 2002. The Sino-Vietnamese approach to managing boundary disputes. *Maritime Briefing* 3(5). Durham: International Boundaries Research Unit, University of Durham.

———. 2004a. Vietnam and ASEAN—A case study of regional integration and conflict management. *Dialogue + Cooperation* 1: 9–22.

———. 2004b. Assessing Sino-Vietnamese relations through the management of contentious issues. *Contemporary Southeast Asia* 26(2): 320–45.

Amer, Ramses and Nguyen Hong Thao. 2005. The management of Vietnam's border disputes: What impact on its sovereignty and regional integration? *Contemporary Southeast Asia* 27(3): 429–52.

British Broadcasting Corporation, Summary of World Broadcasts, Part Three, Far East, 2975 B/6–7 (July 19, 1997); 7074 A3/7–8 (July 10, 1982); 7393 A3/1 (July 23, 1983); 8143 A3/1–3 (December 30, 1985); and 2996 B/4–5 (August 13, 1997) (BBC/FE).

Chin Kin Wah. 1997. ASEAN: The long road to "One Southeast Asia." *Asian Journal of Political Science* (Special Issue on ASEAN) 5(1): 1–19.

China, Viet Nam sign Agreements. *Beijing Review*, 44(2) (January 11, 2001): 9–10. (Beijing Review 2001).

Gay, Bernard. 1995. La nouvelle frontière lao-vietnamienne. Les accords de 1977–1990. Histoire des frontières de la péninsule indochinoise—2, Travaux du Centre d'histoire et civilisations de la péninsule indochinoise publiés sous la direction de P. B. Lafont. Paris: L'Harmattan.

Hoang Anh Tuan. 1993. Why hasn't Vietnam gained ASEAN membership? *Contemporary Southeast Asia* 15(3): 280–91.

———. 1994. Vietnam's membership in ASEAN: Economic, political and security implications. *Contemporary Southeast Asia* 16(3): 259–73.

Kittichaisaree, Kriangsak. 1987. *The law of the sea and maritime boundary delimitation in South-East Asia*. Singapore: Oxford University Press.

Nguyen Hong Thao. 1997. Vietnam's first maritime boundary agreement. *Boundary and Security Bulletin* 5(3): 74–9.

———. 1998. Vietnam and Thailand settle maritime disputes in the Gulf of Thailand. *The MIMA Bulletin* 2: 7–10.

———. 1999. Joint development in the Gulf of Thailand. *Boundary and Security Bulletin* 7(3): 79–88.

———. 2001. Vietnam and the Code of Conduct for the South China Sea. *Ocean Development & International Law* 32: 105–130.

———. 2002a. Les délimitations maritimes concernant le Vietnam: accords conclus et négociations en cours. In *Le Vietnam et la mer*. Edited by Monique Chemillier-Gendreau. Paris: Les Indes Savantes, 47–76.

———. 2002b. Declaration on Parties' Conduct in South China Sea (the East Sea)—A step towards the establishment of the Code of Conduct for the region. *Vietnam Law and Legal Forum* 9(99): 19–21.

———. 2004. The new legal order in the Tonkin Gulf. *Vietnam Law and Legal Forum* 10(119): 9–15, 19.

———. 2005. Maritime delimitation and fishery cooperation in the Tonkin Gulf. *Ocean Development & International Law* 34(1): 25–44.

Nguyen Vu Tung. 1993. Vietnam-ASEAN cooperation in Southeast Asia. *Security Dialogue* 34(1): 85–92.

———. 2002. Vietnam-ASEAN co-operation after the Cold War and the continued search for a theoretical framework. *Contemporary Southeast Asia* 22(1): 106–20.

Paribatra, Sukhumbhand. 1994. From ASEAN Six to ASEAN Ten: Issues and prospects. *Contemporary Southeast Asia* 16(3): 243–58.

Prescott, J. R.V. 1985. *The maritime boundaries of the world*. London: Methuen.

Prescott, Victor. 1998. *The Gulf of Thailand*. Kuala Lumpur: Maritime Institute of Malaysia.

Quang Nghia. 1986. Vietnam-Kampuchea border issue settled. *Vietnam Courier* 4: 8–9.

Valencia, Mark J. 1991. *Malaysia and the law of the Sea: The foreign policy issues, the options and their implications*. Kuala Lumpur: Institute of Strategic and International Studies.

Vietnam-China Joint Declaration. 1999. *Vietnam Law and Legal Forum* 5(54): 13.

VN—China gulf pact to enhance relations. 2004. *Vietnam Law and Legal Forum* 10(118): 8–10.

Zou Keyuan. 2002. Sino-Vietnamese Fishery Agreement for the Gulf of Tonkin. *International Journal of Marine and Coastal Law* 17(1): 127–48.

———. 2005. The Sino-Vietnamese Agreement on Maritime Boundary Delimitation in the Gulf of Tonkin. *Ocean Development & International Law* 34(1): 13–24.

Vietnam's International Commitments upon Entry into the WTO

Limits to Its Sovereignty? A View from Moscow

VLADIMIR MAZYRIN

This chapter explores some of the driving forces, potential benefits of, and challenges to Vietnam's accession to and entrance into the World Trade Organization (WTO). I seek to ask, as Vietnamese policymakers have also asked, whether and how this important shift in Vietnam's external relations will distort its sovereignty in policymaking and the defense of Vietnam's national interests. My aim, in other words, is to define and measure the price that the Hanoi government has agreed to pay for entering this global trading club. I also seek to review the process of accession and harmonization to WTO norms. By the end of 2005, Vietnam had come close to WTO membership since the process began in 1995 with Hanoi's application. Vietnam may indeed achieve the goal of WTO membership considerably faster than China and even Russia, though perhaps not as quickly as it initially expected.

Driving Forces and Incentives

Vietnam's entry into the WTO is an important step on its way toward full integration of its economy into the international business community, in accordance with its open door policy and policy of renovation (*doi moi*), launched in 1986. It may be considered the final act by Hanoi's leadership in adopting the general "rules of the game" in business, rules that are largely exogenous for this transitional country and obligatory for members of the WTO. This step also confirms that Vietnam has begun its transition to a deeper stage of structural reforms that were impeded in the late 1990s and recommended persistently by international experts and donors. This stage of the reforms demands further deregulation of the economy, more active support of the private sector (instead of the state-owned enterprises (SOEs)) and increasing export activities and liberalization of foreign trade. Such changes reflect a deepening of the policy reform agenda.

Therefore entry into the WTO demands that Vietnamese authorities accept common principles in external and domestic economic policies already long institutionalized by the industrialized countries. Many developing states criticize the negative social and economic impacts of these policies. They believe that the global north and transnational corporations use WTO rules together with such institutions as the World Bank and the International Monetary Fund to govern the international trade and financial system in their own interests. They also argue that fulfilling a nation's commitments to the WTO may result in placing the economy of such nations under a form of WTO authority.

It is difficult to ascertain the Vietnamese leadership's apprehensions about these impacts, and their responses. The transnational flows arising from this process help to reduce the importance of national borders (both visible and hidden) and may, in some nations' views, curtail state sovereignty, forcing independent nations to cede part of their power to international or regional organizations, nongovernmental organizations, and transnational corporations as part of the process of reform and resolving domestic dilemmas.

But the Vietnamese government supposes that WTO membership need not harm national interests, and may even promote their realization. No country has quit the WTO system, after all, and every country outside wants to enter it. And at the regional level, Hanoi supports the strengthening of similar organizations, such as the ASEAN Free Trade Area project and the emergence of an East Asian economic community under the "ASEAN plus" format. Another incentive for acceleration of entry into the WTO is the Chinese demonstration effect. China's experience has proven fruitful for its southern neighbor, and has helped Hanoi to better organize, prepare, and negotiate its accession. Growth of trade competition with China helps to stimulate Hanoi's efforts to restore the price advantages of Vietnamese commodities in external markets (VIR 2002). Finally, Vietnam has sought to enter the WTO before the end of the Doha round of multilateral negotiations, for after this round the rules governing the WTO accession package may yet again tighten.

Domestic as well as external forces help push Vietnam toward the WTO. The domestic forces are a result of twenty years of the significant transition in Vietnam toward a market economy, a transition that has overcome doubts and hesitation about pace and method. In short, Hanoi failed to find an alternative path to national development alternative way of national development, and WTO requirements have come to be regarded as consistent with and promoting realization of the nation's transition to a market economy.

Potential Benefits of Vietnamese Accession

Vietnam's decision to join the WTO is based first and foremost on pragmatic concerns—the benefits it may and will receive, both near-term and longer-term, though they are by no means guaranteed.

Comparative Advantage

Full membership in the WTO should allow Vietnam to more effectively employ its comparative advantage in the international division of labor due to the excess supply of manpower in Vietnam (where it is particularly cheap in the countryside). Restrictions on Vietnamese exports that continue to constrain expansion of trade will decrease or be eliminated, especially in light industry and other labor-intensive sectors of the economy. For example, quotas and other non-tariff restrictions on textile exports were removed within the WTO in 2005 (after the expiry of the fibers products agreement under the Uruguay round). Certainly, the delay in Vietnam's accession to the WTO creates difficulties for the local textile industry (BFCI 2004a).[1] Therefore international market access for Vietnam's main manufactures, such as textiles, clothes, footwear, electronics, ceramics, and plastic goods may help to preserve its competitive position. And, according to World Bank and OECD estimates, Vietnam's entry into the WTO will allow it to increase exports significantly within a few years.

Providing Fair Terms in Trade

In my view, and the view of some other commentators, bilateral trade and economic agreements with industrialized countries signed at the turn of this century do not provide fair terms of trade to Vietnam. Many discriminative measures and quantitative restrictions have been imposed on Vietnamese goods. Vietnam expects to be granted unconditional and unlimited most favored nation status in bilateral trade on entering the international trade regime, though full membership in the WTO does not automatically guarantee this regime in trade with all members.

WTO membership will also make accessible to Vietnam the results of many years and many rounds of multilateral negotiations on tariff reduction. It should promote stability in the home market, allow local firms to build their businesses, allow more courageous local and foreign investment, reduce commodity prices, and increase competitiveness. WTO mechanisms may help Hanoi to settle trade disputes with powerful trading partners—disputes that are sometimes, as with the United States, resolved unilaterally and to Vietnam's disadvantage today. In addition, Vietnam especially relies on its status as a developing country to retain some benefits or safeguards once within the WTO. For example, Vietnam presumes that it will be authorized to protect less mature sectors of the domestic economy for some time, and seeks a delay in applying certain WTO rules in particular fields (VWIP 2001).[2] But it can hardly expect the suspension or cancellation of antidumping measures that industrialized countries have frequently applied to Vietnam.

Expanding Export of Services as well as Goods

WTO accession will allow Vietnam to more successfully export not only goods, but services as well. The diplomas and professional certificates of Vietnamese accountants, lawyers, doctors, and others—some of them perhaps less accomplished professionals—may eventually be recognized worldwide. The changing international payments system may create additional opportunities for Vietnamese banks. Vietnam's implementation of international accounting standards and of a national treatment regime for foreign investors will, it is hoped, make the economic environment more equitable and transparent and reduce direct costs both for investors and local manufacturers.

Full WTO membership will also, it is hoped, increase trading partners' trust in Vietnam, improve the overall foreign trade regime, stabilize and expand markets and sales, and help to ensure quality for local commodities. Today, Vietnam is primarily considered a supplier of oil and other raw materials to the world market, and that is a role that Vietnam currently accepts. These goods are traded within the WTO with minimum regulation and without quotas or any special restrictions for developing countries. But if Vietnamese exports continue to diversify, the country's interest in equal participation in global trade should only grow.

Access to International Financial Resources and Modern Technology

Upon entering the WTO, Vietnam should become more attractive for investors in manufacturing and services, and should find access to international capital easier as it accepts transparent rules and norms of global trade. Entry into the markets of WTO member-states should provide greater foreign capital to local export manufactures. And under the TRIMS agreement, Vietnamese investors will receive equal privileges abroad, though currently there is little investment by local businesses outside Vietnam. WTO membership should enable more effective integration of modern technology that may help the modernization and reform of state enterprises.

A Voice in Global Trade Regulation

As Vietnam's economy increasingly depends on global markets and international competition in trade sharpens, WTO membership will give Vietnam an opportunity to participate in elaborating new rules of global trade. Vietnam may also become one of the developing countries' activists within WTO. As the fifth ministerial conference of the WTO in Cancun showed, this group will demand that the global north makes concessions to the south in certain areas.

Questioning the Terms of Accession

Emphasizing the positive effects of WTO accession and foreign trade liberalization on Vietnamese trade and economy reflects the international financial institutions' evaluation of the effects of liberalization on national economic growth for Vietnam. The World Bank and the International Monetary Fund believe that trade barriers prevent optimum distribution of resources and promote rent-seeking activity. Such barriers do not allow Vietnam yet to realize its potential in the sectors in which Vietnam does have certain comparative advantage. Yet some observers have wondered whether the national economy is ready for the strict rules of world trade. They have criticized the attempt to combine growth with fast WTO accession (Nguyen Quoc Khai 2004a).

Weaknesses in the banking system, legislative shortcomings with significant implications for transparency and equality, low competitiveness of Vietnamese goods and services in the world market (WEF 2004),[3] and other factors limit the current potential for integration.

Meanwhile, extracting benefits from WTO membership will depend on Vietnam itself in many respects, including the determination of the Hanoi leadership to accelerate market reforms. Will Vietnam resist deeper structural reforms, and not only in the trade realm? (BFCI 2004a) The recent WTO Working Group that evaluated the last rounds of negotiations on Vietnam's entry appreciated recent concessions but insisted on additional liberalization in the domestic economy. Vietnam is familiar with the opposing viewpoints expressed by international nongovernmental organizations and others. They doubt that Vietnam can enter the WTO on terms favorable for its equitable development; this view is part of a critique of neoliberal economic theory. According to Oxfam International, conforming to WTO rules will result in excessive liberalization of imports and foreign investments, and threaten income sources for many, particularly in the countryside (Oxfam 2004).

WTO Commitments and Challenges for Vietnam

WTO membership envisages establishing transparent procedures in trade, institutional and legal changes, guaranteeing protection of foreign investments in Vietnam, and acceding to northern countries' expansion of the transnational corporate sector. Particularly dangerous for lower-income, developing, and transition countries is extending special terms of trade that are fixed in bilateral agreements such as the Vietnam-US Bilateral Trade Agreement, to all members of this organization (VTC 2004). WTO members agreed in December 2002 to apply a special preferential regime for accession of such countries but it was not fully implemented. And the liberalization of poorer countries on trade in goods and services should be limited in scope. The "non-market economy" designation for Vietnam by more developed countries restricts the access of cheap goods by their markets. For example in 2003–4, the United States suddenly disrupted the successful import of Vietnamese catfish and shrimp. Several major international NGOs considers such bans unfair, threatening domestic (Vietnamese) fisherfolk, and economic stability (McCarty and Kalapesi 2003; Oxfam 2004).

Vietnamese leaders believe that potential economic loss from nonparticipation in the WTO is more severe in the medium and longer term than the dangers from joining the WTO. Hanoi has already made or will finally accept concessions aimed at obtaining consent of the WTO Working Group members on Vietnam's accession, and has had to yield to their pressure in many areas by weakening trade protectionism through reductions or elimination of tariffs, quotas, licenses, and subsidies.

Updating Legislation as Core Institutional Reform

Institutional issues are particularly significant in Vietnam's commitments to the WTO. Vietnam must update and conform its legislation to international norms, particularly in foreign trade regulation. This process began in 2001 with the drafting and renewed implementation of legislation directly relating to the market economy and international trade, including competition and antimonopoly law. By the end of 2005, Vietnam had adopted or revised over 94 statutes and 265 legal acts, but the work is certainly not yet finished. There was an attempt to reform the legal system to minimize corruption, estimated by Transparency International as very high (100 out of 174) in the world's rankings in 2003 (*Business Week* 2003; VIR 2003). Other changes needed are in customs rules, foreign trade, insurance, and a number of other fields. In forcing Hanoi to apply international trade norms, the WTO also gives Vietnam new mechanisms for certain kinds of protection, for it can apply antidumping tariffs under certain circumstances (e.g., VWIP 2001).

From Protectionism to a Liberal Trade Regime

Vietnam will be observed by other WTO nations after it joins the WTO trade regime to see whether it applies the principles of freedom, equality, antidiscrimination, and building a competitive trade environment. Vietnam's trading partners are concerned about direct and indirect support of exports by the Hanoi government, for example, through dumping and subsidizing of manufacturers. It has promised to increase its foreign trade transparency and create a mechanism for judicial review of administrative decisions including independent arbitration of economic disputes in the trade arena. And Vietnam must limit state intervention in the economy, through import restrictions, infringing on the commercial rights of foreign traders, and state control over the economic decisions of local companies.

There is an inconsistent demand for decentralization of state monopolies. Hanoi understands the need for state-owned enterprise (SOE) transformation, but also its complexities, particularly when general corporations and other entities form core elements of the domestic system. Even the Bilateral Trade Agreement affirms the right to retain state monopolies in some strategically important sectors (such as mineral extraction and information resources).

Vietnam has undertaken a commitment to give most favored nation treatment in bilateral trade (MFN) to other WTO members. At the same time, Vietnam will enjoy a special regime for government procurement, sea freight, movie distribution, and a few other fields. Hanoi has agreed to remove remaining protectionist barriers immediately after accession to the WTO. The new foreign trade regime will be based on tariff regulation, and free from quantitative or qualitative restrictions, especially from direct bans on imports and exports. Vietnam has to considerably lower its protection barriers, including freezing tariffs on agricultural produce and manufactures (*VNExpress* 2004). For example, Vietnam agreed to stop impeding the import of medicines, machinery, and other important goods. A new regime for vehicles will come into force in 2007; today import tariffs for locally assembled vehicles are 25% and 80% for produced vehicles (*Thoi bao Kinh te* 2004). But in all probability, Hanoi will be obliged to accept a lower level of protection, perhaps as a result of compromise with Western nations on cutting subsidies for the agricultural sector. These measures force local manufacturers to compete with foreign goods, including the fledgling high technology industries (e.g., assembly of vehicles or electronics) that have huge investment demands. So Vietnam's attempts to defend higher tariffs confirm its hope to maintain its domestic industry that is without sufficient resources or experience and that has often been unprofitable.

Consequences for Domestic Agriculture
and the Rural Areas

Vietnam's basic WTO commitments could seriously affect domestic agriculture and the rural areas by transforming the modes of state activity. The state may maintain monopolies in trading major agricultural products under the WTO agreements, but its regulation of these matters must conform to WTO norms regarding state-trading monopolies. Vietnam has committed to reducing state support for farmers and direct export subsidies, commitments that have become obligatory for WTO newcomers. Vietnam will also eliminate export subsidies for coffee and other products, including goods such as rice, soybeans, vegetables, and sugar. Vietnam has asked for a delay in implementing the agreement on foodstuff safety.

Hanoi has been forced to concede on protection levels for agricultural products on a stage-by-stage basis, as China also had agreed several years earlier. Vietnam sought to point out that Western countries did not follow the rule they were imposing on junior partners such as Vietnam. According to the *Zuddeuche Zeitung* newspaper, the United States and the European Economic Community have spent some US$300 billion to subsidize farmers in their home countries, exceeding by several times their assistance to poorer developing countries (BFCI 2004b). But Vietnam has largely lost these arguments. It has been asked to keep indirect subsidies for farmers and exporters until the country's per capita income achieved US$1,000, as a number of WTO members previously enjoyed. But this concession was available only during the Uruguayan round of negotiations (Thao bao Kinh te 2004), and relies on such indirect assistance as the financing of environment protection, maintenance of food security, and rural development. Such measures are carried out in Vietnam through United Nations and other programs and are welcomed by the WTO. Thus, the implementation of WTO norms is expected to result in direct losses to the Vietnamese agrarian sector. WTO does impose rigid requirements while the world round of negotiations on agrarian issues that began in Doha has not been completed. Vietnam's commitments in this field will have effects in the long run, and WTO restrictions will block attempts to maintain state protection of an ineffective agrarian sector.

Related Investment Measures

Under the WTO TRIMS agreement the Hanoi government should remove various restrictions on foreign investors, such as fixing the shares of joint venture output being exported (now up to 80%), or the amount of repatriated profit. This may make Vietnam more attractive to foreign capital. But at the same time the obligation to cancel special privileges for investment in special economic zones can have a negative impact. These zones have become real engines of national growth; and reducing incentives for them could have negative results. Vietnam's demand for transfer of modern technology as a condition of foreign investors' entry has caused disagreements. Technology transfer is particularly important to Vietnam because its science and technology do not yet sufficiently stimulate manufacture and trade. Backward technology and equipment along with slow infrastructure updating result in high prices and low efficiency, complicating retail and wholesale trade.

Protection of Intellectual Property Rights

Weak protection of intellectual property is a key concern of Vietnam's foreign investors and trading partners. Foreigners registered about 96% of Vietnam's patents in 1995–2002 and illegal reproduction and distribution of software, books, and movies occurred widely (Nguyen Quoc Khai 2004b). When the TRIPS agreement comes into force, WTO members will recognize intellectual property rights, and therefore, Vietnam has begun to bring national legislation on intellectual property into line with WTO standards. But some of the existing problems are so significant that they cannot be resolved quickly. Special attention is being given to strengthening legal and judicial procedures at courts, customs, and state industrial property agencies at the central and local levels. The new Civil Code begins the process of defending intellectual property rights, and Vietnam has adopted a number of normative acts to provide protection beyond the broad provisions of the Civil Code (VNIA 2002).

Opening of the Services Sector

Among the most serious challenges to the local economy arises from the opening of the services sector, in such areas as finance, banking and insurance, legal services, consulting services, transport, and information services. Most of Vietnam's services in these areas are not yet fully marketized and they are vulnerable to competition from industrialized countries. So Hanoi sought to avoid inclusion of nontrade matters in WTO regulation but eventually was forced to grant access to 92 subsectors, more than China (access to 85 services subsectors), Thailand (74), or the Philippines (50) (Oxfam 2004). The process will be gradual, lasting until 2008, as stipulated in the Vietnam–USA Bilateral Trade Agreement.

Most disputed were the terms of foreign access to the financial sector and especially insurance services and retail trade. Foreign companies dealing in life insurance in Vietnam sought to expand their activities in other insurance subsectors. Having agreed to open the insurance market, Hanoi will lose some sources of future investments into the local economy. But Vietnam must make concessions, and the backwardness of its financial services is a major problem, caused by the absence of real competitors. Initial competition in retail trade has already provoked anxiety and protests in the local business community. Afraid of the implications of WTO accession, they criticize the predominance of powerful foreign companies, as in the case of the Saigon municipal trading corporation that complained of local business decline brought about by such Western trading networks as "Metro Cash and Carry" (*VNEconomy* 2004a).

Telecommunications is another vulnerable subsector that is very attractive for foreign capital. Leading global players could easily destroy the VNPT state corporation monopoly in this market. In one sense this would be positive, because it would create equality in competition and increase inflow of new investment in a less monopolized environment. But the telecommunications subsector has strategic importance for the state, and these developments will be especially complex.

Commitments and Impacts in Other Fields

Vietnam must also develop and apply a list of national technical standards corresponding to international norms and WTO requirements. This work should be completed in 2010 and is intended to speed integration into the global economy in such areas as quality certification, human safety, and the environment. This work should also lead to higher spending for standards and laboratories. The WTO also supervises international labor standards, and these will certainly come under discussion in the Vietnamese case as well. Such labor standards could be a problem for many Vietnamese private as well as state-owned enterprises, especially when trade unions are dominated by the Party and state and violations of workers' rights and interests are increasing.

Experts analyzing the consequences of Vietnam's accession to the WTO have not yet paid sufficient attention to social impact. Inequalities between groups and regions have widened and may continue to do so. The opening of markets may worsen the position of farmers and subsidized industries. Manual laborers and those with lower education or the unemployed will be especially vulnerable. Vietnamese scholars warn that adherence to international norms will force keen competition in the labor market, and increase migration and employment in the informal sector (*VNEconomy* 2004a). To counter these dangers Vietnam will seek to restructure manufacturing, decrease structural unemployment, and increase labor force mobility.

The official mass media frequently explains these problems by noting that all WTO newcomers have to pay a rather high price for better opportunities in international trade. That high price will include access for powerful transnational corporations and the growth of their influence on local commodity and services markets. Some believe that they will influence the Vietnamese government in determining some of its economic policies (*VNEconomy* 2004b). A survey carried out by the Vietnam Academy of Social Sciences in 2003 at 160 enterprises revealed the wide discrepancy in expectations with respect to the consequences of the entry into WTO. Ninety-nine percent of respondents expressed hope for improvement in the quality of goods and services, and 90% hoped for acceleration of economic growth. Meanwhile 69% expected unequal growth and a widening gap between the rich and the poor; 46% of respondents were afraid of new bankruptcies; and 23% were concerned with the prospect of rising unemployment (*Financial Times* 2003).

Entry Process Peculiarities

The Schedule and Tactics of Negotiations

The process of Vietnam's entry into the WTO has been long and difficult. The sessions of the WTO Working Group on Vietnam's accession pursued only fact-finding until 2000, as Vietnam's representatives answered more than 1,550 questions from members with the aim of strengthening transparency in the foreign trade regime (AFP 2001; VAW 2002). Domestically, the government organized activities to popularize ideas of economic integration and foreign trade liberalization, explanation of WTO rules and norms, analysis of the impact of WTO entry, and education of government officials. Training courses were held to assist Vietnam in accomplishing its goals, and technical assistance was offered through the United Nations and other donors. Without a precise understanding of the agreements necessary for implementation upon entry into the WTO, Hanoi could not correlate its new commitments with the needs and opportunities of the economy and trade. Effective participation by Vietnam was complicated by the low capacity of the governmental bodies, as well as duplication and uncertainty as to their functions, including a continuation of state patronage and special privileges.

In 2001 and 2002 (during the fifth and sixth rounds of negotiations) the Vietnamese delegation began discussions with Working Group members on the terms for domestic market opening for foreign commodities and services. During the seventh and eighth rounds in 2003 and 2004, progress was achieved on a number of agreements on tariff relaxation. These arrangements took into account not only the economic interests of Hanoi's partners, but also addressed Vietnam's goal of obtaining favorable terms upon entry, even if the benefits of those terms could only be realized in the longer term. In the ninth and tenth rounds in 2004 and 2005, the Working Group and Vietnam worked on the draft report on Vietnam's accession as the major part of the final package of documents. At this point, the multilateral negotiations had entered the decisive stage.

Vietnam achieved some concrete results in the negotiations—for example, the accession protocol provides for a transition period of three to five years, after which Vietnam will be obliged to fully apply all standard international trade norms. The same approach has been used in the Chinese case. At the last WTO biennial conference in late 2005, Vietnam could not secure accession, but the delay was not unexpected for investors who were skeptical of Hanoi's ambitious goals on the schedule for WTO entry. And there must be further domestic consensus in Vietnam before moving to deeper reforms. Thus this delay may help strengthen Vietnam's economy and domestic companies, particularly state-owned enterprises, because the sharpest competition with foreign firms has not yet erupted. Meanwhile, Hanoi has not yet accepted all commitments because some of them have serious effects on the economic and legal system. Not being a world power with the capacity to insist on such beneficial terms of access as China or Russia, Vietnam sought to achieve its strategic goal through tactical maneuvers, and may intend to disregard some obligations after the entry into the WTO if it feels that is necessary (as China did). Vietnam cannot completely give up protectionism, for example in the form of prohibitive import taxes. So in the negotiations Hanoi has sought to determine some priority sectors for further protection and ensure a delay in opening of selected markets.

Partners in Negotiations

Hanoi first achieved trading arrangements with the United States, Japan, the European Union, and Canada through bilateral trade and investment agreements. Their position has particular importance for Vietnam's accession to WTO because they account for up to two-thirds of world trade turnover (BFCI 2004c). This approach—working first with the main partners—is easily explained, for these are primary trade partners of Vietnam; they account for 65% of Vietnam's foreign trade turnover. And Vietnam seeks, where possible, to take advantage of differences among the major trading partners (such as the European Union and the United States) in its WTO affairs. Hanoi officials appreciate the Vietnam-US Bilateral Trade Agreement as a breakthrough, for it helped to open the global north to the Vietnamese market. Many of the agreement's articles exceeded the provisions of the WTO.

Vietnamese membership in ASEAN and regional economic fora of the Asia Pacific, particularly APEC, has substantively facilitated negotiations with other countries, including China, with which Vietnam has signed an agreement as well. This giant neighbor serves as a model of market reforms for Hanoi and a training field for WTO entry. Beijing supports its junior partner in this race while remaining a major trading competitor of Vietnam in attracting foreign investment and gaining foreign markets for labor-intensive commodities (e.g., clothes, footwear, household goods, electronics). The heart of their contradictions is diplomatically left unspoken, and China has special interest in two aspects of Vietnam's WTO accession. First is the preservation of an existing preferential regime for the purchase of Chinese goods for Vietnam's domestic market. Vietnam's desire to constrain the influx of such goods causes come discontent in Beijing, and Hanoi continues to be concerned about the threat of rising Chinese influence in the local market of retail trade and services.

Hanoi also remains worried about potential activity of Chinese firms in areas such as civil construction, insurance, and import and distribution operations. These firms' offensive strategy could result in their domination over such services because of capital and scale advantages. Vietnamese border areas could suffer most in a possible decline of local small industry and trade. In the face of inevitable competition with growing Chinese imports, unemployment will also increase. The second obvious Chinese interest lies in possible access to Vietnamese natural resources through participation in the share capital of domestic companies. Until now China has not been allowed entry directly into oil and other extraction activities.

Japan has also asserted its interests in this process. Vietnam's negotiations with Japan were slow because of Vietnamese resistance (according to Japan) and an emphasis on Russia. But a key reason for the delay appears to be Tokyo's substantial requirements on the reduction of import tariffs, opening of the services sector, protection of intellectual property rights, and other issues.

Main Implications of Accession

The direct domestic impact of WTO accession on Vietnam should be a restriction of power and use of administrative instruments of the state in the economic arena that some might equate to partial loss of sovereignty.

In the short term we could expect greater regional disparities in social and economic development among different groups. This could result in discontent and difficulties in the domestic political situation. The main impact on Hanoi's foreign policy would be the agreement to follow the laws and rules of the global economy. Vietnam may integrate more quickly within the Asia Pacific region in order to escape excessive dependence on stronger and richer partners, including resistance to perceptions of growing interference from Washington in international and regional affairs, and the rising power of China on the Vietnamese economy.

Conclusion

Hanoi did not obtain access to specially facilitated accession procedures available for the transitional or nonmarket economies. Vietnam has failed to achieve this nonstandard status of faster access that was arranged for China (2001) and Cambodia (2004). China entered WTO with up to 200 significant concessions (Oxfam 2004). But Vietnam stands a good chance of achieving rapid entry if it continues in its path of liberal reforms. Hanoi seeks to balance national sovereignty with the realization of development goals. Compromises, even sacrifices to achieve those goals will be needed if WTO membership will eventually strengthen Vietnam's position in world markets and allow the use of WTO mechanisms for the advocacy of Vietnam's economic interests. Yielding to excessive demands could result in negative implications for Vietnam, including serious effects for many regions and sectors of the Vietnamese economy. WTO accession could seriously damage both the state and private companies for some time. But with reasonable commitments, we can also expect certain benefits for Vietnam. In the long run WTO membership may speed up Vietnam's economic transition, increase its prosperity, and enhance its modernization.

Notes

1. The textile sector now employs well over a million workers and is an important source of GDP growth for Vietnam. Until entry into the WTO this sector will remain under quota regulation, weakening the competitive position of Vietnamese manufacturers (BIKI, 22.VII.2004).
2. For example, the European Union agreed to a seven year delay for Vietnam (VNN 2004a).
3. In spite of certain progress, in 2003 international agencies evaluating the factor of competitiveness have placed Vietnam on fiftieth position in the list of 95 countries in the world rating—see World Economic Forum, Global Competitiveness Report (WEF).

References

Agence France Press, November 30, 2001.

(BFCI) Bulletin of Foreign Commercial Information (Moscow), July 22, 2004a.

——— August 12, 2004b.

——— August 28, 2004c.

Business Week. 2003. Vietnam's time is running out, November 24, 2003.

Financial Times. 2003. Trade: Joining WTO will accelerate Vietnam's economic reform, June 6, 2003.

McCarty, Adam and Kalapesi, Carl. 2003. The economics of the NME issue: Viet Nam catfish case study.

Nguyen Quoc Khai. 2004a. Kinh te Viet-Nam truoc nguong cua To chuc Mau dich The gioi. Tap chi Cach mang, No. 40. Online at www.daiviet.org, accessed January 20, 2005.

———. 2004b. Vietnam: Global integration and economic development. Paper presented at the Vietnam Update 2004 Conference, Institute of Southeast Asian Studies (Singapore).

Oxfam International. 2004. Extortion at the gate: Will Vietnam join the WTO on pro-development terms? Briefing Paper No. 67, 1–32.

Thoi bao Kinh te Saigon (Saigon Economic Times), June 26, 2004.

U.S.–Vietnam Trade Council. 2004. Education Forum, May 7, 2004. Online at www.usvtc.org.

Vietnam Investment Review (VIR). 2002. Chinese minister reaffirms WTO bid to support, May 13.

———. 2003. WTO negotiations hit by lagging legal reform, October 27.

Vietnam National Information Agency, May 14, 2002.

Vietnamnet (VNN). June 2, 2003. Online at http://www.vnn.vn/kinhte/2003/06/45250.

———. October 9, 2004a. Online at http://www.vnn.vn/kinhte/2004/10/64630.

———. December 22, 2004b. Online at http://www.vnn.vn/kinhte/2004/12/68350.

Vietnam's Accession to WTO (VAW) (Training course on WTO Implementation). 2002. Country Report. Seoul, April, 2002.

VNEconomy, July 23, 2004a. Online at http://www.vneconomy.com.vn.

———, September 10, 2004b. Online at http://www.vneconomy.com.vn.

VNExpress, July 01, 2004. Online at http://vnexpress.net/Vietnam/Kinh-doanh/2004/07/3B9D406E.

World Economic Forum (WEF). 2004. Global Competitiveness Report. Geneva. Online at http://www.weforum.org, visited December 20, 2004.

CHAPTER SIX

Economic Interdependence within ASEAN

A Perspective on the Vietnamese Strategy for Development and National Security

HIEN DO

During a session break at the UN General Assembly at the beginning of 1990, an American researcher was reported to have said to Nguyen Dy Nien, then Vice Minister of Foreign Affairs: "Some people might consider it a mockery, but we think that only the Vietnamese will be ready to become competitors of the Japanese in the twenty first century; [for this], they will still need a takeoff point" (Nguyen Dy Nien 1995a, 34).

This vision would have been a pure fantasy for those who knew Vietnam earlier. According to the official calculations of the Vietnamese Ministry of Trade (Ministry of Trade 2000, 37), to meet the basic needs for a population whose average yearly growth rate between 1975 and 1985 was 2.3%, Vietnam would have needed a yearly GDP of at least 7%—but in fact it only just reached half that level. The level of dependence on external sources, notably the USSR and other socialist bloc countries, had increased dramatically, and official statistics did not hide that (Institute of World Economics 1995, 157–8). Ten years after reunification, Vietnam's external debt amounted to 8.5 billion rubles with the USSR and US$1.9 billion to the rest of the world, while the Vietnamese budget showed a permanent deficit that the government sought to resolve by printing currency. Even though it was an agricultural country,

Vietnam was importing rice and other agricultural products that its national production should, logically, have supplied. The difficulties and complexities of the American embargo and permanent tensions at the borders exacerbated this state of affairs. The country was politically isolated due to its intervention in Cambodia.

Today's Vietnam is still far from being a formidable competitor of Japan, but it is also an extraordinarily different country from that in the difficult years of the 1980s, with a very different international image. After declaring its policy of "wanting to be friends with all countries of the international community," Vietnam normalized its relations with China and the United States of America and in 1995, it became a full member of the Association of Southeast Asian Nations (ASEAN). As the host country of the fifth Europe-Asia Summit (ASEM) in Hanoi in late 2004, Vietnam has sought to speak for "late joiners," making its voice heard among the new Asian members of ASEM on such topics as Myanmar, always a sensitive topic of discussion. Today's Vietnam is also very different from the Vietnam of the 1980s in economic terms. Now the third largest rice exporter in the world, Vietnam has maintained among the highest growth rates in Southeast Asia in recent years. But it is still unclear whether the seeming regional integration in ASEAN and recent growth will assure Vietnam's takeoff.

The socioeconomic development strategy for the period 2001–10 presented by Vietnam's government in 2001 focused on three key and interlinked objectives—maintaining stability and sovereignty, achieving sustainable, high economic growth rates and achieving sustainable poverty reduction and equity. The government recognizes that economic growth is of vital importance and that among the biggest risks is in not pursuing deeper integration. On the eve of the tenth Vietnamese Communist Party Congress in 2006, the immediate question for Vietnam's political leadership was not primarily "what to do?" but rather "how to do it?" as deeper integration creates new realities and problems for Vietnam.

Economic Pragmatism and National Security: Motors of Vietnam's Regional Integration

Awareness of a More and More Interdependent World

The crisis that shook the Asian economies in 1997 reinforced the Vietnamese political elite's vision of an increasingly fragile and interdependent world. By the end of the 1980s and the beginning of the 1990s, while the national economy was still experiencing difficulties and the political and strategic environment in the Asia-Pacific region was in a state of confusion, the Vietnamese leaders had opportunities to reevaluate the country's regional and international situation. Since the Second World War, Southeast Asia had been a geographical and strategic zone where American influence had been exerted on many states through economic, military, and political means, successive treaties and various organizations, and even simply the strong attraction exerted by the "American model." For Vietnam the emergence of other powers gave the Far East its new economic, political, and strategic configuration, and Japan, the world's second economic power, became an essential partner with significant weight.[1] At the same time, China's territory, demographics, and economic strength made it the center of Asia.

It is now axiomatic that economics occupies a growing place in international relations. From the end of the 1980s, economic development imperatives constituted one of the undeniable driving forces of Soviet—American *détente* that in turn exerted a strong influence on the strategic USSR–US–China triangle. Within the framework of its political objective of the "four modernizations," China too modified its external political strategy in order to create a stable and favorable environment for its economic development and to bring it to the rank of a world power.

In Vietnam these changes were followed cautiously, though Vietnamese leaders could already feel the start of a larger change. As early as the end of the 1980s, Minister of Foreign Affairs Nguyen Co Thach remarked, "Great economic challenges have become the great political, security and defence challenges for all countries. These are the underlying reasons for the great powers' strategic readjustments" (Nguyen Co Thach 1990, 2–8). He went on to specify that world economic interdependence had decreased the risk of war, and that a "strong economy," an "appropriate defence capacity" and "broadened international cooperation" were the guarantors of the country's security. He noted that internationalization of the forces of production had led to the end of the world's division into several separated markets, confined within the framework of political and military alliances (Nguyen Co Thach 1989, 1–8).

Beyond measurable economic factors, interdependence has become a way to justify reinforced links between countries (Smouts et al. 2003, 278–9), because interdependence does not necessarily mean equal relationships (Hassner 1974, 1263). In Vietnam, there was an increasing awareness that autarky and isolation were not the best means to ensure the independence of the country and reinforce the legitimacy of the Party. Is a nation that does not wish to be pushed to the margins of international life a nation that controls its participation in interdependence and uses it in favor of its political interests and objectives? As Pierre Hassner put it:

> We find ourselves on the verge of the political economy of international relations, which find power relations at the heart of exchange, the relations of exchange at the heart of the power phenomenon, the relations between different forms of dependence and different forms of power at the heart of international life which, in economics like politics, seem to be defined more and more by the control and manipulation of interdependence. (Hassner 1974, 1262)

The arguments of Kenneth Waltz are probably the most rigorous: interdependence leads to relationships that are very costly to break down (Waltz 1970, 205–7; Rosecrance and Stein 1973, 1–28). At the beginning of the 1990s, needing to escape from its economic problems, it was clear that Vietnam could not rely only on its internal forces. The country therefore needed to be accepted on the international scene in an era of increasingly complex relationships between countries, regions, and continents. As the Sixth Party Congress observed: "Mankind is facing a challenge involving several new problems of global character. . . . Between countries that are different in their social regimes, the only judicious choice is to participate in a movement of economic emulation" (Vietnamese Communist Party 1987, 35–6).

Regardless of the immediate discourse on interdependence, globalization, or more recently the notion of the shared property of mankind, the Vietnamese Party and state are clearly fully aware of the world in which Vietnam must live. But this awareness does not necessarily provide the tools needed to deal with these trends, nor allay all doubts. Questions about the effects of globalization, its political risks, and the path to follow continue to face the Vietnamese leadership. But there seems no alternative to entering the mainstream in international relations, at least according to a senior official and former Secretary to former Prime Minister Pham Van Dong writing in the late 1990s: "Going against the trend of the time, even though it would be a complex tendency [and] . . . alluding to obscure superpower conspiracies, will never be a sign of consciousness. Barricading oneself in against globalization and relying only on our own strength . . . amounts to depriving ourselves of the conditions and capacity to resist. It's like throwing in the towel before the fight, deluding oneself into believing that staying away from the battle will bring safety, whereas it will only lead to failure, bringing about isolation and exclusion" (Tran Viet Phuong 1999, 13).

The Judicious Decision for Regional Integration

Regional integration in the context of interdependence and globalization was seen in Vietnam as a necessary component of the adaptation to make globalization more acceptable on a national level. Particularly in Southeast Asia, the regionalization process is a tool for the developing countries to improve their position on the international scene, both in the economic arena and in politics. Concerns for economic integration often go together with the desire to affirm national position and status by promoting regional political identity. As then Vice Foreign Minister Nguyen Dy Nien put it in Bangkok early in this process, in 1993, "Integration is not an aim per se. It comes from the vital interests of the countries in the region. It is able to bring about common security and prosperity for all countries, at the same time giving a position for each country in the process of participating in global cooperation" (Nguyen Dy Nien 1995b, 148).

It is important to notice, in the specific case of Vietnam, the striking contrast of the political benefits before and after its entry in ASEAN. At the beginning of the 1990s, by solving the Cambodian imbroglio and ending the boycott inflicted by the international community, the Vietnamese Party and state sought to recover its domestic and international legitimacy and reinvigorate the national economy—for the regime was increasingly dependent on its ability to provide economic growth (De Mesquita and Downs 2005). The crisis of the socialist bloc, the fall of the USSR, and problems in the process of normalizing relations both with China and the United States (Nguyen Hong Thach 2000, 227–53) reinforced Vietnam's judicious choice in linking with its regional grouping through membership, although the leaders hesitated initially in making this decision.

Given the legacy of the Cambodian invasion, the political leadership sought to demonstrate its policy of giving priority to economic development as the best proof of its commitment to peace and stability in Southeast Asia. This strategy was well understood by its partners. In the neighboring countries, it was thought that a well-integrated Vietnam would be able to benefit from collective security and would better contribute to the stability of the shared space than a Vietnam isolated on the regional and international scene (Warren 1995; Tirona 1998, 14–15; Lee Kwan Yew 2000, 312–13).

Within Vietnam, the Communist Party had established its legitimacy in the fight for the national independence, and it continued to promise to preserve that independence. But independence no longer meant autarky; instead, economic development was crucial both for independence and for regime legitimacy. According to a member of the Party Political Bureau, Nguyen Phu Trong, a strong economy was crucial to ensuring independence and national political autonomy. In his words, "Once we have gained . . . independence and political autonomy, the main content of independence and autonomy of a country is characterised by the successful construction of an independent . . . economy" (Nguyen Phu Trong 2004, 149–58).

The realities, however, were far more complex. The launching of the *doi moi* renovation program in 1986, accompanied by a reorientation of foreign policy, posed difficult questions for the regime: how could it initiate significant reforms without questioning or upsetting fifty years of history and the Party and state's political legitimacy? How would the Party and state solve internal economic issues, reinsert the nation effectively on the international scene, and preserve or even enhance its legitimacy? The relationships between China, the United States and Japan, and between those major powers and the Southeast Asia region, as well as between ASEAN members themselves, helped Vietnam to open the door of the largely pro-Western ASEAN group (Do Hien 2004, 171–86).[2] Vietnam had no other alternative but to participate in establishing collective confidence with its neighboring countries and the most important stable environment for Vietnam's economic development and national security was the space most directly related to Vietnam—Southeast Asia.

ASEAN was an economic space in which a country with formerly a centralized and planned economy could familiarize itself with the mechanisms of a market economy. It was also a politically neutral space where Vietnam could consolidate its regional and international position, helping to alleviate the pressure of a more balanced relationship with the great world actors. ASEAN helped to illustrate very well the idea of active neutrality explained by then senior Deputy Foreign Minister Tran Quang Co: "As for countries not belonging to the category of great powers, their problem does not consist in nourishing the ambition to become a pole in the multipolar world, but to learn how to live so that they can obtain the most advantages or the least disadvantages in a totally renewed world environment. Consequently, their interest is no longer to take their place behind a great power or a pole that would make them inevitably the object of attacks from the opposite pole. Their interest is presently to create for themselves an independent position that can give them the possibility to establish cooperative relationships with all sides" (Tran Quang Co 1995, 4).

This neutrality was also welcomed by the great actors, especially the cumbersome Chinese neighbor who saw ASEAN as a "neutral" and "stabilizing" group, practicing a "diplomacy of equal distance from the great powers" and with its own (though relatively soft) regulatory mechanisms (Crombé and Godement 1999, 105–41).

The entry into global interdependence by means of regional integration, treated here as something of a small circle of relative independence, was also seen by Vietnamese leaders as a way of intensifying bilateral relationships and of enriching mutual understanding with Southeast Asia (Hanoi Interview, April 10, 2003). Only two years after entering ASEAN observer status, Vietnam had signed nearly forty cooperative agreements with ASEAN member nations. More than three hundred official meetings every year within ASEAN multiply the additional possibilities of bilateral meetings, giving the countries more opportunities to negotiate on their differences. And integration with and through ASEAN decidedly brings to the Vietnamese elite the possibility of strengthening its lobbying to maximize its economic development, an objective officially set by the government's Decree 08/2003/ND-CP and by Foreign Minister Nguyen Dy Nien (*Phap luat Newspaper*, August 19, 2003).

Vietnam Within ASEAN:
Building an Integration Strategy

New Realities

On the national level, the awareness of and commitment to regional economic integration did not automatically provide Vietnam with the most efficient ways to cope with and handle these complex processes in order to reach its political objectives. The newer realities that Vietnam found through its engagement with ASEAN also helped Vietnam to adjust its policies and those adjustments, in turn, affected internal dynamics.

In the second international colloquium on Vietnamese studies organized in July 2004 in Ho Chi Minh City, for example, differing views on the pace of Vietnam's regional integration reflected the tension between Vietnam's political objectives and the real capacity of the country. The pace of integration is problematic for ASEAN, under development pressure and an economic attraction for East Asia. And ASEAN needs a certain strength to benefit from the advantages of such broader integration circles as ASEAN+1, ASEAN+3, and ASEM. The greater the level of regional integration, the more obvious the shared interests between ASEAN's members. A strong ASEAN strengthens the position of its members on the international scene. But all this also depends on the pace of integration of each state.

At the same time, the compromises afforded to the "group of new members" (Myanmar, Laos, Cambodia, Vietnam) become relatively fixed, and may affect the future of ASEAN and its members. For example, in September 2004, the ASEAN ministers for finance and economy discussed the construction of a "single market" similar to the European model, including the dismantling of custom barriers within the group over eight years (Agence France Presse, September 5, 2004). But the implementation of this project would once more fix two differential dates: 2007 for the six most developed countries of ASEAN and 2012 for the group of new members. Does this sort of "ASEAN way" risk fixing firmly in the minds of ASEAN political decision makers, as well as external observers, the image of an ASEAN divided into two groups with a gap between them? In the context of competition with and pressure from the outside world, ASEAN members realized that the current "positive discrimination" could only be a temporary solution. Equality, though perhaps disadvantageous in the short term for certain members such as Vietnam, could also serve as a basis for the solidarity and durability of ASEAN.

By exposing itself to realities in ASEAN and its member states, Vietnam is forced to an awareness of the gap between external developments, the pace of integration, and its own situation. The lack of competitiveness of the public sector is a good example of the common situation in which ASEAN, with its diverse experiences, provides multiple reference points for "market economy according to the socialist orientation" (Gates 2001). The President of Vietnam's Chamber of Commerce and Industry (VCCI), Doan Duy Thanh, commented on this as a key problem of regime legitimacy: "If the public enterprises continue to lose as much as now, socialism will be destroyed from the inside." He criticized the forced creation of conglomerates of various public enterprises more than ten years ago, in the early 1990s: "The directors do not respect each other, the inferiors do not listen to what the superiors say, most of these conglomerates lose money or just manage to break even" (*Cong luan Newspaper*, June 26, 2002). But, according to

Jordan Ryan, the then representative of the United Nations Development Programme in Hanoi, the accumulation of economic power remains under the control of the state that views these state-owned enterprises as a good compromise that benefits the authority of the Communist Party and thus political stability (Ryan 2005).

Within ASEAN, Vietnam faces as much if not more difficult competition than it perhaps benefits from complementary effects. Vietnam continues to stress its "trump cards": Low cost and hardworking manpower, policies favoring foreign investment, natural resources, and other advantages. And yet these trump cards seem more and more fragile. In addition to the shortage of qualified manpower, labor costs rose in 2001 by 25% over the previous year, while the relative cost of manpower in other ASEAN countries had not changed, and or had even decreased (*Tuoi tre Newspaper*, April 4, 2002). Despite holding the status of a politically stable and friendly country, particularly after September 11, 2001, Vietnam's obstacles include high rates of taxation on personal income (a top rate of nearly 50% versus lower rates in other ASEAN nations, such as roughly 26% in Singapore); a dual structure of prices that does not exist in other countries; and complex, rigid, and long administrative procedures. The results are reasonably clear: in 2001, Japanese investments to Vietnam amounted to $160 million, twice the level of the previous year. Nevertheless this amount corresponds to less than 3% of Japanese investment in China, 8% of investment in Thailand, and 20% of Japanese investment in Malaysia. In 2002, ASEAN investment in Vietnam represented only one-fourth of the foreign investment in the country (with Malaysia, Thailand, and Singapore being the main investors).

Commercial relations have perhaps not yet matched the political hopes of integration, at least in Hanoi. As table 6.1 shows, ASEAN, the second most important market in the region behind China, is not the "favorite destination" of Vietnamese goods. When we look at the geographical distribution of FDI, the economic gains of integration may seem to be distributed more in favor of the south rather than of the center or the north. The ASEAN market is second to last, ahead of the United States only, for exports from southern capital. And this inevitably affects corporate actions in Vietnam and the decisions of the state.

In addition, within ASEAN, a kind of "every man for himself" attitude on the Paracels and Spratlys disputes may have increased the disappointment of Vietnamese leaders, although it probably was not a real surprise for them. The *Declaration of Conduct in the South China Seas*

Table 6.1   Vietnam's exports to the world, ASEAN, China and Hong Kong, Japan, the United States, and the European Union ($ millions) (1992, 1996, 2001, 2004)

Vietnam exports	World	ASEAN	China/ Hong Kong	Japan	USA	EU
1992	2,918	575	298	834	0	250
		19.7%	10.2%	28.5%		8.5%
1996	7,463	1,777	651	1,546	204	1, 001
		23.8%	8.7%	20.7%	2.7%	13.4%
2001	13,562	2,047	1,156	2,367	1,035	3,723
		15%	8.5%	17.4%	7.6%	27.4%
2004	25,625	3,370	2,731	3,507	5,206	6,083
		13.1%	10.6%	13.6%	20.3%	23.7%

Sources: Statistics Yearbook for Asia and the Pacific 2002, Economic and Social Commission for Asia and the Pacific, 2003; Yearbook 2005, Direction of Trade Statistics, International Monetary Fund.

in November 2002 contributed to providing a shared reference point, not a solid legal basis for solving the existing problems. Hopefully the Declaration has moderated the behavior of the actors involved while it has also not prevented them from acting in their own interests.[3]

ASEAN's members often do not share economic, political, and security philosophies and levels of development. More significantly, they have rarely allowed the organization to intrude on their national interests. In many ways ASEAN seems designed to provide an environment in which its members can pursue their national interests. But as a joint instrument of neighbors, ASEAN needs to be strengthened. Economic interdependence within ASEAN, expected to be institutionalized (Kuala Lumpur Declaration) is at present not strong enough to rapidly intensify the links and solidarity between members and therefore it must be consolidated by such pending projects as AFTA and the ASEAN Economic Community.

Vietnam and the Building of an Integration Strategy

For the Vietnamese elite, the question is no longer whether or not to participate in regional integration, but how to benefit most and incur the least risk from integration's advantages. This requires Vietnam to refine its integration strategy as a full member of ASEAN. The relatively weak economic interdependence within ASEAN at present (McKinsey 2002) should not prevent increases in interaction between the members to build a collective identity that will also favor the development of other shared activities. In fact, despite the efforts of the Association, intra-ASEAN trade is not picking up sufficiently. From 1992, when a free trade policy was implemented to ten years later, intra-regional exports as a percentage of total ASEAN exports decreased (-19%) whereas other regions have grown their intra-trade share. In 2004, the intra-ASEAN exports of Malaysia, Singapore and Thailand hardly exceeded twenty percent—the highest rates among the members—and are under fifteen percent with respect to Vietnam (data based on IMF and UN statistics). "Non-ASEAN costs" do not seem, at least for the time being, very high.

ASEAN countries are aware that the level of economic interdependence risks affecting their individual state's efforts to invest in areas of shared cooperation. But they do know that ASEAN is a useful way to reach other markets, that a strong ASEAN is beneficial for all its members in relation to the outside world, and that strong links with the outside world can tighten internal links. In the specific case of the construction of the ASEAN-China FTA, the ASEAN economic and political elite agrees with these internal and external concepts. The framework agreement signed in November 2002 with China pushed ASEAN to strengthen itself by launching the idea of an economic community at the ASEAN summit in October 2003. The ASEAN elite seek to promote a view of the Association as a springboard for entering other economic spaces under more favorable and better conditions.

In Vietnam the seeming commitment of the Party and state to pursue regional and international economic integration does not hide moments of "revision"[4] that can hurt their credibility. They faced ever more pressing external realities that hindered the creation of a coherent strategy. Resolution 07-NQ/TW of the Political Bureau (November 2001) on international economic integration stated both the goals and the means for Vietnam to develop in the twenty-first century. Regional integration was intended to broaden international economic relations, but further integration steps had to be taken, and stronger commitments within ASEAN had to be made.

In Vietnam it is understood that an effective Vietnam on the international scene must first be a regionally competitive Vietnam. In order to maintain its regional competitiveness, Vietnam must strengthen its integration strategy through bilateral relations within and outside ASEAN. Vietnam can reinforce its integration with ASEAN both through extending its ties across Southeast Asia and deepening its cooperation with key partners and key projects within and outside the region. This "regional competitiveness" requires the coordination of national and international projects. And in this framework, the recent

Decision no. 264/2005/QD-TTg by the government (October 2005) concerning the socioeconomic development up to 2020 on Con Dao island in the South China Sea (part of Vung Tau province) is a part of the Vietnamese policy for global development and security, emphasizing the goal of "actively contributing to the open door policy, to the process of international economic integration." The research and preparation aimed at signing free trade agreements with foreign governments and groups of countries outside ASEAN is also a welcome step forward. Vietnam's active participation in the building of triangular growth with Laos and Cambodia and its close cooperation within the development program for the Mekong Delta are further evidences of Vietnam's regional integration and development strategy, particularly in the implementation of regional projects such as the East–West Corridor construction project of ASEAN.

Vietnam's effort to shorten the development distance between new and old members promotes its political position within the Association and may contribute to increasing its "regional competitiveness." Through its own experience, Vietnam is able to contribute to ASEAN consolidation; the admission to Europe–Asia cooperation of the remaining members (Laos, Cambodia, and Myanmar) during ASEM V (Hanoi) is one example. Bilateral relations with the major ASEAN partners can also strengthen Vietnam's position within the group. The United States, China, Japan, and the European Union have an impact as well. The former U.S. Ambassador to Hanoi, Pete Peterson, said (as reported in *Quan doi Nhan dan*): "We are at the beginning of relationships with Vietnam and we promote these relationships. With time, you will see an increased interest on our part with respect to Vietnam because of economic relations and its military and political position. This will enable Vietnam to play a more important role in Southeast Asia" (*Quan doi Nhan dan*, May 28, 2001).

Conclusion

Explaining policies through some sort of economic and commercial determinism is not my goal here. I have simply tried to find some links between the two spheres and to include economic considerations in the analysis of Vietnam's international relations and Vietnam's regional strategies. Vietnam's leaders have presented regional and international economic integration—through the broadening and diversification of external relationships—as a strategy for the strengthening of national security and economic development (Nhat and Ngung 2001), facilitated by economic pragmatism and flexibility in international relationships. If national security in the new international context is a broad concept of which a key substratum is economic, regional integration helps Vietnam to ensure its security through economic action. Strengthened integration brings investment and technology. It also attempts to influence the behavior of actors within and outside the region through the economic and thus the political interests that link them to Southeast Asia.

Vietnam's regional and international strategy for development and national security is a process that needs to be continuously improved because it depends not only on a foreign policy in harmony but also on domestic political compromise. The increasing consideration of the "control and manipulation of interdependence" within ASEAN as well as between ASEAN and the outside world is a political and an economic matter. These links help consolidate Vietnam's position within ASEAN and her interactions with other actors, thanks to the relational networks that ASEAN has built up over time, now with Vietnam as a participant.

Notes

1. Vietnamese Prime Minister Phan Van Khai confirmed in a meeting with French President Jacques Chirac on April 1, 1998 that "until the recent occurrence of the Asia financial and monetary crisis, Japan was always, for Vietnam, a shining economic example to follow." In 2002 Japan was Vietnam's highest ranked trade partner and third ranked investor (UNDP 2004).

2. Only ASEAN perhaps does not weigh heavily in the foreign policy of each great world actor, but ASEAN is important because of economic and political factors. The economic interests that effectively link ASEAN to each power are not negligible. In the case of China, for example, in 1992, between 10 and 15% of foreign direct investment in China come from ASEAN; presently, ASEAN represents 11% of the whole foreign trade of China. In 2003, trade increased by 42.8% to reach US$78.25 billion dollars (Agence France Presse, Beijing, September 6, 2004). For a global vision of China–ASEAN link, see Walter 1998, 37–61; Wang Gungwu 1998, 63–79.

3. News of the agreement between China and the Philippines relating to gas/petroleum exploration in the Spratly zone (September 2004) caused anxiety in Hanoi. The government referred to the Declaration of Conduct, and asked the parties to apply this document (Answer to AFP correspondent by the Spokesman of the Vietnamese Ministry of Foreign Affairs, September 9, 2004). But this matter did not prevent Vietnam from participating in the Tripartite Agreement for Joint Marine Seismic Undertaking in the South China Sea (Vietnam, China, and the Philippines) (March 2005).

4. The ordinance adopted on May 25, 2002 about self-protection on the import of products into Vietnam is perceived as a protectionist measure. This document regulates self-protection measures and their application in the framework of excessive imports of products into Vietnam, declared to be prejudicial to domestic production. Increase of import taxes and setting of import quotas are detailed in it.

References

Crombé, Xavier and François Godement. 1999. La participation de la Chine aux dialogues multi-latéraux de sécurité en Asie-Pacifique. In *Chine, Japon, Asean: Compétition stratégique ou coopération*. Edited by François Godement. Paris: IFRI, Les études de la Documentation française, 105–41.

De Mesquita, Bruce and George W. Downs. 2005. Development and Democracy. *Foreign Affairs* 84 (September–October 2005). Online at www.foreignaffairs.org/2005/5.html, accessed December 4, 2005.

Decision. 264/2005/QD-TTg of October 25, 2005 on the socioeconomic development of Con Dao district, Vung Tau province up to 2020.

Decree 08/2003/ND-CP of the Government on diplomacy at the service of economy.

Do Hien. 2004. Les relations internationales du Viet Nam depuis 1991, la décennie des grands changements au service d'une stratégie pour la sécurité et le développement. In *Viet Nam contemporain*. Edited by Stéphane Dovert and Benoît De Tréglodé. Paris: Irasec, les Indes savantes, 171–86.

Gates, Carolyn L. 2001. The ASEAN economic model and Vietnam's economic transformation: Adjustment, adaptation, and convergence. In *ASEAN enlargement, impacts and implications*. Edited by Mya Than and Carolyn Gates. Singapore: Institute of Southeast Asian Studies, 322–61.

Hassner, Pierre. 1974. Intégration et coopération ou inégalité et dépendance? *Revue française de science politique* (December): 1249–67.

Institute of World Economics, National Center for Social Sciences and Humanities. 1995. *Doi moi kinh te Viet Nam va chinh sach kinh te doi ngoai*. Hanoi: Social Sciences Publishing House.

Kuala Lumpur Declaration on the Establishment of the ASEAN Charter, December 12, 2005.

Lee, Kwan Yew. 2000. *From Third World to the first: The Singapore story, 1965–2000, Singapore and the Asian economic boom*. New York: Harper Collins.

McKinsey and Company. 2002. Studies on ASEAN competitiveness presented at the annual meeting of ASEAN Economic Ministers. Brunei, September 2002.

Ministry of Trade (Bo Thuong mai). 2000. *Viet Nam huong toi the ky XXI*. Hanoi: Hanoi Publishing House.

Nguyen Co Thach. 1989. Tat ca vi hoa binh, doc lap dan toc va phat trien. *Tap chi Cong san (Communist Review)* 8: 1–8.

———. 1990. Nhung chuyen bien tren the gioi va tu duy moi cua chung ta. *Quan he Quoc te (International Relations)* 1: 2–8.

Nguyen Dy Nien. 1995a. The gioi dang thay doi, con chung ta? In *Hoi nhap quoc te va giu vung ban sac*. Edited by the Ministry of Foreign Affairs. Hanoi: National Politics Publishing House, 31–4.

———. 1995b. Tien toi mot Dong Nam A trong the ky XXI. In *Hoi nhap quoc te va giu vung ban sac*. Edited by the Ministry of Foreign Affairs. Hanoi: National Politics Publishing House, 145–50.

Nguyen Hong Thach. 2000. *Vietnam between China and the United States 1950–1995*. Doctoral thesis. School of Politics, University College, The University of New South Wales.

Nguyen Phu Trong. 2004. Construire une économie indépendante et autonome et prendre l'initiative dans l'intégration à l'économie mondiale. In *Le Viêt Nam sur la voie du renouveau*. Edited by Nguyen Phu Trong. Hanoi: The Gioi, 149–158.

Nguyen Quoc Nhat and Nguyen Van Ngung. 2001. *Hoi nhap kinh te voi van de giu gin an ninh quoc gia o Viet Nam*. Hanoi: National Politics Publishing House.

Ordinance on self-protection on the import of products into Vietnam, adopted on May 25, 2002.

Resolution 07-NQ-TW of the Political Bureau of the Vietnamese Communist Party on international economic integration, November 27, 2001.

Rosecrance, Richard and Arthur Stein. 1973. Interdependence: Myth or reality? *World Politics* 24: 1–28.

Ryan, Jordan. 2005. Vietnam goes global. *YaleGlobal*, December 15, 2005. Online at yaleglobal.yale.edu/display.article?id=6633.

Smouts, Marie-Claude, Dario Batistella, and Pascal Venesson. 2003. *Dictionnaire des relations internationales*. Paris: Dalloz.

Tirona, Rosalinda V. 1998. *ASEAN in the 21st century: A Philippine perspective*. Hanoi: Embassy of the Philippines.

Tran Quang Co. 1995. The gioi huong ve the ky 21. *Nghien cuu quoc te* 5: 3–7.

Tran Viet Phuong. 1999. Toan cau hoa va hoi nhap kinh te quoc te. In *Toan cau hoa, quan diem va thuc tien, kinh nghiem quoc te*. Edited by Central Institute for Economic Management. Hanoi: Statistics Publishing House, 5–21.

UNDP. 2004. *Vietnam Development Cooperation Report*. Hanoi: United Nations Development Programme.

Vietnamese Communist Party. 1987. *Van kien Dai hoi Dai bieu Toan quoc lan thu VI*. Hanoi: Truth Publishing.

Walter, Xavier. 1998. Perspectives d'Asie. In *Les relations internationales en Asie-Pacifique*. Edited by Serge Besanger and Guy Schulders Guy. Paris: Alban, 37–61.

Waltz, Kenneth N. 1970. The myth of national interdependence. In *The international corporation*. Edited by Charles P. Kindleberger. Cambridge: MIT Press, 205–227.

Wang Gungwu. 1998. La place de la Chine dans la région Asie-Pacifique. In *Les relations internationales en Asie-Pacifique*. Edited by Serge Besanger and Guy Schulders. Paris: Alban, 63–79.

Warren, Christopher. 1995. Speech on American national interests in the Asia-Pacific region. Washington (July 1995; speech provided by the Embassy of the United States in Paris).

Newspapers and Wire Services

Agence France Presse (Hanoi), September 5, 2004.

Agence France Presse (Beijing), September 6, 2004.

Cong luan, June 21–26, 2002.

Phap luat, August 19, 2003.

Quan doi nhan dan, May 28, 2001.

Tuoi tre, April 4, 2002.

CHAPTER SEVEN

Vietnam's Integration into the World
National and Global Interfaces

EERO PALMUJOKI

For over 10 years, Vietnam's political leadership has faced the dilemma of how to take full advantage of the economic trends of the global system in general and Asia-Pacific region in particular and simultaneously maintain its political structure. Vietnam has, together with the People's Republic of China (PRC), managed to preserve a Communist Party system of political power, developed a market economy, and opened it to the world economy. This process has created obvious contradictions between the political and social system, ideology, and new economic trends.

This chapter examines how Vietnam has sought to integrate into the surrounding world and cope with globalization by analyzing the articulation of different semiotic systems at the interface of Vietnam's political and ideological tradition and international fora. A semiotic system, in this context, refers to the time and space-bound economic, political, cultural, and ideological knowledge bases, practices, institutions, and values that give meaning to political texts. From the point of view of a nation-state, these political and ideological elements form a layer—what we sometimes call political culture—that includes different and contradictory elements (Champagne 1978, 207). My particular interest here is how Vietnam's national identity is constructed at these global interfaces.

National political actors such as the Communist Party have substantial influence on how to meet globalization. Therefore, globalization takes place selectively, and that selection takes place based on political and ideological traditions, and conscious policy choices. This approach relies, in a broad context, on the social constructivist theory of international relations, emphasizing the development of interest and identity in international interaction (Wendt 1999). The formation of identity and interest is closely connected to conscious policy choices: in identity building it is very important to note the distinction between us and them (Virtanen 2003, 2004), the relationship between political and ideological tradition and regional and global discourse. These global engagements are rather limited, to such groups as ASEAN (Association of Southeast Asian Nations) or the WTO (World Trade Organization), the language of which is regulated by world trade law. These discourses are semiotic systems of their own.

Vietnamese Marxism–Leninism
as a Semiotic System

In its conventional meaning, language is understood as an instrument for communication in order to transfer information. But language also has other functions that have very little to do with the content of information but are still very important for social interaction. Political language has an important role in the formation of national identity, both in its expressions of national heritage and its expression of a political system, where the constructions of language may be particularly sophisticated. Marxism-Leninism is a system in which theory must inform our understanding of key concepts, and in which traditional Marxism-Leninism finds few interfaces with the international non-Marxist discourses of international organizations.

For a long time, this was not a problem for Marxist-Leninist discourse in general or for Vietnamese Marxism in particular, because virtually all communication was directed inwards. The issue of *who will win* (or *who will defeat whom*) in the struggle between two camps in the Cold War was, on the one hand, related to internal policies in creating a Marxist-Leninist political system and in carrying out a Soviet-type economic model in Vietnam. On the other hand, that *who will win* formulation helped communicate to the socialist world that Vietnam belonged to the Soviet camp. This concept is still in use in Vietnamese political vocabulary. It and the concept of basic contradictions continue to characterize the elements of orthodox Marxism-Leninism in Vietnamese political culture (Phan Doan Nam 2003). Therefore, Vietnamese rhetoric on international affairs in that era could be primarily understood as communication to itself and its camp, and only secondarily as carrying new information. This is typical, however, for political communication in general and Marxist-Leninist parlance in particular. Marxism-Leninism thus formed a semiotic system in which Vietnamese political texts were understandable and the political sphere was defined.

Soviet *perestroika* in the mid-1980s made it possible for the Vietnamese to alter this language and broaden its own international environment. Crucial for Vietnam's political doctrine was gradual abandonment of the two camps theory and the political language supporting it. More heterogeneous political concepts and discourse appeared alongside orthodox language. Thus from the beginning of the *doi moi* reform process, Vietnam's political and cultural vocabulary took on new elements and new considerations of international and regional relations.

Looking for the Interface with the Global System: Vietnam and Regionalism

Despite the obvious influence of the Soviet reforms, Vietnamese developments took their own path. On the one hand Vietnam's situation resembled China more than the Soviet Union; on the other hand Vietnam aspired to broaden its policy toward ASEAN but was initially unsuccessful due to the Cambodian question. After the Paris agreement on Cambodia, Hanoi was less constrained in approaching ASEAN. The new language involves both ASEAN vocabulary, such as the concept of *regionalism*, and non-ASEAN Chinese elements, such as the continuing use of the concept of *peaceful evolution*.

Confirmation of the adoption of ASEAN language can be found in many documents. One of the most interesting was the report on the ASEAN-Vietnam Conference held in Hanoi in August 1991. This report, and the document that followed from the authorized Vietnam-ASEAN group published in February 1993, indicated that the basic ASEAN vocabulary of regional cooperation was now in wide use in Vietnam's political language (Report 1991; Shared Destiny 1993). The adoption of ASEAN vocabulary and the definition of membership in ASEAN as a key approach at the beginning of the 1990s also implied a reconsideration of the connection in political rhetoric between internal politics and external relations. The *doi moi* tendency in which such Marxist-Leninist concepts as *who will win* and the *two camps theory* were

ousted from their firm position in Vietnamese political language, even at
the central Party level, continued with growing momentum. Such older
political concepts as *who will win* or *basic contradictions* also acquired new
connotations in new contexts. But official foreign policy thinking as well
as concrete policies broke away from older ideology. In semiotic terms,
there was no interface in political terms between global (the new foreign
policy) and national (the continuity of traditional political power and
structures).

This cannot, of course, be the whole picture. One should ask how
important this separation was or whether it took place at all. One answer
is that global tendencies and Vietnam's opening with ASEAN mold the
political vocabulary and thinking in areas of domestic concern as well.
And recent articles by senior Party officials also indicate that the old
vocabulary is still being used for current global analysis (Phan Doan Nam
2003). On a regional level, the Vietnamese Party and government began
to emphasize those elements in ASEAN cooperation that fit Vietnamese
political tradition, particularly the importance of sovereignty as a basis for
ASEAN cooperation. Together with other ASEAN principles emphasizing economic globalization with strong *regional* and *national resilience*,
sovereignty formed a bridge between the national political tradition and
regional cooperation (Busse 1999, 46–7). The policy of regionalism in
the context of ASEAN cooperation also made it possible to separate the
domestic political system from regional cooperation. Since joining
ASEAN, Vietnam has followed the ASEAN mainstream that emphasizes
relations between governments as well as cautious policies in dealing with
the delicate issues of other members. This includes the concept of
constructive engagement, which was introduced to justify Myanmar's membership of ASEAN. Thus regionalism can perhaps be said to have become
a part of Vietnam's identity building. I therefore emphasize the political
nature of identity building in contrast to those views that emphasize the
common cultural values behind regional identity. For Vietnam, the
commitment to regional identity is a result of the political search for a
state identity after the Cold War (Nguyen Vu Tung 2002, 114).

ASEAN's loose political structure offered Vietnam a flexible instrument to help mold its relationships with the region as well as its own
expression of its identity. This does not mean that Vietnamese officials
have ignored problems of the ASEAN structure and the emphasis of
national interests in the regional organization. This dynamic also limits
the use of ASEAN when Vietnam faces global challenges, such as dealing
with and accession to the World Trade Organization (WTO) (Tran
Phuong Lan 2004).

Broad changes in the economy and political administration have taken place in Vietnam in the past decade, as Vietnam's integration into ASEAN and the global economy have reflected. One goal of these changes has been to attract foreign investment, aid funding, and technology to Vietnam. Vietnam had to adopt new practices, including a new vocabulary, when fitting its administrative system to a more open regional economy. This coincided with the ASEAN Free Trade Area (AFTA) process that molded ASEAN cooperation and unified member countries' policies toward other politico-economic forums, such as APEC and the WTO. The general idea behind the free trade area was that the ASEAN countries would have already adjusted to free trade when Asia-Pacific and global trade liberation became a reality. Therefore the instruments of the agreement were relatively effective. The arrangements of AFTA even include some supranational characteristics, although supra-nationalism at the political level has been taboo in ASEAN cooperation (Shared Destiny 1993, 20).

Besides these general political principles of Southeast Asian regional cooperation, the main instrument to promote AFTA and reduce the general tariff level, the Common Effective Preferential Tariff (CEPT) scheme, includes major elements for trade liberalization in Southeast Asia. Although Vietnam was not obliged to follow fast track tariff reductions, the CEPT agreement addressed such other elements as non-tariff barriers (NTB) that Vietnam has encountered in negotiations with the WTO (Palmujoki 2001, 139). At the ASEAN Hanoi Summit in December 1998, the ASEAN governments decided to accelerate AFTA. This decision nullified those benefits that Vietnam and other less developed ASEAN members enjoyed in the earlier CEPT scheme and compelled them to a stricter schedule in tariff reductions (Pham Quoc Tru 2003).

Vietnam and Global Institutions

Vietnam's adoption of a regionalist policy both indicates and reflects new definitions of national interests and regional identity. Together with regional, political, and economic development, Vietnam's interaction with global institutions, multilateral funding institutions (MFI), and various development agencies grew rapidly during the 1990s. In the late 1990s, Vietnam received US$2.0–2.4 billion annually in official development assistance (ODA), about 5% of its GDP. By far the biggest donor has been Japan, providing nearly 30% of Vietnam's foreign aid, followed by the Asian Development Bank and the World Bank. At the same time the role of foreign direct investment diminished due to the Asian economic crisis, from US$2.3 billion in 1995 to US$1.6 billion in 1999 (Overview of Official Development Assistance Vietnam 2000). Nevertheless, ODA continued to be very important.

At the political level in Vietnam, however, dependency on ODA does not seem to be much discussed. The presence of the donors and the MFIs is not substantially reflected in the government's policy statements, nor is it dealt with extensively in Communist Party publications. The Communist Party theoretical organ, *Tap chi Cong san (Communist Review)* has traditionally had the difficult task of reconciling international and domestic developments with Marxist-Leninist ideology. Between 2002 and 2005, *Tap chi Cong san* carried 15 articles on ASEAN, 17 articles on the WTO, and only 1 article dealing with APEC. No article dealt directly with the donors' role in and relations with Vietnam, excluding some general pieces on the role of such major funding institutions as the World Bank and the IMF in the Third World. The focus on ASEAN indicates its importance as Vietnam's main reference group in international forums. *Tap chi Cong san* has also paid significant attention to Vietnam's negotiations with the WTO and to WTO principles and rules, reflecting the political position of the Party and government that have made WTO membership a major step in Vietnam's foreign relations (Phan Van Khai 2003). But all this discussion of Vietnam's WTO candidacy would seem conceivably contradictory from the perspective of Marxist-Leninist ideology.

This seeming contradiction, however, may be illusory. At root, the donors' activities question Vietnam's role as an independent actor and impose conditions that question Vietnam as a sovereign actor. Although the donors may be flexible in their interpretation of the implementation of their conditions, they have a fixed agenda that, in the view of some critics, is not entirely formulated in conjunction with the recipient. To discuss issues on the donors' agenda publicly or even in senior Party circles—issues such as democracy, corruption, and the rule of law—is awkward and at times unpalatable. In that sense Vietnam finds a certain lowest common denominator between donor politics and Vietnam's needs, but not true political partnership with these institutions.

Perhaps contrary to the general relationship with the donors, the WTO negotiations enable the Party and government to appear as a sovereign player on the most serious issues in the relationship between sovereignty and economic development. The multilateral nature of the WTO that is emphasized in its summits would give Vietnam a chance to identify itself as a part of the ASEAN group or as a part of the developing countries group in general in its attempt to defend its sovereignty against developed countries (Nguyen Van Thanh 2003). Vietnam received substantial support from ASEAN in order to help its argument that "as a heavily indebted low-income developing country, with a per capita income of less than $400 per year," "it should be treated leniently, and in particular should be eligible for exceptions under the Subsidies Agreement." The WTO working group majority, however, is perhaps more inclined to consider Vietnam as a vibrant economy with bright prospects (WTO News, June 15, 2004). The intergovernmental nature of the WTO stands out in relief in the accession negotiations, when the organization presents the framework of the negotiations, but important talks are held between the candidate and major members such as the United States and the EU. The most difficult bilateral negotiations are held with the biggest members, particularly with the "Quadrilaterals" (the United States, the EU, Japan, and Canada).

The basic ideology behind the WTO, the emphasis on free trade and neoliberal economic thinking with its conservative view on the division of labor on a global scale, does not match the goals of a developing country such as Vietnam. Recent TRIPS (Trade-related aspects of Intellectual Property Rights) and GATS (General Agreement on Trade in Services) agreements are often regarded as failing to meet the interests of developing economies (Submission 2003; Joint Communication 2003). Similarly, complex trade negotiations call for a broad range of experts who can identify the different interests behind proposed legislation and details in the trade negotiations, for a solitary developing country cannot simply foresee all the consequences of new agreements. Accordingly, the reason to join the WTO is not its rules as such; WTO membership is a guarantee for the donors and funding institutions that the recipient country will conduct proper economic policies and will help certain countries obtain further funding from international institutions. Whether this de facto constraint is behind Vietnam's WTO candidacy is difficult to say. The Vietnamese political texts do not refer exactly to this consideration.

WTO Membership as a Vehicle for Globalization

The established world trade rules have been very important for export-oriented ASEAN economies. Malaysia, the Philippines, Singapore, and Thailand in particular have been active WTO members. It is estimated that ASEAN has formed the most effective bargaining group among the developing countries in the GATT/WTO (Narlikar 2003, 169–76). The ASEAN countries have not hesitated to invoke the WTO (GATT) trade rules when their interests have been threatened, and several trade disputes have been taken to the WTO's dispute settlement body by these countries. ASEAN's development strategy, even from the very beginning of the establishment of organization, was based on the division of world labor. This, however, was not based on the classical economic theory of comparative advantage that divides countries into producers and processors of raw materials, but on a conscious policy to take advantage of world economic trends in order to move from one developmental ladder to another. The relationship between national economies and the global economy is focused on the concept of *interdependence*, which in ASEAN vocabulary had a positive connotation instead of the negative meaning that the concept usually had among the developing countries.

The first apparent signs of a transition from orthodox Marxism to ASEAN strategy can be seen in Vietnamese thinking at the end of the 1980s. Perhaps most important was Foreign Minister Nguyen Co Thach's article in *Tap chi Cong san* in August 1989. Thach reiterated the positive interpretation of *interdependence* earlier suggested earlier by some senior Party officials and connected it to *regionalism* and to the division of world labor. He even touched on a difficult question of participation in the division of labor and *sovereignty* and concluded that the more developed an economy is, the more dependent it is on global economy. He suggested that Vietnam had to make a choice between economic development and an old-fashioned interpretation of sovereignty (Nguyen Co Thach 1989). Hence, some basic ASEAN ideas were already accepted in certain circles of the Party even before the solution of the Cambodian issues that finally provided Vietnam with an escape from its international isolation.

During the 1990s the concept of *globalization* was established in the Vietnamese political vocabulary, as a reference to the economic possibilities of the global economy and participation in it rather than the negative consequences of global economic forces. But this view, in the discourse of the Communist Party, was not entirely without reservation. Although globalization was been considered an inevitable trend that the Vietnamese Party, government, and society had to face, the discourse revealed two views. According to the traditional pragmatic view, globalization offered opportunities, posed threats, and presented challenges to governments (Nguyen Hoanh 2003; Van Quang 2003; Dinh Quang Ty 2004). But a different, doctrinal approach sought to reconcile globalization with

Marxist terminology and to directly justify Communist Party power (Vu Van Phuc 2003; Nguyen Xuan Thang 2004). In fact, classical Marxist theories seem to fit much better into globalization issues than into Vietnam's current domestic situation (Phan Doan Nam 2003; Nguyen Van Quy 2005). There was even the suggestion of examining antiglobalization movements and considering what kind of policies Vietnam should adapt in view of the antiglobalization trends (Pham Dinh Nghiem 2003). The commonality of these differing interpretations was the notion of sovereignty, the protection of which remained a key duty of the Party and state (Do Nhat Tan 2004; Le Huu Nghia 2004).

But basic questions such as WTO membership must enjoy broad support among the Party leadership, not just certain sectors of the Party. The Vietnamese Party has not yet adopted Thach's position. The reluctance of the Party's theoretical journal to deal with the role of MFIs in Vietnam reflects this. And each of these elements—Party power, sovereignty, globalization, regionalism, and others—can be interpreted as part of Vietnamese political culture, not necessarily reflecting deep-seated controversy in the Party itself. Vietnam also moved gradually in the globalization process: first toward ASEAN and AFTA, then APEC in 1998. Together with the applications of some other Asian countries, most importantly China, Vietnam's application to the WTO in 1995 can be seen as a consistent act of this policy.

The Basic Rules of the WTO and Vietnam's Principles of Globalization

Even though the WTO is not the same as world trade governance, it forms a trade regime in which the world trade regulations are drafted, decided, and at least partly controlled. When compared to other sectors, such as health, environment, security, or even finance, the coherence of the trade regime is emphasized. When a trade regime is focused on one organization, other regimes are scattered among different players, which base their policies on roughly accepted norms drawn from different agreements, conventions, and statements without any effective control mechanisms. If the WTO is connected to broader economic governance its importance is not, of course, the same. The financial institutions, the World Bank and the Asian Development Bank (ADB), as well as the International Monetary Fund (IMF) have roles for which WTO membership cannot compensate for a developing country.

But there are aspects of WTO membership that are crucially important. As mentioned earlier, WTO membership can be a guarantee for credit from these funding organizations. Second, a solitary developing country has more formal influence in the WTO than within these originally governmental, but in practice supra-national, institutions. The WTO is a clearly intergovernmental organization, where the decisions are based on formal consensus, and sovereign members have, at least in theory, important roles. How real and concrete this influence, of course, is another question. Some recent studies, however, indicate increasing influence of developing countries along with their growing activities at WTO negotiations (Page 2002, Ford 2003).

At the time of this writing, the WTO includes 149 countries that have signed the agreements negotiated during the GATT rounds and after the establishment of the WTO itself. After the accession of China in 2001, all the world's main trading countries except Russia are members. Thus the WTO's authority rests not only on the ability to draft, decide, and control the world's trade rules, but also on its wide sphere of influence due to the breadth of its membership. Although the WTO's authority is further enforced by its broadly accepted underlying ideology to liberalize world trade, this does not mean that economic liberalism as such is the driving force for countries' decisions to join the WTO. Many countries seek to take advantage of global trade and to support their own exports. Therefore they have acceded to agreements that probably harm their own intentions to protect their own domestic markets. The policy of the trade organization to work toward removal of trade barriers and not economic liberalism as such is an important factor that solidifies the organization and gives it authority in world trade issues.

Finally, the WTO dispute settlement mechanism makes it unique among international organizations. Although the WTO has no instruments to implement its resolutions, the decisions of the dispute settlement body justify its members in reciprocal action against a member who has broken WTO rules. The effectiveness of this mechanism lies in the interests and the trading power of the disputing parties.

In order to implement its policies, the WTO has three principles to promote international trade and the removal of trade barriers: *non-discrimination, transparency,* and *national treatment.* Non-discrimination means that the regulations, tariffs, and other barriers to trade do not give a different position to any exporting countries' products in an importing country. Transparency means that the regulations laid down by every importer country are available and distributed through WTO channels to all producers. National treatment is derived from non-discrimination, but is a stronger instrument for free trade. It posits that national and foreign products or services should be treated equally and that member states will not put forward measures that are more favorable to the domestic business, not even (in its strict interpretation) to the services offered by governments. All these principles emphasise equality between WTO members, but may also be interpreted as posing a threat to national sovereignty in its traditional sense (Nguyen Thanh Nga 2002).

Although these principles—national treatment in particular—pose risks to national sovereignty, in semiotic terms there is an interface between WTO legal jargon and the Vietnamese approach to globalization. Yet it is the differences between these semiotic systems that should be emphasized. The development of Vietnamese thinking from Marxist-Leninist orthodoxy through regionalist ideas to globalization was described above, but these trends do not mean that older elements have totally disappeared; rather new elements have appeared alongside the old elements of political culture.

The formation of the WTO legislation along the lines of major trading nations' interests characterises the other side of this relationship. In recent WTO developments the differences between the rich developed countries and the least developed countries are even more pronounced. Law drafting has usually been done in a small circle of OECD countries, and the proposals are then offered to the majority of the member countries, mostly developing countries. The trading interests of developing countries are articulated at UNCTAD and among different developing countries groupings, such as Group 77 (Vu Van Hien 2004). Those interests emphasize the duty of developed countries' preferential treatment of developing country exports without reciprocal concession by the developing countries.

Vietnam's situation in this respect is controversial. It is a poor developing country, and the WTO principles include risks to its social and political system by limiting political authority, as well as enlarging market access for imports against which Vietnam's domestic production cannot compete. Therefore the traditional claims of the developing countries on preferential treatment also tempt Vietnam to protectionist policies. On the other hand, when it identifies itself as a developing export-oriented Southeast Asian country seeking to take advantage of the global economy, the WTO principles (perhaps particularly non-discrimination and transparency) may open up new possibilities to defend its global interests. This contradiction is obvious in Party officials' discussions of WTO accession (To Huy Rua 2004).

Non-discrimination particularly meets Vietnam's and ASEAN's preferred concept of globalization with sovereignty. ASEAN countries have invoked this and other positions derived from the *transparency* principle, while developed countries (especially the United States) have imposed environmentally related trade barriers. The less developed countries have appealed to these principles when developed countries, led by the United States and the European Union, have called for International Labour Organization agreements and other social issues to be included in the WTO legislation. In most cases, this policy of appealing to the WTO rules has been successful and the WTO's dispute settlement mechanism has supported the ASEAN countries' petitions.

Therefore, poorer and weaker countries may at times chalk up victories in trade disputes with richer countries. These victories may be vital to certain sectors, even if they are not to an entire economy. But they are also important for political identity when countries emphasize national sovereignty as a basic point of departure in their external relations. The WTO principles cut both ways for Vietnam. National treatment calls for cutting subsidies for Vietnam's economy and transparency calls for remarkable changes in legislation and administration, particularly in the area of technical barriers to trade. But the advantages have been arguably even more important, including freer access to such markets as the United States after WTO membership is achieved (Nguyen Thanh Nga 2002; Directorate for Standards and Quality 2004; Le Danh Vinh 2005).

When reporting domestically on Vietnam's accession negotiations, the Vietnamese government has emphasized technical matters, though it has certainly encountered the disparity between developing countries and developed countries in its membership negotiations. Although these talks may emphasize its role as a sovereign actor, Vietnam has had to assent to such developed country initiatives as GATS and TRIPS (Dinh Trong Thinh 2004). These issues have been emphasized in its negotiations with the "Quadrilaterals." Most of the members, including the European Union, have been satisfied with Vietnam's concessions and have expressed their support for Vietnam's membership (Vietnam Communist Party 2004). Bilateral talks, however, offer strong WTO members an opportunity to press the acceding country in a way that is not possible between the WTO member countries—for example, the United States requests for "WTO plus" obligations, which assumes requirements that exceed the WTO rules (Extortion at the Gate 2004; Luong Van Tu 2005). Dealing with these issues implicates Vietnamese politics, economic affairs, and sovereignty as well as non-commodity trading laws such as intellectual property that remain very difficult issues for Vietnam's economy in this developmental phase.

Conclusions

The WTO basic principles have formed a broad interface between global and Vietnamese national policies. Their key point of departure, intergovernmental negotiations between sovereign states, supports Vietnam's identity both as a player in a group of developing countries and as an ASEAN country. The WTO principles of non-discrimination, national treatment, and transparency emphasize equality among trading states. These principles have been proven to be important to export-oriented Southeast Asian countries and Vietnam expects to take advantage of these basic rules in its export efforts. These principles, however, are a double-edged sword when combined with more recent agreements concerning non-commodity trade, investments, and services. In these cases these principles may be perceived as a threat to national sovereignty in economic policy, social welfare, and other traditionally important issues in a socialist country.

It seems obvious, nonetheless, that Vietnam is also trying to take advantage of these threats. This means that Vietnam identifies with those developing countries that are cautious about developed countries' attempt to decide on world trade currents. This provides commonality both to regionalist vocabulary as well as with more traditional Vietnamese political culture. Both sides of the Vietnamese attempt—to adapt to globalization as well as to maintain older political structures—are clear. In its attempt to make use of the growing trade volume around the world, regional integration and ASEAN membership have been an important springboard for a broader and deeper globalization processes. The other side of the discourse with the WTO sheds light on an important notion of sovereignty. The defense of sovereignty in international fora gives legitimacy to the political leadership and, if the benefits of globalization have been successfully exploited, reinforces the political system.

References

Bibliographical note: This chapter uses *Tap chi Cong san's* (TCCS) electronic versions, www.tapchicongsan.org.vn (except Nguyen Co Thach 1989), in which the page numbers are missing and the issue numbers start from the year of 2001.

Busse, Nikolas. 1999. Constructivism and Southeast Asian security. *The Pacific Review* 12(1): 46–7.

Champagne, Roland A. 1978. A grammar of the languages of culture: Literary theory and Yuri M. Lotman's Semiotics. *New Literary History* 9(2): 205–10.

Dinh Quang Ty. 2004. Toan cau hoa va kha nang canh tranh cua nen kinh te ve Viet Nam hien nay. *Tap chi Cong san (Communist Review)* 54, www.tapchicongsan.org.vn.

Dinh Trong Thinh. 2004. WTO voi cac nen kinh te yeu. *Tap chi Cong san (Communist Review)* 55, www.tapchicongsan.org.vn.

Directorate for Standards and Quality. 2004. Online at http://www.tcvn.gov.vn/wtovn/english/information.html, accessed February 2005.

Do Nhat Tan. 2004. Hoi nhap kinh te quoc te tren co so doc lap tu chu va dinh huong xa hoi chu nghia. *Tap chi Cong san (Communist Review)* 72, www.tapchicongsan.org.vn.

Extortion at the Gate. 2004. Will Viet Nam join the WTO on pro-development terms? Oxfam Briefing Paper 67, October.

Ford, Jane. 2003. *A social theory of the WTO trading cultures.* Basingstoke: Palgrave Macmillan.

Joint Communication. 2003. Joint Communication from the African Group, World Trade Organisation, IP/C/W/40426 June.

Le Danh Vinh. 2005. Cac vu kien thuong mai va viec chu dong phong chong trong qua trinh hoi nhap kinh te quoc te. *Tap chi Cong san (Communist Review)* 85, www.tapchicongsan.org.vn.

Le Huu Nghia. 2004. Bao cao de dan. *Tap chi Cong san (Communist Review)* 56, www.tapchicongson.org.vn.

Luong Van Tu. 2005. Vietnam's chief negotiator in the WTO accession process, Luong Van Tu's statement at the 10th Session of the Working Party on the Accession of Vietnam to the WTO, Geneva, www.wto.org/english/news_e/news05_e/vietnam_15sep05_e.htm.

Narlikar, Amrita. 2003. *International trade and developing countries: Bargaining coalitions in the GATT & WTO.* Abingdon: Routledge.

Nguyen Co Thach. 1989. Tat ca vi hoa binh, doc lap dan toc va phat trien. *Tap chi Cong san (Communist Review)* 8: 1–8.

Nguyen Hoanh. 2003. Xanh cac giai phap tang cuong kha nang hoi nhap kinh te quoc te. *Tap chi Cong san (Communist Review)* 44, www.tapchicongson.org.vn.

Nguyen Thanh Nga. 2002. Toan cau hoa—hai mat thuan va nghich doi voi thuong mai cua Viet Nam. *Tap chi Cong san (Communist Review)* 25, www.tapchicongsan.org.vn.

Nguyen Van Quy. 2005. Tim hieu tu tuong cua C. Mac ve toan cau hoa. *Tap chi Cong San (Communist Review)* 82, www.tapchicongsan.org.vn.

Nguyen Van Thanh. 2003. Can-Cun sup do: Thu tim nguyen nhan cua that bai. *Tap chi Cong san (Communist Review)* 48, www.tapchicongsan.org.vn.

Nguyen Vu Tung. 2002. Vietnam-ASEAN co-operation after the Cold War and the continued search for a theoretical framework. *Contemporary Southeast Asia* 24(1): 106–20.

Nguyen Xuan Thang. 2004. Ve hiep dinh thuong mai to do song phuong. *Tap chi Cong san (Communist Review)* 57, www.tapchicongsan.org.vn.

Overview of Official Development Assistance Vietnam. 2000. UNDP, Hanoi, October.

Page, Sheila. 2002. *Developing countries in GATT/WTO negotiations.* London: Overseas Development Institute.

Palmujoki, Eero. 2001. *Regionalism and globalism in Southeast Asia.* Palgrave: London and New York.

Pham Dinh Nghiem. 2003. Phong trao cong toan cau hoa. *Tap chi Cong san (Communist Review)* 47, www.tapchicongsan.org.vn.

Phan Doan Nam. 2003. Mau thuan va phuong thuc giai quyet mau thuan trong quan he quoc te ngay nay. *Tap chi Cong san (Communist Review)* 47, www.tapchicongsan.org.vn.

Pham Quoc Tru. 2003. Thuc tran va trien vong cua trinh lien ket kinh te ASEAN. *Tap chi Cong san (Communist Review)* 49, www.tapchicongsan.org.vn.

Phan Van Khai. 2003. Interview with Prime Minister Phan Van Khai. Far Eastern Economic Review. March 20, 2003, 16.

Report. 1991. Report of the International Symposium on Interaction for Progress, Westlake Guest House, Hanoi, August 20–23, 1991.

Shared Destiny. 1993. Shared Destiny—Southeast Asia in the 21st Century. Report of the ASEAN–Vietnam Study Group.

Submission. 2003. Submission by Bolivia, Brazil, Cuba, Dominican Republic, Ecuador, India, Peru, Thailand, Venezuela. World Trade Organisation, IP/C/W/403, 24 June.

To Huy Rua. 2004. Viet Nam tren lo trinh gia nhap To chuc Thuong mai the gioi. *Tap chi Cong san (Communist Review)* 62, www.tapchicongsan.org.vn.

Tran Phuong Lan. 2004. Vietnam voi 'y tuong cong dong kinh te ASEAN' cua ASEAN. *Tap chi Cong san (Communist Review)* 65, www.tapchicongsan.org.vn.

Van Quang. 2003. An ninh kinh te toan cau hoa kinh te. *Tap chi Cong san (Communist Review)* 41, www.tapchicongsan.org.vn.

Vietnam Communist Party. 2004. EC supports Vietnam's joining WTO, www.cpv.org.vn.

Virtanen, Pekka. 2003. Local management of global values: Community-based wildlife management in Zimbabwe and Zambia. *Society and Natural Resources* 16: 179–90.

Virtanen, Pekka. 2004. The politics of law: Customary authority and changing premises of legal reform. *International Journal for the Semiotics of Law* 17: 53–75.

WTO News June 15, 2004, www.wto.org/english/news_e/news04/ cc_vietnam_15june04_e-htm.

Vu Van Hien. 2004. Mot so van de ve hoi nhap kinh te quoc te. *Tap chi Cong san (Communist Review)* 59, www.tapchicongsan.org.vn.

Vu Van Phuc. 2003. Cac to chuc kinh te, tai chinh, thuong mai quoc te lon voi toan cau hoa hien nay. *Tap chi Cong san (Communist Review)* 44, www.tapchicongsan.org.vn.

Wendt, Alexander. 1999. *Social theory of international politics*. Cambridge: Cambridge University Press.

PART II

———

Law, Legal Reform, and the Vietnamese State

Understanding Legality in Vietnam

JOHN GILLESPIE

Introduction

The history of legality in Vietnam is inextricably bound up with the adaptation of foreign ideas. Legality is broadly conceived to mean state rule through law. This chapter argues that contemporary approaches to legality are based on precepts, practices, and habits initially derived from China, France, the former Soviet bloc, and more recently from Western capitalist economies. Legality in Vietnam has never precisely mirrored the teachings of conquerors, colonists, and patron-states, but rather it reflected different systems of knowledge—the new overlaying and interacting with the old (Rambo 1987, 115–22). Efforts by contemporary lawmakers to build a law-based state (*nha nuoc phap quyen*) follow this centuries-old pattern.

Understanding the changing notions of legality provides valuable insights into legal development in Vietnam, because legality acts as a litmus test for assessing whether states take laws seriously. Without legality, political, moral, economic, and social constraints still function, but laws provide poor signposts of state power. Since different approaches to legality have been debated in Vietnam for at least a thousand years, it provides an analytical focus that is unencumbered by the Western ideological aspirations that complicate more ambitious legal projects such as the "rule of law" and "constitutionalism." The study in this chapter of continuity and change in the meanings ascribed to legality provides a framework for understanding the rich and detailed accounts of legal development throughout this volume.

Conceptualizing Legality

The proposition that radically different systems of knowledge from China, the former Soviet bloc, and the West have shaped Vietnamese understandings about legality raises many questions. How did ruling elites reconcile new ideas about legality with preexisting knowledge systems? Why did new ideas influence ruling elites more rapidly than those at the periphery of state power? How did new ideas become accepted as universal truths? A common theme in these questions is understanding how different systems of knowledge interact—will one set of intellectual/cultural traditions engage or subordinate another?

Discourse analysis provides a useful way to understand how different systems of knowledge interact (Black 2002). Its many methodological threads share the common belief that people are not simply passive receivers of information from an external reality. They are actively involved in producing their own reality. As Robertson (1999, 417) observed, "being embedded in a background context of beliefs, practices and goals is what makes the perception of anything possible and what gives that perception shape." Discourse analysis produces insights that contrast sharply with conventional legal positivist explanations for legality. It holds that laws appear the way they do because people interpret them from particular sets of beliefs, practices, and goals, and not as legal positivism would have it, because laws compel people to arrive at certain conclusions (Rorty 1997). What follows is that people understand new systems of knowledge from the interpretive traditions in which they are embedded. The deep beliefs of an interpretive tradition or community form "a lattice or web whose component parts are mutually constitutive" and determine what ideas, arguments, and facts members find compelling (Fish 1999, 280). Legality, for example, may appear logical and desirable for those embedded in one interpretive community but inappropriate and alien to members of a different interpretive community.

If people find it difficult to look beyond the epistemological assumptions in which they are embedded, then how do knowledge systems change? Discourse analysis posits that people's ideas change because they are influenced by multiple interpretive communities. As discussed below, many contemporary lawmakers in Vietnam were trained as lawyers in the former Soviet bloc, belong to the Party, but work daily in foreign aid programs that promote neoliberal legality.[1] Each interpretive community provides different, sometimes incompatible perspectives about the possibility and desirability of introducing neoliberal legality to Vietnam. Ideas, arguments, and facts contained in one such community discredit beliefs and practices privileged in another interpretive community.

Self-interest and external pressure forces such as the market economy, globalized culture, and ideological teachings undoubtedly influence the selection and adaptation of new knowledge systems. But if discourse analysis is correct, and people can never entirely extricate themselves from their epistemological assumptions, then they evaluate, prioritize, and strategize new ideas from the perspectives of pre-existing interpretive traditions. There is no fixed definition about what constitutes an interpretive community (Fish 1989, 141–60). Most theorists agree, however, that members of interpretive communities share common epistemological and tacit understandings about the meaning of law. Factors that differentiate communities include different validity claims, epistemologies, and tacit understandings. Much of what interpretive communities think about the law is expressed in discourse. For this reason this chapter uses discourse—in all its forms—to examine the ways different interpretive traditions have constructed legality in Vietnam. The discussion so far suggests the need to understand the interaction between different knowledge systems by examining their validity claims and willingness to engage new ideas. What follows is a brief overview of the epistemological approaches to legality in the three knowledge systems that dominated the pre-*doi moi* era.

A Brief Overview of Pre-*Doi Moi* Approaches to Legality

Three main systems of knowledge—neo-Confucian, colonial legality, and socialist legality—influenced understandings about legality before *doi moi* reforms in 1986 opened Vietnam to new ideas.

Neo-Confucian Virtue-Rule

China provided much of the moral, political, and legal thinking that has informed elite perceptions of legality over the past 2,000 years. Yet it was not until the Lê Dynasty (1428–1788) that Vietnamese rulers systematically embraced the neo-Confucian orthodoxies underlying Chinese laws and governmental structures (Woodside 1998, 206–8). Confucian scholars believed that if people were persuaded by education, social pressure, and virtuous example to live morally, laws were unnecessary (Peerenboom, 1998, 234–60). Self-perfected people were expected to know the difference between right and wrong and promote harmonious exchanges (Chuong Thau and Phan Ngoc 1994). As in China, the Confucian elite in Vietnam saw no inconsistency in championing rule through ritual principles (*duc tri*), while controlling social behavior with draconian penal laws (*phap tri*). Legalist (*phap gia*) thinking promoted by Confucian scholars such as Hsun-tzu saw state law as a means of codifying, though never replacing, virtue-rule (Ta Van Tai 2001, 130–5). That legalist thinking influenced Lê and Nguyen rulers in Vietnam is shown in the attention given to legal codes and procedures.

Legalists urged strict legal compliance to minimize bureaucratic adventurism and promote community acceptance of law (Pham Diem 2001). But they did not countenance universal legality. Mandarins (*quan vien*), for example, reasoned from analogy in the numerous cases where laws did not directly apply to social problems. Where analogy failed, catchall provisions allowed them to criminalize "doing what should not be done," or those "committing wicked acts." It did not matter that such behavior was not otherwise proscribed by statute.[2] There was little attempt to develop doctrines and principles to enable mandarins to systemically draw on accumulated legal experiences. On the contrary, the practice of *thoa dang* (situational validity) of law and morality encouraged decision makers to syncretically select from moral and ethical sources to find ethical solutions to specific problems.[3] Exogenous normative sources such as laws were not considered absolute, universal, or immutable but rather alternative sources of guidance. The chief aim of legality in this system was to maintain moral order notwithstanding gaps and contradictions in the written law.

Even this situational understanding of legality only remotely touched the lives of most Vietnamese who lived in villages at the periphery of the imperial knowledge system. The familiar injunction *phep vua thua le lang* ("the laws of the emperor give way to the customs of the village") implies resistance by village-based knowledge systems to imperial legality. The limited interaction between the mandarins and village rulers ensured that neo-Confucian orthodoxies and legalism only slowly engaged with egalitarian Buddhist, Taoist, and animistic village beliefs.

French Colonial Legality

For almost 90 years (1867–1954), French colonialists imported Western legality into Vietnam (Roberts 1929, 64–75; Nguyen The Anh 1985). They not only transplanted French laws and institutions, but they also seconded French legal personnel including judges, court officials, and lawyers to administer the system. Colonial law expounded liberal ideology promoting legal equality, positive liberty (only laws can remove liberty), religious freedom, free speech, and, most importantly, the notion that laws encode universal values. For colonists surrounded by the language, architecture, manners, and cuisine of metropolitan France, liberal legality seemed plausible and desirable. At least initially, colonial legality only applied to Europeans and the tiny indigenous bourgeoisie who came to believe that Western legality promised an orderly and predicable world.[4] In a complex development pattern, colonial legality was slowly extended to Cochin-China, and urban centers in Annam and Tonkin (Murray 1980, 160). By default most indigenous Vietnamese remained embedded in village customary practices and imperial rule.

In time perhaps, liberal legality would have spread beyond colonial enclaves. But in practice colonial rule amplified long-standing tensions between elite urban and rural values and beliefs. Those on the periphery had long regarded the elite as belonging to a different knowledge system, but under colonization this perception strengthened (Grossheim 2004, 59–73). Unlike imperial legality, however, the principles underlying liberal legality were unrecognizable to those living outside the Francophone world and colonial economy. A governance system that placed law above morality and promoted universal solutions over situational validity seemed inflexible and immoral.

Ironically, the most radical challenge to French legality came from nationalists such as Phan Boi Chau and Phan Chu Trinh who were familiar with European philosophy and Constitutional legality (Marr 1981, 15–23). They enlisted liberal legality such as "the right to life and freedom" to prosecute the anticolonial struggle (Ho Chi Minh 1961, 96). Radicalized by contradictions between the harsh implementation of colonial law and its lofty idealism (liberty, equality, and fraternity), socialist leaders discarded liberal legality in favor of the Marxist-Leninist view that rights are contingent on class background, revolutionary contributions, and economic conditions (the base-superstructure metaphor).

Independence and Revolutionary Morality

Just as premodern ideas continued under French rule, there was no clear line marking the end of the colonial era and the beginning of the socialist period. Vestiges of colonial legality lingered for over a decade after the 1946 Constitution declared Vietnam independent of French rule. By the 1960s, however, the Democratic Republic of Vietnam began to comprehensively adopt the legal doctrines and institutions of the Soviet Union.[5]

Two fundamentally different approaches toward legality emerged during this period that continue to influence contemporary thinking. The Party ruled by moral example and edict, while the state systematically constructed a Soviet-inspired legal system. From its inception, the Party commingled neo-Confucian moral principles with Marxist-Leninist political–legal ideals to "sweep clean" (*quyet sach*) the old morality and make the Party line appear universal, rational, and desirable (Ho Chi Minh 1988, 7–8). Coming from scholar-gentry families, prominent Party leaders such as Ho Chi Minh and Truong Chinh initially studied classical Chinese texts to prepare themselves to rule as virtuous Confucian "superior men" (*quan tu*). From this epistemological background, neo-Confucianism and Marxism appeared to share similar frames of reference that transcended doctrinal differences (Nguyen Khac Vien 1974, 50).

The first generation of Party leaders were attracted to socialist ideas, because neo-Confucianism was considered unequal to the task of organizing resistance to French colonialism (ICP 1930, 58–9). They harnessed the motivating symbols in the old system of knowledge by depriving them of their original content and basic identity. Even so, they never entirely jettisoned the old system of knowledge and viewed concepts of socialist legality from both Confucian and Marxist-Leninist perspectives. These conflated ideals: exalted public needs over individual interests, privileged rule through moral virtue, and treated laws as tools to maintain social order.

Party leaders used a revolutionary morality (*dao duc cach mang*) synthesized from these knowledge systems to interpret and project state power. Ngo Van Thau, a professor teaching in the Judicial Training School from the 1960s until the 1980s, remembers how Party and state officials were required to interpret laws from five moral perspectives: *can* (diligence), *kiem* (thrift), *liem* (honesty), *chinh* (loyalty), and *chi cong vo tu* (social needs first).[6] These "traditional" values that "everyone understood" assumed different shades of meaning according to their application. For example, diligence and thrift retained their everyday meaning when applied to work practices within the justice system, but honesty, loyalty, and "social needs first" were reborn as obedience to Party policy—a sort of "new wine in old bottles."

Party leaders used revolutionary morality to lead the state and society (Young 1979, 774–5). Ho Chi Minh frequently stressed the importance of Party leadership (*su lanh dao cua dang*) by moral example (virtue-rule) (Nguyen Khac Vien 1974, 45). He said that "if one does not have morality, one can hardly lead the people however talented one can be"

(Ho Chi Minh 1995, 338). Party leaders were expected to "display higher knowledge than ordinary people, must act with lucidity and clear sightedness and must look farther and wider than others" (Song Thanh 1995, 6).

The Party could not rely on morals alone to induce change. It also needed cadres infused with the correct viewpoint (*quan diem dung dan*) and Leninist mass organizations to mobilize popular support. Mass organizations functioned as "instruments of top-down control, despite paying lip service to being representative of group interests" (Tran Thi Thu Trang 2002, 12). Though nominally configured as a Leninist organization, the Party and state functioned as a neo-Confucian-Leninist hybrid (Weggel 1986, 418–19).

Implementing Socialist Legality

At the First Congress of the Vietnam Workers Party (*Dang Lao Dong Viet Nam*) in September 1951, Party leaders instructed legal cadres to "build up socialist law" (Hoang Quoc Viet 1962, 14–15). At this time officials still used the French civil law concept *phap che dan chu* (democratic legality) to characterize the legal system. It was not until the Third Party Congress in 1960 that the Party formally adopted the Soviet *sotsialisticheskaia zakonnost* (socialist legality) doctrine, which translated into Vietnamese as *phap che xa hoi chu nghia* (Tran Hieu 1971, 8).

Socialist legality is defined in Vietnamese writings as a tool of proletarian dictatorship (*chuyen chinh vo san*) to defeat enemies, protect the revolution, and the collective democratic rights of people to organize and to manage and develop a command economy (Lesnoi 1961, 30–34). It reasoned from Marxist theory that worker-controlled societies require legal systems that reflect proletarian aspirations. The connection between law and class is explained by the metaphor that law is part of the "superstructure," which reflects the "will of the ruling class" (*y chi cua giai cap thong tri*) and their domination over the means of production. Vietnamese writings also linked socialist legality to "state discipline" (*ky luat nha nuoc*)—rule through law. In the minds of elite lawyers, socialist legality came to mean that law is not above the state but rather emanates from the state. As an extreme manifestation of legal positivism, there was no space for customary rules or natural rights. Socialist legality also invested the Party and state with prerogative powers to choose not to follow state laws. Legality thus facilitated, but never constrained, state power.

Tensions between socialist legality and Party virtue-rule were not entirely avoided by allowing the Party and state to flexibly apply the law as a "management tool" (*cong cu quan ly*). Soviet-trained lawyers complained that "vestiges of the Confucian conception of virtue-rule (*duc tri*) make our cadres and people not fully conscious of socialist legality and lack a full understanding of the necessity to apply the law and this prevents the building of a socialist jurisdiction" (Vu Hoa 1994, 74). Legal officials made numerous attempts to tame virtue-rule with legal rules.

The divergent streams of thought within the Party and state about the importance of legality are partially explained by the different ways virtue-rule and socialist legality developed in Vietnam. Contrasting with the highly syncretic processes that produced revolutionary morality and virtue-rule, socialist legality did not meaningfully engage with the old knowledge systems. The purge of most French-trained lawyers in the 1960s and their replacement by thousands of state officials trained in Soviet bloc universities undoubtedly accelerated the shift toward socialist legality (Ginsburgs 1979). This transformation gained further momentum with a campaign against colonial legality and Sino-Vietnamese legal words associated with the colonial regime (Dinh Gia Trinh 1965, 24–6).

The comprehensive assimilation of Soviet legal thinking took place within an epistemological framework that discouraged comparison with preexisting systems of knowledge. As a holistic philosophy, Marxist-Leninism could only accommodate other viewpoints from a Marxist perspective. An extensive review of Vietnamese legal literature over this period has failed to find a single article analyzing local political, economic, and cultural barriers to the transplantation of Soviet legal thinking, though a few articles considered minor procedural differences between Vietnamese and Soviet practices (Ta Thu Khue 1963, 13–14).

Soviet training encouraged Vietnamese legal officials to think of themselves as belonging to an international socialist family (*gia dinh xa hoi chu nghia*) that deemphasized cultural differences. For those embedded in this interpretive tradition, Soviet legal thinking and institutions appeared compatible with Vietnamese conditions because they originated from a similar "political system" (*he thong chinh tri*). In the socialist family, the Soviet Union was considered the "elder brother" and "family members" followed what they were told. Local adaptations of Soviet law were condemned as "dangerous nationalism" (*chu nghia dan toc cuc doan*) (Lesnoi 1963, 26–8).

Yet elite officials were not entirely isolated from preexisting systems of knowledge. As members of state organizations and local communities, they realized that imported egalitarian socialist rules could not easily displace traditional values and hierarchical practices. Some officials "used reason and sentiment in carrying out the law" (*ly va tinh trong viec chap hanh phap luat*) to selectively apply Party edicts and laws to localized problems. This practice resembled premodern *thao dang* situational decision making.

Through osmosis socialist legality gradually acquired meanings from premodern and French legal epistemologies. Take, for example, the Sino-Vietnamese term *phap che*, which was used to translate the Soviet word for "legality" (Dinh Gia Trinh 1964, 28–9). While *phap che* retained its Soviet meaning in legal discourse, in political discourse it reverted to its premodern legal meaning to "ensure legal compliance" through mass legal/moral education campaigns. Apart from these small-scale, localized, and pragmatic adjustments, elite lawyers did not meditatively theorize a distinctly Vietnamese version of socialist legality.

In the 1970s Party theorists were still debating whether "the Party-line and policies are enough and that building the laws will only set self-imposed limits that impede production and work" (Dam Van Hieu 1976, 20–1). Soviet-trained lawyers had not yet convinced most Party leaders to normalize state structures with laws—a minimum prerequisite of any type of legality. Fundamental issues vital to the development of legality remained unresolved. For example, it was unclear whether the Party or the legislature should enact laws. Up until this point the distinction was unimportant, because the Party line, state laws, and planning directives were considered interchangeable. Legality also had little practical relevance. So few laws were passed by the National Assembly that one commentator opined that "in such a situation even a semblance of legality became superfluous or just a formality" (Hoang The Lien 1994, 34). Finally, the question of whether Party committees or state administrators should run the country rarely surfaced, because Party leadership was "direct, unified and detailed."

To summarize, the first wave of Party leaders straddled the neo-Confucian and socialist worlds. They filtered socialist legal thinking through neo-Confucian beliefs that valued virtue-rule more highly than strict conformity to legal rules and processes. Even at the zenith of socialist orthodoxy, Party leaders could not escape from the old systems of knowledge, which partially explains why socialist legality did not easily displace virtue-rule.

The next generation of Party leaders grew up in a society influenced by both socialist and neo-Confucian interpretive beliefs. For them, the order and discipline promised by socialist legality seemed more socially appropriate and desirable than virtue-rule. That premodern modes of government remain important today suggests an ongoing interplay between neo-Confucian and subsequent approaches to legality.

(Re)Introducing Western Legality

After compressively rejecting French colonial legality during the 1950s and 1960s, following *doi moi* reforms in 1986 the state began reintroducing Western notions of legality. With previous legal changes, Western legality is filtered through the pre-existing systems of knowledge.

Scholars studying social change in Vietnam during the 1960s and 1970s observed a quiet, sometimes covert, process of resistance to the centrally planned economy (Fforde, 1984, 317–19). Entrepreneurs and spontaneous markets had survived decades of official suppression and by 1986 state officials estimated that more than 60% of consumer goods passed through illegal private trading networks (Vo Van Kiet 1986, 9). Rather than leading social change, these studies suggest that Party leaders struggled to control a vibrant entrepreneurial economy with revolutionary morality and Party edicts (Fforde and de Vyldes 1996).

The emerging gap between the stagnant command economy and booming regional economies further amplified the perception that command regulation could not deliver industrial and technological development. Party leaders worried that without unleashing the private sector the country would fall further behind those of its neighbors (Tu Tuan Anh 1994, 15–26). Like the first generation of Party leaders, the leaders in the mid-1980s looked for a new system of knowledge to revitalize the country.

Law Reform Discourse

Profound questions raised during the Fifth and Sixth Party Congresses, held in 1982 and 1986 respectively, queried the effectiveness of using central planning to regulate the economy. In addition to formally recognizing a mixed market economy, reform-minded leaders such as Truong Chinh also argued for the replacement of virtue-rule with legal regulation (Carlyle Thayer 1991, 23). The 1982 *Party Report on Economic Guidelines and Tasks* stated that "the power to rule the state must be reflected in the systems of laws. The law, as it is boiled down, is the institutionalisation of the Party line and policies. But there must be no confusion among the line, policies and law."[7] In other words, the Party should use legislation rather than extra-legal prerogative powers to regulate the economy.

Political Constraints to Developing a Commercial Legislative Framework

Lawmakers faced a conundrum in drafting market-oriented laws. Socialist economic laws were unsuitable as templates, but lawmakers could not wait the decades needed to codify laws from domestic commercial practices. They were compelled to search for inspiration beyond Vietnam's borders. Lawmakers could not use Soviet legal templates, because the Soviet Union had not yet embarked on market reforms. Under the "open door" (*mo cua*) policy they wanted Western investment and technology, but they did not want Western social and political systems. Above all else, the long-standing tradition of national self-reliance, vindicated by victories in the French and American wars, convinced them that legislative solutions lay in home-grown institutions and strategies.

Lawmakers also rejected proposals from some French-trained Vietnamese lawyers to recycle commercial laws from the past.[8] Colonial laws were the closest facsimile in Vietnam to a usable legal past. The laws had been translated into Vietnamese, taught in the Saigon Law School, and applied in Republic of Vietnam courts by a generation of Southern judges and lawyers. But for Northern lawmakers colonial law arose out of and was designed to regulate capitalist economic relationships and was considered inimical to Vietnam's "socialist-oriented market economy." To make matters worse, the adoption of southern legislation bestowed too much legitimacy on the discredited ancien régime.

Having begun economic reforms earlier than the Soviet Union, Chinese law influenced the first wave of Vietnamese commercial laws such as the Foreign Investment Law 1987. Lawmakers believed that similar cultural beliefs, economic structures, and, above all else, political system made China an appropriate legislative source. Because the Chinese lacked appropriate experience in many commercial areas, lawmakers were eventually compelled to import some laws directly from the capitalist West.

Case Study: Drafting the Ordinance on Economic Contracts 1989

The debates informing the drafting and subsequent amendments to the Ordinance on Economic Contracts 1989 reveal much about contemporary attitudes toward legality. The following discussion positions the drafting debates in three distinct developmental periods. Command economic thinking strongly influenced the first drafting committee convened during the early stages of *doi moi. Nha nuoc phap quyen* (law-based state) doctrines introduced in 1991 opened lawmakers to new Western thinking about legality. After the Party endorsed international economic integration in 2001, many of the remaining epistemological objections to Western legality evaporated.

The Early Doi Moi *Period*

For decades Vietnamese lawyers used "state economic management" (*quan ly nha nuoc kinh te*) to link central planning and economic production (Pham Thanh Vinh 1964, 120). This regulatory formula gave Party and state authorities extra-legal discretionary powers to "fine-tune" the implementation of state plans. Inconsistencies between laws, plans, and Party edicts did not especially matter in the command economy, because the Party and state primarily used prerogative powers to order society. But in a mixed market economy regulators could not simply suppress market pathologies. They needed a legislative framework to establish acceptable commercial norms and practices.

In 1987, the Party Central Committee instructed the Ministry of Trade to appoint a drafting committee to prepare an ordinance regulating contracts for profit-making activities (economic contracts).[9] Drafting commenced at a time when the Council of Ministers was still undecided about the role of state planning. In fact the entire legal infrastructure still exhibited Marxist-Leninist antipathy to private ownership of the "means of production." The Constitution and the Penal Code criminalized private commercial activity. Compounding these attitudes, drafters were trained to administer a centrally planned economy, and with the limited exception of two French-trained lawyers, they understood few of the theoretical and cultural tenets of mixed market systems (Sidel 1993, 226–8).

Drafters expressed a cultural disdain for entrepreneurs that echoed premodern beliefs. Official attitudes during the precolonial period are epitomized by the Confucian saying "emphasise agriculture, commerce is peripheral" (*trong nong mat thuong*), by prohibiting large-scale commercial organizations. After independence, neo-Confucian antimercantilism merged with socialist class theory to profoundly shape bureaucratic attitudes toward private commerce. During the high socialist period state officials were rewarded for reviling the private sector and respecting the state sector (Dang Phong 1999, 78–80). Small-scale household producers were tolerated, but large-scale private producers were suppressed because they exploited their workers' surplus value. Contemporary surveys suggest that these values are still uppermost in the minds of many state officials (Dang Phong 1999, 15–16).

Reflecting tensions between orthodox socialism and the desire to attract foreign investment, the Party Central Committee instructed drafters to prepare an ordinance that preserved "state economic management" over the economy; established contract rules to facilitate autonomous business transactions among state and private businesses; and provided contractual guidance to inexperienced business players. Both the scope and structure of the ordinance were based on the Soviet-inspired Decree No. ND-54/CP, the Regulations on Economic Contracts 1975. For example, the ordinance retained the distinction in the command economy between economic contracts for profit and civil contracts for personal consumption. Only commercial entities with business licenses (*giay phep kinh doanh*) (state-owned enterprises, private companies/enterprises, and cooperatives) were permitted to enter economic contracts for profit (Duong Dang Hue 1994). Provisions also based economic contracts on the "state plan" (Article 10) and gave state economic arbitrators powers to intervene and adjust contractual rights (Article 8).

Drafters gave regulators "state economic management" powers to create a *co che xin cho* (asking-permitting) market-entry system (Pham Duy Nghia 2005, 84–5). Rather than clearly defining the areas where entrepreneurs could conduct business, the licensing system gave regulators broad discretionary powers to "fine-tune" the scope of business activities. Infractions of these vague and protean guidelines were punishable with administrative and criminal penalties.

Also reflecting command thinking, drafters wanted to dictate how transactions were handled and the terms that were incorporated into written contracts. In part this longing for specificity is attributable to ingrained habits learned from the command economy when regulators told enterprises what to do. Drafters also had little confidence in the capacity for the judiciary to resolve cases without highly prescriptive lists of what proper contracts should entail. But more than this, drafters thought Vietnamese entrepreneurs were inexperienced and often dishonest and required detailed legislative guidance backed by tight supervision. Discretionary "state economic management" powers gave regulators powers to adjust private contractual rights to preserve the "state benefit" (*loi ich cua nha nuoc*) (Nguyen Thi Khe 1996, 23–4).

Despite their misgivings about Vietnamese entrepreneurs, drafters also adopted provisions that championed autonomous contractual rights. Article 4 of the ordinance protected signatories from duress; Article 5 introduced the concept of voluntary commercial relationships; and Article 6 guaranteed state protection for contractual promises. Private rights directly contradicted the state-dissected legality contemplated in socialist legality.

Nha nuoc phap quyen (Law–Based State) and the New Legality

In 1999 the Party Central Committee directed the Supreme People's Court to redraft the Ordinance on Economic Contracts 1989. Contrasting with the clear instructions given to the original drafting committee, the Court was ordered to make the ordinance more relevant to current economic conditions. Behind this cryptic injunction lay an unresolved dispute about the role of "state economic management" in Vietnam's mixed market economy.

Much had changed in both the regulatory views of the state and the political economy since the ordinance was enacted in 1989. The Seventh Party Congress in 1991 enlarged the socialist political-legal canon by adding law-based state (*nha nuoc phap quyen*) concepts to socialist legality (Do Muoi 1992, 6). *Nha nuoc phap quyen* stressed the need for stable, authoritative, and compulsory law; equality before the law; and the use of law to constrain and supervise enforcement and administration. It also proposed a separation of Party and state functions where the Party was supposed to formulate socioeconomic objectives, leaving state apparatus to enact and implement the Party line. Taken together these precepts constituted a liberal form of legality. But *nha nuoc phap quyen* did not abrogate socialist legality and once and for all eliminate the Party's prerogative powers to substitute policy for law. It is still uncertain whether the Party unequivocally accepts that its policy needs state legislation to acquire coercive force (Gillespie 2004, 169–172). Rather than a coherent legal doctrine, *nha nuoc phap quyen* is treated by commentators as a conceptual umbrella for new legal thinking. Its main contribution is to open the narrow epistemological conventions permitted by socialist legality and allowing commentators to smuggle new ideas about legality into official discourse (Tran Dinh Huynh 1999, 3–5).

New thinking about legality surfaced in the debates about the role of "state economic management" in regulating economic contracts. Foreign legal advisers to the drafting committee argued for a neoliberal facilitative law that deregulated "asking-permitting" (*co che xin cho*) discretionary licenses. Underlying this approach was the view that entrepreneurs can do anything that is not expressly prohibited by law. Advisers thought the best way for entrepreneurs to take full advantage of private rights was to confine the state to a minimalist, "night watchman" role.

There is little discernable support for neoliberal legal thinking in the Vietnamese legal literature. Many commentators advocate the liberal legalist view that "law should be attached to politics but is not a servant of the state" (*Nha nuoc va Phap luat* 1996, 116–17). In other words, laws implement political policy but are not "management tools" (*cong cu quan ly*). But only a small group go further to argue that "state economic management" compromises market rights, such as freedom to conduct authorized business activities (Pham Duy Nghia 2002, 53–6). And even they, however, remain skeptical about whether the sweeping deregulation promoted by neoliberal legality is an appropriate regulatory policy for a poor country experiencing uneven wealth creation.

Some commentators support an East Asian developmental model that reserves a proactive role for the state (Tu Tuan Anh 1994, 253–4). They agree with neoliberal theorists that transparent legal systems encourage market stability and predictability, but believe that economic growth requires "Rhine capitalism" where proactive states regulate economic producers. They support an ongoing role for "state economic management" in controlling large state-owned enterprises and micromanaging the private sector.

More typically, commentators argue that "state economic management" is needed to ensure that resource allocation in society complies with Party socioeconomic objectives. For them the "state managerial role in the market economy is extremely important. It ensures stable growth and efficiency for the economy, particularly social equality and progress. No one else but the state can reduce the gap between the rich and poor, the towns and the countryside, industry and agriculture and among regions in the country" (Mai Huu Thuc 2001). A lingering preoccupation with class conflict is also suggested by the use of "state economic management" to ensure that entrepreneurs do not accumulate too much wealth in the mixed market economy.

These competing ideas influenced the drafting committee. Drafters disagreed on two fundamental issues that directly concerned the role of "state economic management" in regulating private contracts. Should the conceptual distinction between economic and civil contracts be abolished so that unregistered household entrepreneurs could enter into economic contracts? At issue was the state's power to proactively determine the type of entrepreneurs permitted to form economic contracts and engage in large-scale commerce.

The Ministry of Justice led opposition to fundamental change. According to Hoang The Lien, a key Ministry official, "parties to economic contracts should be business persons (i.e. individuals or units that the government has allowed to carry out business). Not all people are allowed to participate in business processes and conduct business activities" (Hoang The Lien 2000, 21). In other words, divisions between economic and civil contracts are necessary to proactively ensure that the "right type" of entrepreneurs enter business transactions.

Duong Dang Hue (2000, 14–18), the Ministry of Justice representative on the drafting committee, used class-based arguments to block reforms. He opined that businesses are operated by "rich people" who enjoy many privileges over "ordinary citizens." Breaches of economic contracts have the potential to generate wide-ranging social harm by causing business failure and unemployment. Civil contracts, in contrast, produce highly particularized harm to consumers and families. "State economic management" over market entry is needed to protect the economy and "working-class" interests.

Judges on the drafting committee argued for a unified economic and civil contract system. While not opposing "state economic management" as an ideal, they found that the dual contract system was conceptually confusing (Tran Van Su 2000, 9–13). The Supreme Court Annual Report (2000, 40), for example, showed that most contractual cases reviewed by higher courts involved procedural irregularities, such as filing actions in the wrong court division. Judges attributed these irregularities to the dual contract system. Judges also found the dual system troublesome because it prevented them from using provisions from the comprehensive Civil Code to cover the numerous regulatory omissions and ambiguities in the ordinance and the Commercial Law. They maintained that a comprehensive legislative response was needed to unify and harmonize the doctrines governing economic and civil contracts.

As a comparatively weak institution, the Supreme Court struggled to mobilize support from conservative ministries for a unified contract law. But drafters from the Ministry of Trade agreed that separate economic and civil contractual regimes had outlived the economic conditions in which they had risen and gave provisional support for the removal of "state economic management" over private contracts.

It is difficult to explain the divergent approaches to state economic management solely in terms of self-interest and "palace wars" between different institutions. As a commercial regulator the Ministry of Trade had the most to gain by retaining "state economic management," yet it was the most in favor of a neoliberal rights-based law. Counterintuitively, the Ministry of Justice and Ministry of Interior, with no direct stake in the outcome, led the opposition to change. In supporting a unified contract law, only the Supreme Court argued a position that clearly advanced its own interests. For a fuller explanation it is necessary to examine how the drafters responded to changes in the interpretive environment.

International Economic Integration

The next significant change in legal thinking slowly gained momentum from the mid-1990s, when Party leaders decided that Vietnam's future lay in international economic integration. In return for the market access gained by joining international treaties such as APEC, AFTA, and especially the Vietnam-US Bilateral Trade Agreement (BTA) and WTO, Vietnam agreed to harmonize its commercial laws with international standards.

Opposition by conservative ministries to imported neoliberal legality dissolved when the Politburo issued Resolution No. 7-NQ/TW on International Economic Integration in 2001. The Legal Needs Assessment sponsored by the Ministry of Justice (2002, 25), for example, concluded that "the concept of proactive international economic integration must be instilled in the development and completion of the legal system of Vietnam in all fields, from law making and implementation, to legal education and dissemination." The lawmaking agenda from this time has overwhelmingly reflected the legislative harmonization required for BTA and WTO membership.

The shift toward international economic integration directly affected the committee redrafting the ordinance on economic contracts. Both the BTA and WTO required Vietnam to enact a contractual regime that did not discriminate between the economic sectors (VNS 2003). As pressure mounted to enact the laws required for WTO accession, the ministries of Justice and Interior moderated their support for "state economic management." By March 2004, the drafting committee decided to abolish the Ordinance on Economic Contracts and relocate the contractual provisions in a redrafted Commercial Law and Civil Code. The third draft of the new Commercial Law contained provisions that permitted any entity with legal capacity to form economic contracts.

Drafters from the Supreme Court failed, however, in their bid to remove the confusing doctrinal distinctions between civil and economic contracts (Dinh Thi Mai Phuong 2005, 15–16). The new Commercial Law, which passed the National Assembly in 2005, removed "state economic management" powers that had enabled officials to decide which type of entrepreneurs were permitted to form economic contracts. But it retained the divisions between civil and economic contracts.

Changing the Interpretive Architecture

It is possible to infer a nexus in the case study between pressure forces in the political economy and legal reform. After all, it was not until the Party threw its weight behind international economic integration that recalcitrant ministries abandoned their objections to an open contractual regime. Efforts by foreign investors and donors to remove "state economic management" powers were greatly assisted by the Party's decision to join the BTA and WTO. There is less evidence that domestic entrepreneurs pressured for contractual reforms (Gillespie 2006, 320–45). They knew only too well that when "state economic management" powers are reduced in one area, they rapidly regroup in another. That the political economy generated pressure for regulatory change does not explain, however, why members of the drafting committee responded in different ways. A more complete understanding must take into account the interpretive environment from which they understood and reacted to external factors.

Luu Van Dat, the leader of the drafting committee in 1987, was elevated from decades of comparative obscurity in the command legal system to advise the state about capitalist law. Despite receiving French legal training during the colonial period, 30 years of working in the command system had eroded his knowledge of, and attachment to market laws. Other drafters who had been trained in Soviet bloc countries, knew and cared even less for market principles and rights-based contracts.

During the early stages of *doi moi*, drafters had few contacts with Western lawyers. With the limited exception of French-trained lawyers, they lacked the linguistic skills needed to communicate meaningfully with foreign legal advisers or to read and comprehend market laws. They were deeply embedded in an interpretive tradition that privileged state powers over individual rights and tacitly assumed that private businesses could not function without proactive discretionary controls.

By the time the newly constituted committee began redrafting the ordinance in 1999, clear epistemological differences were emerging between drafters. Judges on the committee gained exposure to neoliberal legal ideas while participating in various legal assistance projects and from junior officials who were trained in Western law schools and could translate and explain market laws. But their understanding about this knowledge system was filtered through deeply entrenched Soviet-inspired precepts and practices. They interpreted their instructions to upgrade contractual rules in a way that did not fundamentally disturb "state economic management" powers. Their approach to legality was more consistent with socialist rather than neoliberal perspectives.

Drafters from the Ministry of Trade were much more strongly influenced by neoliberal legality. Most were Western-educated and had acquired an understanding, even sympathy for neoliberal legality through prolonged treaty negotiations (especially for the BTA and WTO) and from numerous foreign donor-sponsored study tours and workshops. Their fluency in English enabled them to directly access and comprehend neoliberal legal literature. They were prevented from overtly identifying with the neoliberal position, because these beliefs were too closely associated with foreigners. Nevertheless, as a group they championed deregulation, market access, and other neoliberal ideas. This epistemological shift was made possible by the relaxation of socialist orthodoxies that followed *nha nuoc phap quyen* debates, and especially by Party support for international legal harmonization. Both reforms opened the epistemological settings and allowed new legal responses to changes in the political economy.

The case study suggests that Ministry of Trade drafters were embedded in a loosely constituted neoliberal-oriented interpretive community. They quickly assimilated complex neoliberal legal principles because they understood the conceptual language and shared many of the same regulatory goals. They diagnosed regulatory problems from neoliberal perspectives and drew legal solutions from neoliberal ideas. Constantly repeated principles, doctrines, and strategies played a central role in constituting and directing the way the members of this community selected and adapted neoliberal legal principles.

Drafters were not only members of a neoliberal-oriented interpretive community; they also belonged to Party and state-institutional interpretive communities. In order to function within multiple interpretive environments, they used neoliberal ideas strategically. Rather than passively following neoliberal orthodoxies, Ministry of Trade drafters actively debated and selectively used imported ideas to realize institutional objectives. They were careful to use foreign knowledge and skills in ways that did not offend the hierarchies and policies in their host institution and in other politically powerful communities. Over time the perceived success of international economic integration in securing off-shore markets increased the drafters' prestige and influence, allowing their ideas to spread further into the organizational hierarchy.

Conclusion

Consistent with the proposition that new systems of knowledge overly engage with but rarely entirely displace preexisting systems of knowledge, neoliberal legality has not swept aside socialist legality. The case study about the Ordinance on Economic Contracts suggests a much more complex interaction between new and old ideas. Since lawmakers belonged to many interpretive communities, new understandings of legality had to negotiate and accommodate preexisting approaches to legality. As other chapters reveal, neoliberal legality is encountering more resistance in some interpretive communities than others. Its progress has been especially rapid in the commercial arena, but socialist legality and the extra-legal prerogative powers remain much more deeply entrenched in politically sensitive areas.

This leaves the important question: what factors are likely to broaden the reach of neoliberal legality within the state? If it is correct that lawmakers formulate responses to social change from the precepts, habits, and practices in which they are embedded, then a change in these beliefs will alter their perceptions about legality. But how do belief structures change?

Discourse analysis points out that preference convergence, of the kind required to change beliefs, is most likely to occur when lawmakers discuss ideas in a sustained and unmediated environment. These conditions are evident in the collaborative structures formed between foreign donors/lawyers and key Vietnamese consultants and state officials. Legal projects inculcate neoliberal legalism by bringing foreign advisers into a close working environment with a growing number of local legal consultants and officials. They know each other, work on the same projects, and increasingly share similar educational backgrounds and worldviews. Common social interests and professional ideas encourage an enclave-like and self-referential approach to policy alternatives. This in turn generates a propensity for foreign-funded projects to exclude or minimize critical legal and political perspectives.

The incentive to conform is provided by access to donor-funded projects, foreign travel, and education. If tendering rules standardize methodological, analytical, and presentational formats, then friendships and networking provide access to the unwritten "rules of the game." Projects are awarded to consultants who have learnt how to approach problems and prescribe solutions from neoliberal legal perspectives. Neoliberal interpretive communities are sometimes difficult to identify, because members deploy new ideas strategically so as not to offend power brokers within their institutions. But in working closely with foreign donors, members are constantly exposed to particular story lines or narratives about the correct approach to regulatory problems. By providing detailed explanations for solving economic problems, neoliberal legality frequently gives members an edge over lawmakers struggling to make "state economic management" apply to market conditions. As neoliberal legality spreads, members gain in status and their ideas penetrate further into organizational hierarchies.

Because Vietnamese lawmakers belong to many interpretive communities, neoliberal ideas are not imported in their entirety, but rather they are strategically deployed to accommodate preexisting knowledge systems. Nevertheless, the extent to which neoliberal legalism has infiltrated Vietnamese state institutions is probably underestimated. It suits both foreign and local interests to downplay the influence of new ideas, because the specter of foreign interference is easily used to discredit reforms. Donors also frequently miscalculate the extent of their influence. They conflate legal reforms that are amenable to resolution in the short- to medium-term with reforms that address transactional practices that are so deeply rooted that they are only likely to respond to long-term historical changes. This leads them to underestimate their influence in changing attitudes to legality.

Notes

1. The term neoliberal legality is the legal analogue of neo-liberal economic theory, which is based on a philosophy whose basic units are individuals that make rational decisions according to prevailing circumstances and available information (Cooter 1996, 142–46).
2. "Whoever commits an act that should not be done shall be condemned to penal servitude or exiled for a major wrong and demoted or fined for a minor one." Lê Code, Article 642; Nguyen Code, Article 351.
3. Interviews with Hoang Ngoc Hien, sociologist at the Nguyen Du Institute, Hanoi, 2001–2004.
4. Colonial legal pluralism was rather complex. But by the late colonial period criminal law applied to everyone, though a modified version of the Nguyen Code still governed the rural population in Annam and Tonkin (Hooker 1975, 226–30).

5. Interviews with Le Kim Que, President of the Bar Association of Hanoi, Hanoi, June 1997, October, 1999; Nguyen Thuc Bao, former Legal Adviser to Ministry of Agriculture, Hanoi, September 2000. See also see George Ginsburgs (1979), The Genesis of the People's Procuracy in the Democratic Republic of Vietnam, 5 *Review of Socialist Law* 5: 187, 191–2; Penelope Nicholson (2000), Borrowing Court Systems: The Experience of the Democratic Republic of Vietnam, 1945–1976, unpublished PhD Thesis, University of Melbourne, Melbourne, chapter 5.
6. Interview with Ngo Van Thau, former professor, Judicial Training School, Hanoi, 2001.
7. Circular No. 3831/TP 1983 on Some Immediate Work to be Done by the Judiciary Sector to Implement the 5th Party Congress Resolution, Ministry of Justice.
8. The most influential French trained lawyers were Luu Van Dat, the former director of the Law Department of the Ministry of Trade and Tourism, Pham Huu Chi, the former chief adviser to the Minister of Justice, and Tran Cong Tuong, head of the *Uy ban Phap che*, the precursor of the Ministry of Justice.
9. Information concerning the initial drafting of the Ordinance on Economic Contracts 1989 was gleaned from interviews with two members of the drafting committee: Luu Van Dat, legal adviser to the Minister of Trade, Hanoi, January 1990, and Phan Huu Chi, legal adviser to the Minister of Justice, April 1992.

References

Black, Julia 2002. Regulatory conversations. *Journal of Law and Society* 29(1): 163.

Chuong Thau, and Phan Ngoc. 1994. Confucianism in Vietnam seen from an historical tradition. *Vietnamese Studies* 10.

Cooter, Robert. 1996. The theory of market modernization of law. *International Review of Law and Economics* 16: 141.

Dam Van Hieu. 1976. Some ideas about building a unified legal system in the SRV. *Luat Hoc* 4 (October): 35. Translated in Joint Publications Research Service (JPRS), 69122 May 19, 1997, 20.

Dang Phong. 1999. The private sector in Vietnamese industry from 1945 to the present. In *Vietnam's undersized engine: A survey of 95 larger private manufacturers*. Hanoi: MPDF Discussion Paper No. 9.

Dinh Gia Trinh. 1965. May y kien ve tinh dan toc va tinh khoa hoc cua thuat ngu luat hoc—Nhan xet phe phan ve mot so thuat ngu thong dung (Nationalistic and scientific use of legal terminology: Criticisms of common legal terms). *Tap san Tu phap* 3: 24.

Do Muoi. 1992. *Sua doi Hien phap xay dung Nha nuoc Phap Quyen Viet nam, Day manh su nghiep Doi moi (Amending the Constitution, Establishing a Law-Based-State and Promoting doi moi Achievements)*. Hanoi: Nha xuat ban Su that.

Dinh Thi Mai Phuong. 2005. New provisions on contract in the new Civil Code and Commercial Law. *Vietnam Law and Legal Forum* 12(135): 15.

Duong Dang Hue. 1994. Phap luat ve viec cap giay phep thanh lap doanh nghiep dang ky kinh doanh o Viet Nam: Thuc trang va mot vai kien nghi (Legal regulations in relation to issuance of permits to establish enterprises and business registration on Vietnam: The present situation and some recommendations). *Nha nuoc va Phap luat* 4: 20.

———. 2000. Nhung co so cua viec xay dung Phap lenh hop dong kinh te (sua doi) (Foundation for building up Ordinance on Economic Contracts (amended)). In *Kien nghi ve xay dung phap luat hop dong kinh te tai Viet Nam (Recommendations on building up the economic contract legislation in Vietnam)*. Hanoi: Ministry of Justice VIE/95/017.

Fforde, Adam. 1984. Law and socialist agricultural development in Vietnam: The Statute for Agricultural Producer Cooperatives. *Review of Socialist Law* 10: 315.

Fforde, Adam, and de Vylder, Stefan. 1996. *From plan to market: The economic transition in Vietnam*. Boulder: Westview.

Fish, Stanley. 1989. *Doing what comes naturally: Change, rhetoric and practice in literary and legal studies*. Durham: Duke University Press.

———. 1999. *The trouble with principle*. Cambridge: Harvard University Press.

Gillespie, John. 2004. Conceptions of rule of law in Vietnam. In *Asian discourses of rule of law*. Edited by Randall Peerenboom. London: Routledge, 54–89.

———. 2006. *Transplanting commercial law reform: Developing a "rule of law" in Vietnam*. Aldershot: Ashgate.

Ginsburgs, George. 1979. The genesis of the People's Procuracy in the Democratic Republic of Vietnam. *Review of Socialist Law* 5: 187.

Grossheim, Martin. 2004. Village government in pre-colonial and colonial Vietnam. In *Beyond Hanoi: Local government in Vietnam*. Edited by Benedict Tria Kerkvliet and David Marr. Singapore: Institute of Southeast Asian Studies, 54–89.

Ho Chi Minh. 1961. *Selected Works*. Vol. II. Hanoi: Foreign Languages Publishing House.

———. 1988. *Ve tu cach nguoi Dang vien Cong san* (On the behavior of Communist Party members). Hanoi: Nha Xuat Ban Su That.

———. 1995. *Complete Works*. Vol. 5. Hanoi: National Politics Publishing House.

Hoang Quoc Viet. 1962. Viec xay dung phap che xa hoi chu nghia va giao duc moi nguoi ton trong phap luat (Building up socialist legality and educating people to respect laws). *Hoc Tap (Study Review)* 16: 14.

Hoang The Lien. 1994. On the legal system of Vietnam. *Vietnam Law and Legal Forum* 1(1): 33.

———. 2000. Xac dinh doi tuong va pham vi dieu chinh cua Phap lenh hop dong kinh te (sua doi) (Identification of governing objectives and scope of the Ordinance on Economic Contracts (amended)). In *Kien nghi ve xay dung Phap luat hop dong kinh te tai Viet Nam (Recommendations on building up the economic contract legislation in Vietnam)*. Hanoi: Ministry of Justice-UNDP VIE/95/017.

Hooker, Michael Barry. 1975. *Legal pluralism: An introduction to colonial and neo-colonial laws*. Oxford: Clarendon Press.

Indochinese Communist Party (ICP). 1930. Political Thesis of Indochinese Communist Party. Reproduced in *Vietnam Documents and Research Notes* 1970, no. 103.

Lesnoi, V. M. 1961. Phap che xa hoi chu nghia Xo viet (Soviet socialist legality). *Tap San Tu Phap* 4: 30.

Lesnoi, V. M. 1963. Nen tu phap cua Nuoc Viet nam Dan chu Cong hoa (The judiciary of the Democratic Republic of Vietnam). *Tap San Tu Phap* 11: 26.

Mai Huu Thuc. 2001. Characteristics of market economy with socialist orientation in Viet Nam. *Vietnam Social Sciences* 1: 24.

Marr, David. 1981. *Vietnamese tradition on trial, 1920–1945*. Berkeley: University of California Press.

Ministry of Justice. 2002. Report on the Comprehensive Needs of Developing Law Making Bodies, Law Implementation and Enforcement, International Treaty Reception and Dispute Resolution. Hanoi: Ministry of Justice.

Murray, Martin. 1980. *The development of capitalism in colonial Indochina (1870–1940)*. Berkeley: University of California Press.

Nguyen Khac Vien. 1974. *Tradition and revolution in Vietnam*. Berkeley: Indochina Resource Centre.

Nguyen The Anh. 1985. The Vietnamese monarchy under French colonial rule 1884–1945. *Modern Asian Studies* 19: 153.

Nguyen Thi Khe. 1996. Cac bien phap bao dam thuc hien hop dong kinh te trong nen kinh te thi truong o Viet Nam (Measures to ensure the implementation of economic contracts in the market economy in Vietnam). *Nha nuoc va Phap luat* 9: 17.

Nha nuoc va Phap luat. 1996. *Nhung van de ly luan co ban ve Nha nuoc va Phap luat (Basic theoretical issues about State and Law)*. Hanoi: Nha xuat ban Chinh tri Quoc gia.

Peerenboom, Randall. 1998. Confucian harmony and freedom of thought. In *Confucianism and Human Rights*. Edited by William Theodore de Bary and Tu Weiming. New York: Columbia University Press, 234–60.

Pham Diem. 2001. Judiciary offences under Vietnam's ancient laws. *Vietnam Law and Legal Forum* 7(82): 20.

Pham Duy Nghia. 2002. Tiep nhan phap luat nuoc ngoai—Thoi co va thach thuc moi cho nghien cuu lap phap (Transplantation of foreign laws—Chances and challenges for legislative studies in Vietnam). *Nghien cuu Lap phap* 5: 50.

———. 2005. Confucianism and the conception of the law in Vietnam. In *Asian socialism and legal change: The dynamics of Vietnamese and Chinese reform*. Edited by John Gillespie and Pip Nicholson. Canberra: Asia Pacific Press, 76–90.

Pham Thanh Vinh. 1964. Tinh chat phap lenh trong ke hoach 5 nam lan thu nhat (1961–1965) (Legal nature of the First Five Year Plan 1961–1965). In *Nghien cuu Nha nuoc va Phap quyen (Studies on state and legality)*. Hanoi: Nha xuat ban Su hoc, 111–23.

Rambo, Terry. 1987. Black flight suits and white ao-dais: Borrowings and adaptations of symbolism of Vietnamese cultural identity. In *Borrowings and adaptations in Vietnamese culture*. Edited by Truong Buu Lam. Honolulu: Center for Southeast Asian Studies, University of Hawaii, 115–23.

Roberts, Stanley. 1929. *The history of French colonial policy 1870–1925* (new impression 1963). London: Frank Cass.

Robertson, Michael. 1999. Picking positivism apart: Stanley Fish on epistemology and law. *Southern California Interdisciplinary Law Journal* 8: 401.

Rorty, Richard. 1997. Justice as a larger loyalty. In *Justice and democracy: Cross-cultural perspectives*. Edited by Ron Bontekoe and Marietta Stepanints. Honolulu: University of Hawaii Press, 9–22.

Sidel, Mark. 1993. Legal reform in Vietnam: The complex transition from socialism and Soviet models in legal scholarship and training. *UCLA Pacific Basin Law Journal* 11: 221.

Song Thanh. 1995. President Ho Chi Minh laid the foundation for a law-governed state. *Vietnam Law and Legal Forum* 1(9): 3.

Supreme Court Annual Report. 2000. Bao cao Tong ket, Cong tac Toa an Nam. Hanoi.

Ta Thu Khue. 1963. Can than trong trong viec ap dung kinh nghiem Lien-Xo vao trinh tu phuc tham (We need to be cautious in applying Soviet experience in appellate procedures). *Tap San Tu Phap* 2: 12.

Ta Van Tai. 2001. The rule of law in the traditional law of traditional China and Vietnam: Traditional East Asian legal practice in the light of the standards of the modern rule of law. *Vietnamese Studies* 4: 128.

Thayer, Carlyle. 1991. Renovation and Vietnamese society: The changing role of government and administration. In *Doi Moi: Vietnam's renovation policies and performance*. Edited by Dean Forbes et al. Canberra: Australian National University, 21–33.

Tran Dinh Huynh. 1999. Moi quan he giua tri luc—dao duc—phap luat trong quan ly dat nuoc cua Chu tich Ho Chi Minh (Relationship Between intelligence, morality, and law in Ho Chi Minh's thoughts on administration). *To Chuc Nha Nuoc* (5): 3–5.

Tran Hieu. 1971. *25 nam xay dung nen phap che Viet Nam (25 years of building Vietnamese legality)*. Hanoi: Nha xuat ban Lao dong.

Tran Thi Thu Trang. 2002. Politics in rural Vietnam: Local democracy or local autocracy? (Unpublished paper, Hanoi).

Tran Van Su. 2000. Nhung vuong mac trong che do hop dong kinh te hien hanh (Problems in the current economic contract regime). In *Kien nghi ve xay dung Phap luat hop dong kinh te tai Viet*

Nam (Recommendations on building up the economic contract legislation in Vietnam). Hanoi: Ministry of Justice-UNDP VIE/95/017, 9–13.

Tu Tuan Anh. 1994. *Vietnam's economic reform: Results and problems*. Hanoi: Social Sciences Publishing House.

Vietnam News Service (VNS). 2003. Fast reform for commercial law. Vietnam News June 11. Online at www.vietnamnews.vnagency.com.vn/2003–11/06/Stories/04.htm, visited February 11, 2006.

Vo Van Kiet. 1986. Report to the National Assembly on the 1987 Socio-Economic Development Plan. Hanoi Domestic Service, December 26. Translated in FBIS Asia and Pacific Daily Report, December 30, 1986, 9.

Vu Hoa. 1994. The ideological heritage of Confucianism is unimportant. *Vietnamese Studies* 1: 71.

Weggel, Oskar. 1986. The Vietnamese Communist Party and its status under law. In *Ruling Communist Parties and their status under law*. Edited by Dietrich Loeber. The Hague: Martinus Nijhoff, 411–19.

Woodside, Alexander. 1998. Freedom and elite political theory in Vietnam before the French. In *Asian freedoms*. Edited by David Kelly and Anthony Reid. Cambridge: Cambridge University Press, 205–22.

Young, Stephen. 1979. Vietnamese Marxism: Transition in elite ideology. *Asian Survey* 24(8): 770.

CHAPTER NINE

Lawyers and Prosecutors under Legal Reform in Vietnam: The Problem of Equality

NGUYEN HUNG QUANG

In 1995, Prime Minister Vo Van Kiet learned that a criminal organization controlled the entertainment industry in the southern commercial center of Ho Chi Minh City. The main activity of this organization was gambling, with a number of big casinos directly run by the gang, and smaller casinos of other criminal organizations under their patronage (*bao ke*). The organization also managed restaurants, hotels, karaoke bars, and acted as "patrons" of other such establishments, along with such activities as murder, betting, blackmail, usurious lending, and so on.

The Prime Minister instructed the Ministry of Interior to undertake an investigation. The case was considered top secret. Nam Cam, the godfather of this gang, was arrested several months later. But thanks to the intervention of some high-ranking government officials, he was released two years later without being convicted. After further investigation, Nam Cam was re-arrested in December 2001 along with 155 associates following a request from the Political Bureau of the Vietnamese Communist Party.

The Nam Cam case was the largest and most serious criminal case in Vietnam's history (Quang and Steiner 2005) because Nam Cam was the *Bo gia* (Godfather) of Vietnam's largest "black society" (*xa hoi den*), an organization that included hundreds of criminals and operated on a national basis. In order to hold the trial of Nam Cam and his associates as "a public and democratic hearing, in line with . . . legal reform"

(Judge Bui Hoang Danh, cited in Cohen 2003), the Ho Chi Minh City court spent some hundreds thousands of dollars for the first instance trial to upgrade its facilities (*Nhan Dan*, June 13, 2003). The trial was to be a model, reflecting the state of judicial reform in Vietnam after several years of implementation of the Party's Resolution 8 on Forthcoming Principal Judiciary Tasks promulgated in January 2002 (Quang and Steiner 2005, 191–211).

Indeed, Vietnam desires to construct a socialist law-based state that is appropriate to Vietnamese conditions. Beginning in 2001, the Political Bureau of the Vietnamese Communist Party has issued a number of resolutions regarding legal reform and judicial reform with an orientation toward 2020 (Resolution 8, 2002; Resolution 48, 2005; Resolution 49, 2005). These resolutions are of great importance for legal development of Vietnam in the coming decades.

Reforming courts, procuracy (state prosecutors), and the activities of lawyers are all key points in the legal and judicial reforms. The role of lawyers has been targeted by the Party and government of Vietnam for strengthening and consolidation—for the first time in Vietnamese legal history the role and status of lawyers was recognized in a constructive manner by specific legal documents (Quang and Steiner 2005, 191–211). In the past several years, also for the first time, lawyers have been discussing openly and publicly in the mass media, in workshops, and at presentations, the role, status, and rights of lawyers vis-à-vis prosecutors in litigation, and particularly in criminal cases.

This chapter asks whether, under present circumstances, lawyers in Vietnam can now be considered—by government officials, judges, or ordinary citizens—to have the role, status, and position equal to that of the prosecutor in the judicial arena. The chapter begins with a brief outline of the history of the formation and development of the role of Vietnamese lawyers to enable Western readers to understand why this particular career has not attracted much attention in the past. This is followed by a discussion on the regulations that have created the roles and positions of the lawyer and prosecutor in litigation and criminal process. Further, the chapter describes the different, often conflicting viewpoints and attitudes on the role of lawyers and prosecutors held by Party and government agencies, courts, and individuals working in those organizations. And finally the roles played by lawyers and prosecutors in the largest criminal trial in Vietnam's history—the trial of Nam Cam and his associates—are analyzed.

The Formation and Development of the Role
of Lawyers in Vietnam

The lawyers' (*luat su* or *luat gia*) profession, also known as *thay cai* or *thay kien* (defense counsel), appeared in Vietnam in 1862, at the same time as the French colonial court system (Tuan 2001; Hanh 2002; Hoai 2004). Traditionally, Vietnamese preferred to resolve disputes by amicable settlement or traditional mechanisms. The principles of *chin bo lam muoi* (even fault deserves pardon) and *di hoa vi quy* (an injury forgiven is better than an injury avenged) symbolized earlier preferences for settlement. There is a tradition of avoiding bringing disputes to courts, giving rise to the saying *nhat dao dung dinh* (trial is the last choice) (Dung 2004). If forced to bring dispute to feudal courts, people hoped for justice, God willing (*den gioi soi xet*) (Que 2003). But the feudal system did not recognize the role of the defense counsel, especially under a Confucian social order, where "the King is the son of God," and "the mandarin is the parent." In Vietnam during some eras, however, persons who possessed certain legal knowledge at times helped people draft their claims, consulted with them on petition procedures and answers in court—what is today seen as an early form of the lawyers' profession in Vietnam (Tai 2002; Hoai 2004).

The French colonial government conquered southern Vietnam in 1862 and went on to control the remainder of Vietnam by 1883 (Kim 1946; Que 2003), bringing Western-style courts to Vietnam. The French judiciary in Vietnam was organized in two systems. One resolved matters involving French citizens in Vietnam, and the other had jurisdiction over the Vietnamese, also under the surveillance of the French government (Nguyen Dang Dung 2004). In the late nineteenth and early twentieth century, lawyers were generally French or Vietnamese who held French citizenship. By order of May 25, 1930, the French colonial government recognized the profession of lawyers in Vietnam (Tuan 2001; Hanh 2002).

Immediately after the 1945 revolution, the new Vietnamese government began reorganizing the judicial system. In October 1945, only a month after the revolutionary takeover, President Ho Chi Minh issued an order on the "organization of lawyers" (Order 46 1945). This order was the first document of the new government to recognize the existence and role of lawyers in its judicial system. One year later, in 1946, the role of lawyers was also addressed briefly in the new Constitution of the Democratic Republic of Vietnam, which provided a right to counsel (Constitution 1946).

Only a few lawyers followed the revolutionary government. Others changed jobs or continued to work for the French colonial government when it returned to occupy southern areas in 1945 and northern areas in 1947 (Tuan 2001; Que 2003; Hoai 2004). In response to the shortage of lawyers, Ho Chi Minh issued another order in 1949 allowing defendants to choose a non-lawyer citizen for representation if needed, as long as that advocate was acceptable to the local Chief Judge (Order 69 1949). This order was the origin of the concept of non-lawyer "people's advocates" (*bao chua vien nhan dan*), and may have some conceptual origins in the *certificat de citoyenneté* issued during the French Revolution to help provide poor people with defense counsel (Que 2003) as well as Soviet and Chinese revolutionary practice.

A new Constitution promulgated in 1959 reestablished judicial and procuratorial (state prosecution) systems and eliminated the Ministry of Justice. Responsibility for judicial work, including the work of advocates, was assigned to the Supreme People's Court (SPC). In 1963, a Hanoi Lawyers Office (*Van phong Luat su Ha Noi*) was established under the SPC to ensure the right to defense under the Constitution, though at its formation the office was staffed by people's advocates (Thu 2001; Hanh 2002). These advocates acted only in cases that were dealt with in the regular court system. In cases adjudicated by the considerably less formal tribunals that were set up to punish resisters, deal with land reform issues, and under administrative committees, there is no mention of participation by people's advocates. The operations of those tribunals were often and unfortunately far more forceful than the courts. This is one reason why Vietnamese society tends to think of lawyers as limited to work in criminal defense in the court system (Thu 2001).

The management of Hanoi Lawyers Office was transferred from the Supreme Court to the Law Committee of the Government in 1972 when that office was established. The revised 1980 Constitution reaffirmed a role for lawyers in the Vietnamese criminal and civil justice system. In 1981, when the Ministry of Justice was reestablished after a break of more than 20 years, the Hanoi Lawyers Office was transferred to the Ministry (Tuan 2001; Hanh 2002). The Ministry of Justice then consulted with the Supreme People's Court, the Supreme People's Procuracy, and other state authorities in drafting the first major legal document of the reform era on the work of advocates. This document served as the legal foundation for the establishment of "people's advocate agencies" (*doan bao chua vien nhan dan*) in a number of provinces. By the end of 1987, more than 30 Vietnamese provinces and large cities had set up such advocate agencies and they comprised over 400 people's advocates.

These continued to operate until the promulgation of the 1987 Ordinance on the Organization of Lawyers (Tuan 2001).

The Ordinance on the Organization of Lawyers, promulgated in December 1987, detailed the 1980 Constitutional reaffirmation of the role of lawyers' organization. In the years since, the 1987 Ordinance has been considered a moment of revitalization for the lawyer profession (Thao 2001), laying the foundation for the formation and development of professional lawyers and their general role in the Vietnamese reform process (Loc 2001; Tuan 2001). Within two years, 16 bar (lawyers) associations had been established around the country, replacing the people's advocate agencies. In the next 12 years, between 1989 and the enactment of a new Ordinance on Lawyers in September 2001, 61 bar associations had been established, covering all Vietnamese provinces and major cities with 82 branches consisting of about 2,500 practicing lawyers. In 1989, 60% of recognized lawyers held university law degrees; by 2001, this had risen to 85%. The educational level of lawyers (at least as measured by rates of university law degrees) was considerably higher than that of judges and prosecutors (Nicholson and Quang 2005); in 2003, for example, only 48% of prosecutors held university law degrees or the equivalent (*HCMC Law Newspaper* 2003a).

The Ordinance on the Organization of Lawyers (1987) was in some ways contradictory. It sought to affirm the independence and self-governance of the profession while, at the same time, providing mechanisms that hindered the realization of those principles. The lawyers' profession was still regarded as part of the state administrative structure, not independent (Thao 2001). The state administrative structure maintained control over lawyers' activities, part of the broad domination of "state-run" business and other activities in the late 1980s and into the 1990s. The lawyers' profession was no exception to that mode of thinking.

It must also be noted that there was a long history of a murky attitude toward the role of lawyers in court proceedings. Neither the political leadership nor ordinary people fully understood what might be the appropriate role of lawyers in a socialist society. At one level, there was a strong ideological sense that the socialist state, which maintained legislative, executive, and judicial mechanisms but denied the notion of "checks and balances," effectively guaranteed the civil rights of citizens, making it unnecessary for lawyers to protect people's rights.

In addition, a concept of "collective determination" *(quyet dinh tap the)* permeated the political and legal system, leaving little room for aggressive advocacy. Once a judgment or decision had the unanimous acceptance of the investigation body, the procuracy and the court and the unanimous internal views of judges and political officials, how could a lawyer or even a group of lawyers effectively oppose that collective view? Collective determination was also at work within each procuracy and investigation agency. This ideology led to the practice of returning case files to the procuracy for further investigation if proof was insufficient, rather than acquitting the defendant—such acquittals were extremely rare. This melange of ideology, history, and organization limited the activities of lawyers to a very narrow range—almost entirely to defense of criminal suspects in which acquittals were rare (Hoai 2004).

The new Ordinance on Lawyers was promulgated in 2001, around the time that the Communist Party released Resolution 8 on the reform and strengthening of legal and judicial work. The 2001 Ordinance considerably expanded the rights and roles thereby enhancing the position of lawyers, providing greater detail on the scope of lawyers' practice, and expanding permissible practice to include legal consultation as well as litigation. The 2001 Ordinance was a positive development for the profession in Vietnam, but it remains necessary—as we shall see below—to continue improving the role of rights of lawyers in procedural and litigative matters so that lawyers can play appropriate roles in protecting rights (Hanh 2002; Hoai 2004; Hai 2003; Quang and Steiner 2005, 191–211). A Law on Lawyers was adopted in mid-2006; it is expected to continue expanding the scope of permissible activities available to lawyers.

Presently there are 3,500 lawyers in Vietnam registered in 64 bar associations, practicing law at 839 lawyer offices and 149 office branches (www.vietnamnet.vn, July 2005; www.vnlawfind.com.vn, January 2006). But there are constraints to growth as well: lawyers who are full-time civil servants are not allowed to practice law as of September 30, 2004, according to the 2001 Ordinance on Lawyers, and that accounts for about 26% of the 3,500 lawyers currently in practice. And another group of lawyers will not be able to practice law beyond the next five years due to their age (Quang and Steiner 2005).

Lawyers and Prosecutors in Court: Regulation and Structuring of the Legal Profession

According to the Constitution and the Law on the Organization of the People's Procuracy, the procuracy has two separate functions: conducting prosecutions and supervising judicial activities, with no contradiction recognized between those functions. But in court proceedings, the independence of those two functions is not always clearly identified, and this has greatly affected the quality and independence of judicial activities. It has also created substantial inequality between procurators and lawyers, both in criminal and noncriminal cases.

Issues in Criminal Cases

In criminal cases, under the Criminal Procedure Code (1988), the procurator and defense counsel have equal status of "introducing evidence, filing requests and arguing the case at the court hearing" (Criminal Procedure Code, Art. 20). In formal terms, defense lawyers may participate in proceedings that begin when a suspect is formally accused. But in practice these indicia of equality are not implemented. For example, when the procurator wants to interrogate an accused, he or she obtains a letter of introduction from his or her procuracy office to enter the detention center and deal freely with the accused. On the other hand, the defense counsel must find the exculpatory evidence entirely by himself or herself. There is no institutionalized mechanism for requesting assistance in defense from state or private entities, and so defense lawyers often tend to use private relationships to obtain such assistance. That is particularly difficult, however, because defense lawyers often face "diplomatic denial"—people do not want to become involved with the judiciary, and/or are reluctant to provide information or give testimony. And even if defense counsel is able to find exculpatory or new evidence, investigators, prosecutors, and courts sometimes merely refuse to recognize it (Hai 2003).

In some ways these circumstances are slowly changing. The process by which defense counsel meet with accused defendants in detention is one example. Prior to the 2001 Ordinance on Lawyers, defense lawyers were required to produce a letter of introduction from the relevant provincial bar association, because detention officers understood at that time that bar associations were the local administrative agencies responsible for administering the activities of lawyers. In some localities the process was even more cumbersome: detention facilities required that defense counsel seek the approval of the procuracy before allowing the defender to meet his client. What is most serious is that this process—requiring prosecutor approval before defense lawyers may speak with their clients—remains the informal law of a number of localities, regardless of the changes incorporated in the 2001 Ordinance on Lawyers.

In preparing for a major court hearing, interagency meetings among the court, procuracy, and investigative agency (police) still take place. This process has existed for many years, well before 1988 when Vietnam first adopted a Criminal Procedure Code (Hai 2003), and it reflected the close relationship between the procuracy and the court. A number of Vietnamese scholars have claimed that this pretrial process violated the Constitution's provision that "at trial, judges and people's assessors are independent and subject only to the law" (Hai 2003). But it still existed, and was even "legalized" (Joint Circular 06 1990; Joint Circular 01 1994). Such pre-trial decisional meetings are entirely inappropriate, even unconstitutional, and severely hamper defense counsel in representing defendants. Defense counsel need to be able to speak with and represent clients at the investigation, interrogation, and other stages. But although the law seems to provide that right to defense counsel, it also reserves the right to the procurator to "give consent" or "not to give consent" to such participation (Criminal Procedure Code, Art. 36). In practice, police and prosecutors generally refuse to allow lawyers to represent clients during investigation and interrogation stages, although such refusals elicit vigorous protests from the community of lawyers and are frequently discussed at bar association meetings.

At pleadings, the law allows opposing counsel to express their views on the case. The presiding judge is not allowed to limit the time for arguing, but is allowed to put a halt to irrelevant arguments (Criminal Procedure Code, Art. 192). Prosecutors are not required to answer the arguments of defense counsel, and they hardly ever do; prosecutors usually just produce and read the indictment, disregarding the statements of defense lawyers. Arguments are limited to "one round," and therefore presiding judges generally do not allow defense counsel to expand arguments, expound on new grounds, or provide additional information (Hai 2003; Hoai 2004). Judgment is rendered based on the evidence and material examined by the judges under the concept of "judgment based on the dossier" *(an tai ho so)* (Criminal Procedure Code, Art. 196). This further serves to limit the significance of the defense counsel's role in criminal matters; judgments are often based only on the indictment and the dossier prepared by the procuracy.

In reality, many people within and outside the justice system believe that the fact that a court decides to hear a case is in itself an expression of its consent to the views of the procuracy, and that it is a foregone conclusion that the case constitutes a crime (Hai 2003; Hoai 2004). This attitude seriously affects the independence of the judicial system, and, of course, the role of defense counsel.

The role of the procurator in noncriminal cases has not changed substantially in recent law, including in the Civil Procedure Code 2004. Before the adoption of the Civil Procedure Code, separate ordinances governed the procedure applicable to civil, economic, labor, and administrative cases (Ordinance on Civil Cases 1989; Ordinance on Economic Cases 1994; Ordinance on Labor Cases 1996; Ordinance on Administrative Cases 1996). Under the new Civil Procedure Code, the role of the procurator is quite blurred, particularly when compared with his role in criminal proceedings (Civil Procedure Code, Art. 21; Joint Circular 03 2005). In part this is because civil, economic, labor, and administrative proceedings are initiated by parties rather than, generally, by the state.

From a theoretical perspective, the role of the procurator in noncriminal proceedings is confined to "supervising the proceedings" because of the broad function granted to the procuracy in protecting state interests and preserving social order. Under this principle the procuracy is responsible for ensuring compliance with law and has the right to participate at any stage it deems necessary. These procedures were reconfirmed in the earlier ordinances on civil, economic, labor, and administrative cases cited above.

In reality, the procuracy generally participates right from the start of the case, and generally throughout the process. If the procurator is absent, hearings are often adjourned (Thuc 2002). So the procuracy's role in noncriminal proceedings is similar to the role played in criminal cases. The procurator reviews and participates in the case from the time the case is received by the court to the end of the proceedings, and gives his conclusion and assessment of the case to the court. But unfortunately, the procuracy's assessment of noncriminal cases generally cannot be argued by the parties because it is usually rendered after oral arguments. The earlier ordinances, still followed, generally require the procurator to give only broad directions for completing the case, and do not require him to enter into any discussion with the parties. The real consequence of this process is that the procurator becomes the second lawyer for any party gaining his support. The procuracy's assessment has a strong effect on the judicial panel deciding the case, because it is the attitude of the agency responsible for supervising and inspecting the judiciary.

The Role of Defense Counsel in Appellate and Review Procedures

The criminal and civil procedure codes, as well as other relevant legislation, provide that appellate and review hearings are based on documents submitted by the parties and that the presence of parties (including counsel) is not required except where the court finds it necessary to seek their opinions before rendering a decision. This means that lawyers are usually unable to protect the interests of their clients at the appellate and review stages (Criminal Procedure Code, Art. 249; Ordinance on Labor Cases, Art. 77; Ordinance on Economic Cases, Art. 79; Ordinance on Civil Cases, Art. 76; Ordinance on Administrative Cases, Art. 71). But—and this will not surprise readers who have been following the special role of the procuracy throughout this discussion—the procurator has the right to participate in and present his opinion on the adjudication of the case, largely unconstrained by opposing views (Law on the Organization of the People's Procuracy, Art. 17).

Viewpoints and Attitudes

We can reach the conclusion from the examination of the roles of lawyers and prosecutors that while, in theory, "at trial judges and people's assessors are independent and subject only to the law" (1992 Constitution, Art. 130) reality is quite different. Many factors influence the independence of judges, but it is not easy to parse them (Hai 2003). The problem, however, is clear, as table 9.1 indicates: virtually no one is acquitted, a fact that directly reflects on the actual quality of current judicial work.

We should note that the procuracy, with its 7,400 procurators, has participated in virtually all adjudicated cases, while Vietnam's 3,500 lawyers were not able to participate in all of the cases. This is one reason for the weakness in lawyer representation. But another key reason—probably more important, and now well recognized—is the viewpoint and attitude (the legal culture) of Party and state officials, judges, prosecutors, and citizens toward lawyers.

Table 9.1 Acquittals in the Vietnamese judicial process, 1999–2002

Courts/year	1999	2000	2001	2002
Provincial courts	48	53	13	11
Appellate tribunals of the Supreme People's Court	6	45	14	14
Supreme People's Court Justice Committee and Judicial Council	249	21	80	5

Source: Annual Reports of the Supreme People's Court, 1999–2003

History has left its impact on the development of the legal profession. As we noted above, courts were considered an agency serving the political task of the new government beginning in 1945. Between 1946 and 1954, the key political task of the revolutionary government was to drive out the French, and revolutionary courts were basically military-style courts trying military deserters or shirkers, "counter-revolutionaries," capitalists, and landlords. Judicial decisions were determined before hearings were held. Defense lawyers were often cadres or soldiers belonging to local revolutionary committees or administrative committees, who had to obey higher officials or the judge. Their role was largely to demonstrate that the judgment of the revolutionary court reflected democracy and fairness. And the fear of being blamed for defending "counter-revolutionaries" further hampered any significant or independent role. The principle of democratic centralism *(tap trung dan chu)* guided the operations of courts and all other state agencies, and defense counsel dared not violate that principle. There were lawyers who refused to serve as defense counsel when they knew that the opposing party was a state agency (as often occurred in administrative cases). And when lawyers did play this role, they accepted it subject to "guidance" (*Sunday Law Newspaper* 2003a).

The legal provisions and mechanisms governing the role of lawyers, discussed in the earlier sections, further contributed to the difficulty people had in understanding the role that lawyers should play in court proceedings. These problems have continued, in many cases up to the present day. Lawyers' arguments have not received attention and are often only briefly noted in the judgments. In many cases, hearings have been a kind of performance of a "play" *(dien kich)* in which all knew the outcome before the final act (Hai 2003; Hoai 2004). Lawyers have been regarded as of little help, and a waste of money. Some citizens consider lawyers as playing the role of a "broker" *(nguoi moi gioi* or *thay co)* (Hoai 2004; Quang and Steiner 2005, 191–211). And many enterprises, especially state-owned enterprises, do not use lawyers in their business affairs. They prefer to take advantage of the administrative relationships between state agencies, or state privilege, in handling their disputes. And they are concerned that lawyers may make a dispute more complicated, annoying the state officials responsible dealing with it (Quang and Steiner 2005).

These sorts of issues were all reflected in one of the most important cases in Vietnamese history—and one of the most important cases for the development of a new role of lawyers, the trial of Nam Cam.

Lawyers and the Trial of the Godfather Nam Cam

To prepare for the trial of Nam Cam, the Ho Chi Minh City People's Court established an adjudication group of six judges, five people's assessors, and three court secretaries to work with a case dossier of 118 volumes (consisting of 20,000 pages). A 600-page color printed indictment was distributed to all the defendants and their lawyers. The trial lasted 57 working days, with 83 lawyers participating for the defense, and 238 individuals summoned to give testimony. Over 300 police officers were mobilized to preserve order for the proceedings. And for the first time in the history of the Vietnamese courts, the trial was televised live throughout and a press conference was organized each day. The proceedings attracted the attention of people from all social classes, some out of curiosity and some—particularly lawyers—concerned for how a spirit of judicial reform would be reflected in the trial. Lawyers and scholars expected the court to follow "democratic adversarial" proceedings in accordance with the spirit of Party Resolution 8, and that the judgment would be based on the adversarial proceedings at the court, with the rights of defense counsel respected.

In fact, the defense counsel were given some favorable conditions, including access to documents necessary for defense. This was quite different from past practices, when defense lawyers who wanted to read the case dossier or the indictment had to go to the court to read them, and take notes of the important points. Courts had never previously allowed copies to be made or records taken out of the court office. The lawyers in the Nam Cam trial were also given favorable conditions to meet their clients. They argued with prosecutors. They were allowed to use secretaries at trial sessions, and to use pictures and tape recorders in their arguments and to present evidence. But among the most remarkable events at this trial was that defense counsels were allowed to express their arguments without interruption. And, as the trial proceeded, an even more remarkable event occurred: Courageous defense lawyers were not prevented from claiming in court that the investigators and the procurators had violated the law during the investigation (*HCMC Law Newspaper* 2003a, 2003b, 2003c; *Sunday Law Newspaper* 2003a, 2003b, 2003c).

Despite these advances, the question of equality came to the forefront most clearly in the events surrounding Mr. Dang Van Luan, one of the most prominent lawyers working on the case. Mr. Luan was the defense lawyer for a particularly prominent defendant accused of bribery and of disclosing state secrets. The defendant, who was a member of the Central

Committee of the Communist Party, consistently denied both charges. The first days of the trial passed without startling events, but when it came to the pleadings Mr. Luan boldly stated that his client was innocent, and that the investigators and procurators had violated the law during the investigation and indictment processes. Luan supported his statements with logical argument, and taped records of testimony. And, even more daringly, he alleged that there was a hand behind the scene controlling the trial of his client and seeking to kill his client's "political life." Mr. Luan asked the prosecutors to formally answer his claims, but they declined (*Phap Luat Newspaper*, May 21, 2003). Many other defense lawyers for Nam Cam trial defendants also requested formal answers from prosecutors to their arguments, but in most cases the prosecutors also refused to respond (*VnExpress* 2003c).

Luan's act shocked everyone following the trial, for while this may sound commonplace to Western lawyers and legal scholars, such daring advocacy was new in Vietnam. Newspapers covered it intensively and expressed different views; some called it an "abuse of democratic rights" *(lam dung quyen dan chu)* and others supported Luan's strategy (*HCMC Law Newspaper* 2003a, 2003b). The Supreme People's Procuracy and the Ministry of Public Security strongly opposed it. One of the procurators said that Luan had "offended the agencies conducting the proceedings" and asked that the presiding judge sanction Luan during the trial (*VnExpress* 2003b). The Ministry of Public Security sent official letters to the Ho Chi Minh City People's Court, the Supreme People's Procuracy, the trial panel, the Ministry of Justice, and the Party committee of the bar association of which Luan was a member, requesting that disciplinary measures be taken against him (*VnExpress* 2003a).

Protesting the attitude of the procuracy and the Ministry of Public Security, Luan denied that he had deliberately "offended or slandered" any legal institution, but said that he was merely performing his "heavenly mandate" *(then chuc)* and "mission" *(su menh)* as a barrister (*VnExpress*, May 22, 2003b; *Lao Dong*, September 5, 2003). But he further charged that the prosecutors were "applying pressure" *(gay ap luc)* against the defense lawyers (*VnExpress* 2003e), and he consistently reaffirmed his attitude and his conclusions well after the trial was over. The trial itself, however, did not end as Luan and the other defense lawyers wished. The court's judgment did not recognize any of the arguments or requests of the defense (*VnExpress* 2003e). And the judgment even implicitly criticized Luan, saying that he had merely "subjectively deduced" *(suy luan chu quan)* his views. There was little difference between the punishment imposed by the court and the request by the prosecutors. The alleged acts of the prosecutors and the police came as a shock to some concerned with judicial reform in Vietnam.

Conclusion

Legal and judicial reform in Vietnam began in 1986 and has developed more rapidly since the promulgation of Party Resolution 8 in 2002 (Lien 2002). But much more work needs to be done, and among those steps are the recognition and strengthening of the role of lawyers in society, and more particularly in legal procedure. Vietnamese people believe in the concept of "social order" *(trat tu xa hoi)*, and that the socialist state reflects some aspects of that principle. But social order also requires truth, and there is an increasing awareness that it requires real adversarial proceedings to discover the truth. The position of Vietnamese lawyers has not improved as quickly as many Vietnamese lawyers and scholars would like to have seen, but further improvements must and will be made if Vietnam is to be successful in its mission of constructing a socialist law-based state, and eventually in building a society under the rule of law. Redressing inequalities between lawyers and prosecutors is one important task in those reforms, so that lawyers can become the defenders of rights and justice and of law that Vietnam needs.

References

Legal and Policy Documents

Constitution of the Democratic Republic of Vietnam (1946).

Joint Circular 06/TTLN (1990) of the Supreme People's Court, Supreme People's Procuracy and Ministry of Police dated September 12, 1990 (on settlement of serious cases).

Joint Circular 01/TTLN (1994) of the Supreme People's Court, Supreme People's Procuracy and Ministry of Police dated October 15, 1994 (on settlement of serious cases).

Joint Circular 03/2005 of the Supreme People's Court and Supreme People's Procuracy Providing Guidelines for Implementation of the Civil Procedure Code on Checking Legal Compliance in Civil Procedures and the Participation of the People's Procuracy in the Settlement of Civil Cases (September 1, 2005).

Official Letter 071/C16 of the Ministry of Public Security dated May 14, 2003, VnExpress, May 16, 2003, vnexpress.net.

Order No. 46/SL of President Ho Chi Minh on Lawyer Organization (October 10, 1945).

Order No. 69-S of President Ho Chi Minh with respect to accused persons requesting a citizen who is not a lawyer to defend them before ordinary courts and special courts (June 18, 1949).

Ordinance on Procedures for Settlement of Civil Cases (Ordinance on Civil Cases) (December 7, 1989).

Ordinance on Procedures for Settlement of Economic Cases (Ordinance on Economic Cases) (March 29, 1994).

Ordinance on Procedures for Settlement of Labor Cases (Ordinance on Labor Cases) (April 20, 1996).

Ordinance on Procedures for Settlement of Administrative Cases (Ordinance on Administrative Cases) (June 3, 1996).

Resolution No. 8 of the Political Bureau of the Communist Party on Forthcoming Principal Judiciary Tasks, January 2, 2002.

Resolution No. 48 of the Political Bureau of the Communist Party on the Legal System Development Strategy to 2010 with an orientation toward 2020 (2005).

Resolution No. 49 of the Political Bureau of the Communist Party on the Judicial System Development Strategy to 2010 with an orientation toward 2020 (2005).

Secondary Sources

Cohen, Margot. 2003. Rare move targets gangs, protectors in government. *Asian Wall Street Journal,* June 6, 2003, A4.

Hoang The Lien. Quan diem cua Dang va Nha nuoc ve cai cach tu phap tu nam 1986 cho toi nay (The viewpoint of the Communist Party and state on judicial reform from 1986 until the present) (Unpublished conference paper).

Le Hong Hanh. 2002. *Dao duc va ky nang cua luat su trong nen kinh te thi truong dinh huong xa hoi chu nghia (The ethics and skills of lawyers in the socialist oriented market economy).* Hanoi: Education Publishing House.

Le Kim Que. 2003. Nguon goc nghe luat su (Origin of the lawyer profession). *Lawyer Today Magazine* (Hanoi Bar Association).

Nguyen Dang Dung. 2004. *The che tu phap trong nha nuoc phap quyen (The judicial branch in a rule of law state).* Hanoi: Nha xuat ban Phap ly.

Nguyen Dinh Loc. 2001. Ve Phap lenh luat su 2001 (Comments on the Ordinance on Lawyers 2001). *Law and Democracy Magazine* (Special issue for Ordinance on Lawyers), 7.

Nguyen Hung Quang and Kerstin Steiner. 2005. Ideology and professionalism: The resurgence of the Vietnamese bar. In *Asian socialism and legal change: The dynamics of Vietnamese and Chinese reform.* Edited by John Gillespie and Pip Nicholson. Canberra: Asia Pacific Press, 191–211.

Nguyen Van Thao. 2001. Mot so van de can quan tam khi thi hanh Phap lenh Luat su (Several concerns when the Ordinance on Lawyers is implemented). *Law and Democracy Magazine* (Special Issue on Ordinance for Lawyers), 26.

Nguyen Van Tuan. 2001. Su hinh thanh va phat trien nghe luat su o Vietnam (Formation and development of the lawyers profession in Vietnam. *Law and Democracy Magazine* (Special Issue on Ordinance for Lawyers).

Nicholson, Pip and Nguyen Hung Quang. 2005. The Vietnamese judiciary: The politics of appointment and promotion. *Pacific Rim Law & Policy Journal* 14(1): 1–34.

Pham Hong Hai. 2003. *Mo hinh ly luan Bo luat to tung hinh su Vietnam (The theoretical model of the Criminal Procedure Code of Vietnam).* Hanoi: People's Police Publishing House.

Pham Tri Thuc. 2002. Ve Du an Luat To chuc Vien Kiem sat nhan dan sua doi (About the project for amendment of the Law on the Organization of the People's Procuracy. *Nghien cuu Lap phap* 2: 33.

Phan Huu Thu. 2001. Dao tao, boi duong luat su trong thoi ky doi moi (Training and professional improvement of lawyers in the doi moi period). *Law and Democracy Magazine* (Special Issue on Ordinance for Lawyers).

Phan Trung Hoai. 2004. *Van de hoan thien phap luat ve luat su o Vietnam (Issues for completion of legislation on lawyers in Vietnam).* Hanoi: National Politics Publishing House.

Ta Van Tai. 2002. Phap quyen trong phap luat truyen thong cua Vietnam va Trung quoc co—Tap tuc phap ly Dong A truyen thong duoi anh sang cua cac chuan muc phap quyen hien dai (The rule of law in the traditional legislation of ancient Vietnam and China—Traditional legal customs of East Asia in the light of modern rule of law standards). In *Foreign researchers discussing Vietnam (Vol. II).* Hanoi: The Gioi Publishing House.

Tran Trong Kim. 1946 (reprint 2003). *Viet Nam Su luoc (Summary of Vietnamese history).* Da Nang: Da Nang Publishing House.

Periodicals

Ho Chi Minh City Law Newspaper. 2003a. Demonstrating and illustrating in the hearing; can that be done, May 8, 2003, 7.

———. 2003b. Tran Mai Hanh is not guilty, May 13, 2003, 11.

———. 2003c. Defending the methods of lawyer Luan and lawyer Tri, May 15, 2003, 10.

———. 2003d. July 17, 2003, 7.

Law Newspaper (Bao Phap Luat). 2003. Thai Binh Bar Association holds meeting to study the experience of the Nam Cam case, July 21, 2003, 5.

Sunday Law Newspaper. 2003a. Lawyers with invisible pressures, No. 166, June 13, 2003, 7.

———. 2003b. Rising legal pressure, No. 118, May 18, 2003, 11.

———.2003c. Different application of law?, No. 124, May 25, 2003, 11.

Vietnam News Agency, I did not disparage the investigation body, I just perform my heaven mission, September 5, 2003. Online at www.laodong.com.vn, accessed February 1, 2005.

Vnexpress. 2003a. Barrister Dang Van Luan slandered the investigation body, May 16, 2003, vnexpress.net.

———. 2003b. Procurators request to sue Mr. Dang Van Luan, May 20, 2003, vnexpress.net.

———. 2003c. Procurators! No doubt means agree? May 22, 2003a, vnexpress.net.

———. 2003d. Barrister Dang Van Luan reserves his arguments, May 22b, 2003, vnexpress.net.

———. 2003e. Most of the arguments of the barristers in the Nam Cam trial have been rejected, June 4, 2003, vnexpress.net.

CHAPTER TEN

Vietnamese Courts

Contemporary Interactions between Party-State and Law

PENELOPE (PIP) NICHOLSON

Vietnamese courts have recently seen radical reforms that retain the status quo in certain vital respects, but concurrently enable incremental change. The question is how does Vietnam, with socialist legality as its foundational tenet, deal with the tension between the asserted independence of the court system and its traditional instrumentalism? Put another way, how is the tension between Party-led institutions and "law-based state" (*nha nuoc phap quyen*) to be resolved?

The Leading Role of the Party-State

At the 1991 Seventh Party Congress, the Communist Party of Vietnam (CPV) adopted the policy and goal of *nha nuoc phap quyen*, variously translated as "State-legal-rights" or "law-based state." In effect, this means that the state will not only be the source of law, but will also be bound by it. This ideal helped to produce fundamental changes to the 1992 Constitution in 2001, especially the amended Article 4 that characterized the Party as "the force leading the state and society" and noted that "[a]ll Party organizations operate within the framework of the Constitution and the law."

In the past there was no commitment that the Communist Party would be bound by law. Rather, the Party led through its policies: "The underlying notion of law [was] not so much that of an immutable order to which all should bow, but rather that of an important element of the way in which the Party line [was] implemented" (Fforde 1986, 62). This earlier characterization allowed the Party and its functionaries to operate according to policy and law, where it existed. In the event of a clash between law and policy, policy would, and did, prevail (Nguyen Nhu Phat 1997, 398).

It has been difficult to conceive of the Vietnamese state as separate from the Party: hence the use of the term Party-state. For example, the most recent round of Constitutional amendments did not change the leadership role ascribed to the Party (Constitution 1992 as amended in 2001, Art. 4). Moreover, as we shall see, Resolution 8, On Forthcoming Principal Judiciary Tasks (Resolution 8), introduced in 2002, also restates the Party's leadership role (Nicholson 2005) as do the recent legal and judicial reform Resolutions 48 and 49 of 2005. So in Vietnam today the Party leads the state and determines the political choices and policy orientation of the nation. Further, the Party relies on its members to give effect to its policy choices (Statute of the Vietnam Communist Party 2001, Art. 2[1]).

Thus the structure of the contemporary court system needs to be read and understood within the broader structure of the Party-state. Figure 10.1 sets out the classic formulation of the Vietnamese state. It has the Party that "leads," a state that "manages," and mass organizations that "represent," all simultaneously sitting apart and dependent.

As figure 10.1 makes clear, the Vietnamese court system is (and has always been) formally subordinate to the National Assembly. What the diagram does not show is that Party members hold the majority of positions within courts and most other organizations and departments within the administrative arm of the state.[1] In broad organizational terms, the Party-state relationship is therefore highly integrated.

The meaning of the term "law-based" is more problematic. One possible interpretation is that the Vietnamese Party-state has repositioned law as the "highest" source of Party-state edict. This view is supported by the fact that the Party, through the Constitution, is to be bound by law. More particularly, the Party-state envisions law as ultimately becoming superior to policy (as Party Resolution 8 seems to envision), in contrast to the former instrumental role of Vietnamese law (Gillespie 2004, 2005).

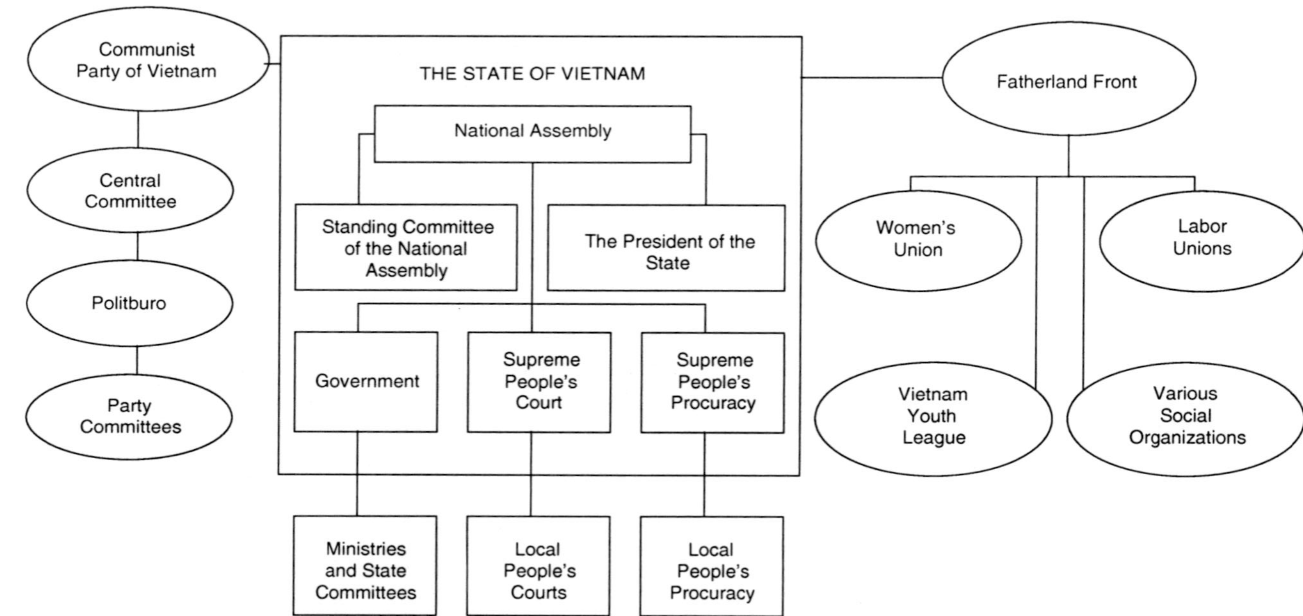

Figure 10.1   Formal political and administrative structure of Vietnam.

Note: This diagram is based on one produced by Phillips Fox solicitors.

Mark Sidel (2002) has argued persuasively that it is too crude today to denote the Vietnamese legal institutions, in particular the National Assembly, as absolute tools or instruments of the Party-state. Nonetheless, the Party-state has not yet been prepared to shift the Party's control of courts to independent courts. As a result of apparently radical reforms courts, at least in part, now manage themselves. However, by retaining the strong leadership role of the Party-state, the courts remain intrinsically political, and not legal, institutions.

Contemporary Court Reform

Since 2000, a series of policies and laws have been introduced to reform the Vietnamese courts. Reforms commenced with changes to the 1992 Constitution made in late 2001, with effect from January 2002. In the same month, the Politburo of the Communist Party issued Resolution 8, which although not a blue print for legal reform, was, until mid-2005, the leading discussion paper on the shortcomings and reforms needed for contemporary legal institutions. Resolution 8 has since been supplemented by two other important Party resolutions on legal and judicial reform, Resolutions 48 and 49 of 2005. The National Assembly has also adopted the *Law on the Organization of the People's Courts* (2002) and the *Ordinance on Judges and People's Assessors* (October 11, 2002). Resolutions have also been passed to provide for implementation.[2] When these diverse sources are read together, the Party has restated its leading role, and at the same time stipulated that courts ought to judge cases independently.[3]

The tension between the Party's leadership of the state and the independence of the courts resonates throughout Resolution 8.[4] Early in Part A of the "Directions" section, the Resolution states that it is the role of the courts (and other agencies) to follow and implement Party policy. In particular, court-related agencies must give effect to the current period's political tasks (*cac nhiem vu chinh tri trong tung giai doan*) and ensure that state power is united (*bao dam quyen luc nha nuoc la thong nhat*). All court-related institutions are also required to implement legislative, executive, and judicial instructions to give effect to the Party line. Readers are reminded that the Party "shall lead" (*lanh dao*) all court-related agencies.

Nevertheless, reading these injunctions in context suggests either that Party policy will be found in laws or, alternatively, that policy will be defined as law or as relevant to the interpretation of law by the court.

Therefore it is possible technically to resolve the stated roles of the Party and the courts. But Resolution 8 still describes courts in terms that require them to be both subservient to Party leadership and independent. John Gillespie (2002, 26) reconciles these principles by writing that the courts are to remain under Party leadership, but free from Party interference. But he also notes that the dividing line between leadership and interference (or intervention) remains unclear.

The legislative reform package following Resolution 8 dealt in much more detail with court reforms, especially those affecting judicial offices. Essentially the Law on the Organization of the People's Courts (2002) provided that judges must hold a bachelor of laws degree, have legal experience, and have attended adjudication training (Art. 37). With the exception of the Chief Justice and judges of the Supreme People's Court (SPC), all judicial appointments, removals, and dismissals to provincial and district courts will be made by the Chief Justice on the advice of especially constituted Judicial Selection Councils (Arts. 25, 40). Court budgets are to be determined by the National Assembly (acting on the advice of the Chief Justice) (Art. 44) and the number of judges will be determined by the Standing Committee of the National Assembly, again on the advice of the Chief Justice (Art. 42[1]). The changes also give the SPC, in conjunction with local people's councils, responsibility for the management of local people's courts (Art. 17).

These reforms suggest two fundamental changes.[5] First, the Party-state commits to fostering higher levels of educational and professional qualifications for staff and empowers the SPC to appoint and remove personnel. Second, the budgetary reforms suggest that court autonomy is to be increased. Rather than be dependent on the Ministry of Justice for funds, as in the past, the court system will now have its own budget settled with the National Assembly. Similarly, management of local courts is no longer within the purview of the Ministry of Justice, but a matter for the SPC acting with local bodies. Finally, the numbers of judges is also a matter for the SPC working with the National Assembly, rather than a matter for the Justice Ministry.

The legislative reforms suggest that the courts are to be decoupled from the Ministry of Justice and will be led and managed by the SPC (Law on the Organization of People's Courts 2002, Arts. 44–6), working with local bodies as appropriate. This is ostensibly a great shift: moving the courts from direct political control via the ministries to self-management or quasi-autonomy. However, what is not articulated is the continuing interconnection between the Party-state and courts.

Structure, Role, and Reality in Vietnamese Courts

As we noted above, the Vietnamese Communist Party relies on its members to give effect to its policies. In courts, 90% of judges are Party members (Nicholson and Quang 2005). This means that personnel owe duties both to the Party and to the law (Statute of the Vietnam Communist Party, 2001, Art. 2[1]). Where Party policy and law conflict, Party policy has traditionally prevailed. Therefore, although the recent reforms suggest a movement of the courts away from the political arm of the Party-state through the conferral of greater independence from the Ministry of Justice, courts, in fact, remain subordinate to Party influence generally and the National Assembly in particular.

Official Court Functions

To understand the shape of courts in contemporary Vietnam it is necessary not only to look at the recent reforms, but also to consider what remains from the past. To this end, the recent statutory articles dealing with the official tasks and functions of the courts are compared very briefly with those of the equivalent 1960 law.[6] Article 1 of the most recent *Law on the Organization of People's Courts* (2002) makes it clear that the courts have several jurisdictions, have the mandate to resolve cases, must educate the people about law, and finally ought to protect the state. The jurisdiction of the courts has been increased when compared with that of the pre-unification courts in the North (Law on the Organization of People's Courts 1960, Art. 1).

The official pronouncement on court roles has changed in two further respects. First, the courts are no longer charged with assisting national unification and socialist construction. Second, from 2002, courts are charged with fostering strict compliance with law (*chap hanh nghiem chinh phap luat*) (Law on the Organization of People's Courts 2002, Art. 1). This is a shift from the less formal encouragement made in 1960 for citizens to be consciously law-abiding (*tu giac tuan theo phap luat*) (Law on the Organization of People's Courts 1960).

The most striking difference is that the 2002 law is more detailed and deals with the responsibilities of the Supreme People's Court before it turns to the duties of the lower courts (Law on the Organization of People's Courts 2002, Arts. 18–26). In contrast, the 1960 law first deals with local level courts before briefly turning to outline the role of the SPC (Law on the Organization of People's Courts 1960, Arts. 20–3). In addition, there are changes in the details of who manages courts at any one level and how the Supreme Court will coordinate and oversee the work of lower courts. In particular, the Supreme People's Court is charged with responsibility to oversee all lower courts, and as we shall see later, this includes the appointment and dismissal of staff (Law on the Organization of People's Courts 2002, Arts. 18–26, 29[1]). The later legislation, although similar, is much more detailed and more specific about which agencies will be responsible for what aspects of court work.

The more recent legislation is also much more explicit about what judges must not do: they must not contravene existing laws affecting officials and public employees; provide consultancy to parties to cases; illegally intervene in the settlement of cases or attempt to influence others settling cases; take dossiers out of their offices except for appropriate purposes; or meet with defendants or parties to cases except in "prescribed places" (Ordinance on Judges and Jurors of People's Courts, October 11, 2002, Art. 15). This is a much clearer statement of the need for judges not to deal with parties or attempt to influence their colleagues' determination of cases than previously existed (Ordinance on the Organization of the People's Supreme Court and Local Courts, March 23, 1961).

Appointment, Qualifications, Term, and
Remuneration of Judges

Vietnamese judges (*tham phan*) have at various times been appointed (and by different bodies) and elected (Anonymous 1961). Further, the criteria by which judges are appointed have changed (Quinn 2003). In the early days, after the revolution, judges were, at least in theory, appointed by the Ministry of Justice in the case of primary courts (now known as district courts). The President appointed secondary court (now known as provincial court) judges.[7] "Political dignity and professional skill" were the criteria upon which appointments were based (Interview with Barrister A 1999). Although the legislation stipulated that judges were to have law degrees and have completed judge-specific training (Order 13, On the Organization of Courts and the Status of Judges in the DRVN 1946, Arts. 54, 55), these requirements were not enforced, with the state introducing temporary provisions requiring only that judges have finished school or worked as a clerk or middle bureaucrat (Arts. 58–64).

The court reforms of 1959 and 1960 introduced the election of most judges to office (Nicholson 2000, 141).[8] The National Assembly was to elect the Chief Judge of the Supreme People's Court and the National Assembly's Standing Committee appointed the remainder of the Supreme

Court judges. Within local courts the People's Councils were to elect all judges to the relevant court. Those working in courts at the time note that the quality of judges varied widely and, further, that the Supreme Court tried to educate local councils in how to appoint appropriate personnel (Le 1961, 13–17).

As noted previously, recent reforms to the court suggest that the criteria for appointment have shifted to reflect a focus on professional skills (Nicholson and Quang 2005). Furthermore, while the President has most recently had the power to appoint all judges, with the exception of the Chief Justice of the Supreme People's Court who was nominated by the President and then elected by the National Assembly, the recent reforms have moved the power to appoint all local (provincial and district) level judges to the SPC. The President now appoints only the Supreme Court judges. As suggested above, if these are read together it appears that judges will be both better trained and potentially more independent of political influence. However, the specific approvals needed for appointment (Circular 01 of 2003) and the reintroduction of a waiver of the educational requirement (Resolution 131 of 2002) undermine the reforms in two significant ways.

First, it remains the case that the Party vets all judicial appointments. This is done in several ways. The Party requires that all applicants for judicial position produce political theory diplomas (Circular 01 of 2003). The Circular provides no definition of political theory diplomas, but in the prior circular, candidates had to furnish a "political knowledge certificate" (*chung chi trinh do ly luan chinh tri*) (Joint Circular 05 of 1993, Part III, Item 1) obtained from the Party school, the Ho Chi Minh National Political Academy. A person must either be a Party member or a candidate for membership to obtain such a certificate (Nicholson and Quang 2005, 12). Moreover, candidates must have been "[t]rained in politics effectively and strongly to implement judicial responsibility and to protect against the phenomenon of 'mechanical and simple legalism, without politics' (*may moc, don thuan, vo chinh tri*)" (Nguyen Van Hien 2001, 4).

Commentators suggest that Circular 01 (2003) will be interpreted consistently with its predecessor. More particularly, the provision of political theory diplomas will require candidates to supply a "political knowledge certificate" (interview with Barrister B 2003). Maintaining this requirement therefore enables Party institutions to provide statements about the appropriateness of candidates for judicial office.

An applicant's dossier must also include support from the "collective leadership of the provincial-level People's Court" and the Head of the Organization and Personnel Section of the provincial-level institution to which an applicant seeks appointment (Circular 01 of 2003, Chapter III, Art. 2, sec. 3). Thus local Party functionaries within the court where an applicant seeks office have direct input into the recruitment process.

The effect of these practices is to ensure that the Party, at both the local and central level, continues to be decisive in the recruitment of judges. This explains why the recent reforms are characterized as decoupling the Supreme People's Court from the Ministry of Justice, and to a certain extent the National Assembly, but not from the Party itself. And, as noted above, these recruits are therefore doubly obligated: they are to be bound by law, but also owe loyalty to the Party.

The dominance of the Party becomes clear in two crucial aspects of court work. First, Quinn (2002, 240) notes that the Party, through the local People's Committee, is usually instrumental in determining whether a case will be pursued. Interviews confirm that the Party is often intimately involved with the determination of at least certain cases. The corruption case of Judge Bui Van Tham, who in 1997 was charged with exerting undue influence on a person holding an official position, serves as an example of how a judge's twin loyalty to law and Party operate (Nicholson 2002). Senior Party functionaries of the court and procuracy usually meet with judges responsible for trials and "together" they resolve how cases are to be determined (Interview with Lawyer W 2001). More particularly, when a judge faces trial for corruption, the Judges' Council would meet with the trial judge to determine together an appropriate course of action (Interview with state-employed Lawyer Y 2001). To characterize this as interference misunderstands the Vietnamese court system: the case illustrates how Party leadership is effected within courts.

The second way in which the recent reforms are undermined has been with the introduction of Resolution 131 (November 3, 2002), which has the primary purpose of waiving the requirement that judges have law degrees. Resolution 131 replicates an earlier Resolution that introduced the concept of a "legal knowledge debt" (*no kien thuc phap ly*) (Resolution 37, 1993, May 14). In effect, a candidate can seek appointment on an undertaking that s/he will subsequently obtain a law degree. Since the introduction of "legal knowledge debt" in 1993, judges have generally undertaken legal training after their appointment, but not necessarily bachelor of laws degrees. Reports suggest that as many of 85% of the judges and 70% of the court officers admitted on an undertaking to obtain legal qualifications do not complete bachelor degrees (Tran 2003, 34–9); rather they attend law-training institutions such as those run by the courts, the procuracy, and the police. It is unclear whether the earlier practice of substituting the lesser qualifications for law degrees will continue.

Judges' terms remain five years (Law on the Organization of People's Courts 2002, Art. 40; Ordinance on Judges and Jurors of People's Courts, 2002, Art. 24). Currently, if a judge seeks reappointment, s/he must submit a fresh application. This practice is much criticized by commentators (Mai 2000, 3). It means that judges who have been viewed favorably by the central and local branches of the Party will receive the needed supporting documentation. Those who have displeased Party organizations cannot expect to be supported.

Judges remain civil servants. This means that promotion, or at least salary increase, flows from time spent in the job. Further, if a judge moves to a higher court there may be additional financial benefits, depending on how long the judge has served at the lower level. As we have seen there is no mechanism for transferring judges between courts other than application to a particular court for a particular position.

As civil servants, judges are not well paid. For example, a Supreme People's Court judge who has served for three years will be paid (in Vietnamese currency, of course) the equivalent of about US$77.00 a month. A district court judge with no experience will receive the Vietnamese equivalent of about US$29.00 a month. More generally, judicial salaries are on a par with other civil servants. This suggests that there are much more lucrative careers elsewhere in the law, even given that judges may acquire additional funds through extra-judicial payments (Nicholson 2002, 201–18). Certainly official reports note trouble recruiting judges, with many rural district courts having only one judge (BC TANDTC 2002, 46–7).

It appears that senior court judges are ordinarily recruited from the pool of lower court judges, court clerks, and personnel (Interview with Lawyer W, 2001; State-employed Lawyer Y, 2001). Further, new recruits are to have law degrees or be prepared to undertake the legal knowledge debt. Whereas in the past political credentials were the primary determinant of suitability for judicial office (Nicholson 2000), there is now a trend away from morality being the basis of appointment, toward a combination of Party approval and technical competency. There is insufficient public information to know quite how this plays out across the diverse courts that make up the Vietnamese court system.

Vietnamese judges are officers and employees of the Party-state. Further, their qualifications are usually fairly limited. They live and work in a politically charged culture where the local Party cell of their employment controls their reemployment prospects. This characterization is not a critique of Party control, but merely a statement of it. As noted earlier, the official documents relevant to courts, particularly

Political Bureau Resolution 8, supports the organic relationship between Party and state institutions, including legal institutions.

The Shape of Judicial Work

As we have seen, courts are charged with deciding cases, introducing and implementing legislation, educating citizens, and fostering and protecting the socialist state. The ensuing discussion focuses on the volume of the courts' work, both in terms of the number of cases they decide and the number of legal instruments introduced, to enable a snapshot of how judges spend their time today. It can be argued that the court's educational role has remained largely constant (Nicholson 2003). The jurisdiction of the court has radically expanded since the pre-unification period. An economic court was introduced in 1994 and an administrative court in 1996. While not particularly busy, these tribunals are entirely new areas of court work requiring judges to develop new expertise. Thus the jurisdictions in which the court can potentially be active has increased.

One of the primary tasks of the court is to determine disputes. Figure 10.2 shows the total caseload of the courts for the period 1999–2001, drawn from the Supreme People's Court reports to the National Assembly. At the time of writing, comprehensive statistics were not available for other years. Overall, there was a marked decline

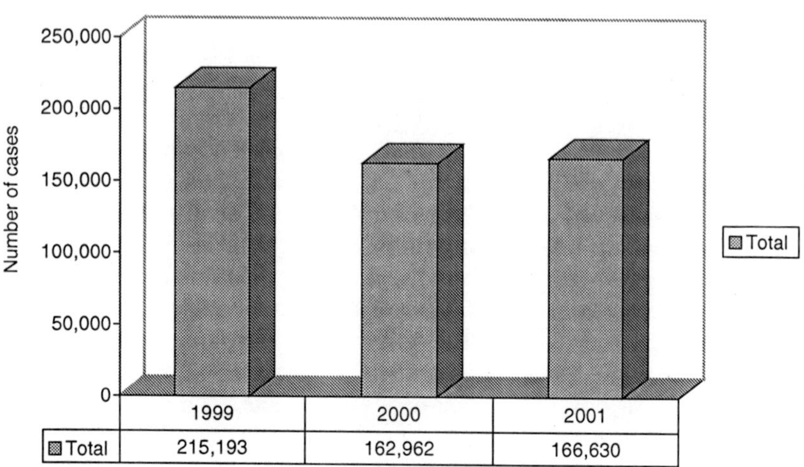

Figure 10.2   Total number of cases accepted by the courts.

Source: Data from Reports of the Supreme People's Court, 2000, 2001, 2002.

in case numbers: in 2001 there were 166,630 cases accepted by the courts across all jurisdictions and all locations, representing a reduction of 48,563 or 23% on the total figures for 1999. The number of cases accepted by the administrative and labor divisions of the court rose slightly over the period 1999–2001. In the civil, economic, and criminal jurisdictions, caseloads dropped. The most striking decrease in case volume was in the civil jurisdiction where the number of cases accepted dropped from 129,215 in 1999 to 111,721 in 2000: a decrease of 17,494 cases or 13.5%. In 2001, the number of civil cases increased slightly to 115,632, reflecting an overall decrease of only 10.5% from the 1999 figures. The single greatest decrease in percentage terms arises within the economic work of the courts. In 1999, there were 1,280 economic cases accepted by the courts. In 2001, that dropped to 690 cases or a decrease of 590 (46%). Finally, criminal cases were down 5,344 cases over the same period: a decrease of approximately 10%.

The reduction in case numbers in the contemporary period is hard to explain. The decrease in economic cases, which is the most striking, has been attributed to forum testing. The economic courts were introduced in 1994 and although its work increased in its early years (Nicholson and Minh 2000, 13), the current downward trend indicates no great embrace of that forum.

The reasons for the sharp decline in the number of civil cases from the year 1999 to 2000 are perhaps less clear. The slight increase in 2001 suggests that numbers are shifting in this jurisdiction and that perhaps a variation within 10% should be taken as not abnormal. It may be that the introduction of the Civil Code in 1997 prompted a litigiousness that has not continued. It may also be that as the law has become more concrete, particularly as it relates to land, fewer parties seek the courts' assistance. In other words, forum testing is again a likely explanation, albeit not here of a new forum, but of the ability of new law to afford claims within an old forum. On the criminal side, criminal caseloads have always fluctuated and a decrease of 10% might be within the margin of differences from year to year.

In terms of the volume of court work generally over the last three years there has been a decrease in some jurisdictions. In particular, the courts' new labor and administrative jurisdictions have seen small growth in case numbers. The crime, civil, and economic case numbers are all down over a three-year period, although the civil cases decreased in 2000 and then increased in 2001. Although this data is drawn from a very compressed time-frame, it suggests that the volume of the courts' work has not radically increased over the last three years.

Court as Source of Law

In addition to resolving cases, the Supreme People's Court amends laws and introduces subordinate laws necessary to the implementation of legal instruments. A study of a major Vietnamese law database (Lawdata) indicates that, while this function of the courts has remained constant over time, the Supreme Court has become much more legislatively active in recent times (Nicholson, 2003). Indeed, a Lawdata search over the period 1945–2003 suggests that the Supreme People's Court has produced many more decisions (*quyet dinh*), circulars (*thong tu*), official letters (*cong van*), and resolutions (*nghi quyet*) in the 1990s than in the 30 years between 1960 and 1990 despite incomplete statistics for the 1990s.[9]

However, the substantial increase in Supreme Court legislative activity has been in evidence throughout the 1990s, particularly after the constitutional changes introduced in 1992. This suggests several things. First, the role and relevance of the courts, and law more generally, have been emerging over the last decade.[10] Second, although the legislation relating to courts might not indicate a great shift in court roles and responsibilities, there is evidence of new patterns of behavior. More particularly, the courts are now more active in contributing to the formation of implementing laws, perhaps in turn reflecting the greater need for law as the basis of judging.

Guiding the Work of the Lower Courts

The Supreme People's Court is responsible for guiding the work of lower courts (Law on the Organization of People's Courts 2002, Art. 19), a function it has been performing since 1959.[11] This has always been considered a significant function and it is perhaps even more the case today. Certainly, grave concerns have been expressed about the ability of lower court judges and therefore the need for effective leadership from the Supreme Court. In 2002, the National Assembly refused to endorse a proposed reform to increase the criminal jurisdiction of district courts because, in the view of the national legislature, judges at this level were incapable of handling more complex cases (AFP, June 14, 2001).

However, particular litigants' use of appeals suggests that this is one method by which the senior courts influence decision making. For example, of the 46,946 criminal cases that were resolved in 2000, 15,399 or 33% were appealed (BC TANDTC 2001, 2–3). In the same year, the rates of appeal were higher in the administrative (63%) and labor courts (37%), but lower in the economic (15%) and civil courts (12.5%) (BC TANDTC 2001, 37–80).

In addition, the Supreme Court plays a far greater advisory role in the work of lower courts. As we saw previously, the Supreme Court is also much more proactive in recent years in the drafting of subordinate legislation. Much of this is directed at lower courts. In addition, the Supreme Court has increased the number of official letters (*cong van*), which respond to local court inquiries on how to determine specific cases. In 2001, 43 such letters were produced (BC TANDTC 2001). While the Court continues to vary its reporting, a comparison of Court reports to those of the National Assembly suggests it generated more official letters in 2001 than in 2000 or 1999.

In the past, the Supreme Court's "guiding" work of lower courts was implemented in a number of ways: through an annual conference, and through articles published in the Supreme People's Court's journal, *Tap san Tu phap* (*Justice Journal*), renamed *Tap san Toa an Nhan dan Toi cao* (*Supreme People's Court Journal*) in 1972. These strategies continue today, but are augmented by the use of expanded publications and summaries of similar facts (*tong ket chuyen de*) (Gillespie 2003, 36). The limited available evidence suggests these are used most in civil and economic cases (Gillespie 2003, 36). In 2005, limited public reporting of cases was also commenced, with the publication of case summaries of many of the judicial review decisions of the Council of Judges between 2000 and 2004 (Vietnam Legal Update, September 2005).

Further, in the past, courts were actively encouraged to seek advice from relevant local authorities—in particular, local Party committees—on how to determine cases (BC TANDTC 1977, 50–1). Today's Supreme Court reports do not refer local courts to local Party committees. Instead, the reports of 1999, 2000, and 2001 suggest that local courts are encouraged to seek the assistance of the Supreme People's Court in Hanoi. Finally, increasing the role of the SPC in the selection of provincial and district court judges may also have afforded the Court more scope to appoint judges sympathetic and responsive to centrally based leadership.

Read together, these changes, coupled with the most recent reforms that reemphasize the leadership role of the Supreme People's Court, suggest that the contemporary court system is moving gradually to institute the Supreme Court as the most significant guide on determining cases. And, the Supreme Court has been entrusted to develop implementing documents. However, this needs to be viewed in the context of the entrenched regionalism that pervades Vietnam and the lack of technical legal skills within courts.

While this characterization of the Supreme Court would appear to
have it sitting at the apex of decision making in Vietnam, and increasingly guiding lower courts to emulate its reasoning, this needs to be
distinguished from a shift in the type or nature of reasoning. This chapter
does not argue that the judgments are becoming increasingly legalistic or
that they will become so in the short term. As Gillespie (2003, 29–36)
has argued, judges are still motivated to resolve cases by "reason and sentiment in carrying out the law" (*ly va tinh trong viec chap hanh phap luat*).
Rather, the bases of judgments may ultimately come to reflect more
consistency, as lower courts come to echo the strategies and inclinations
of higher courts even if that strategy is to determine cases on the basis of
"reason and sentiment."

The Educational or Propagandist (Tuyen truyen)
Function of Courts

Finally, as we saw earlier, courts still have the responsibility to inculcate
loyalty to the Party-state, to encourage people to live according to law,
and to contribute to the struggle to prevent and combat crimes and
offences (Law on the Organization of People's Courts 2002, Art. 1). The
court's propagandist function to foster loyalty and to help eradicate social
evils was traditionally discharged through limited press coverage and the
use of mobile courts (Nicholson 2000, 159). For example, in 1964 the
Court Journal reported the use of over 600 mobile court hearings before
more than 20,000 people (BC TANDTC 1964, 8). This practice saw
court hearings held in factories and in housing estates before workers and
neighbors.

It is beyond the scope of this chapter to undertake an analysis of the
use of the media by the courts. However, without doubt the courts have
radically increased their use of the press to promote understanding of
the types of cases that come before courts and the decisions made. Court
work is now regularly reported in several newspapers including the main
national Party newspaper, *Nhan Dan,* and *Lao Dong, Cong an Nhan dan*
(*People's Public Security,* the main police newspaper), *Quan doi Nhan dan*
(*People's Army,* the main Army newspaper), *Saigon Giai phong* (*Liberated
Saigon,* the main Ho Chi Minh City Party paper), and the *Saigon Daily
Times.* Much of the courts' propagandist work is today carried out by
using the media (radio, television, and print) to report on cases. Further,
the press has taken a keen interest in reporting court news. Today there

is regular reporting of court cases not only in the police daily, *Cong an Nhan dan*, but also in the business, labor, women's, and other media. For example, in 1996 the *Saigon Daily Times* created its first page dedicated to reporting law and business and appointed a legally qualified reporter, Nguyen Hien Quan, to work part-time on relevant stories.

The manner in which the court uses or manipulates the press and vice versa is complex, all the more so because the media remains state controlled. However, it is too simplistic to see the press as entirely controlled by the state (Sidel 1998, 97–119; Heng 2001, 213–37). This chapter cannot speculate upon the delicate court-media relationship mediated by the Party-state, except to note that it is complex and presumably the balance of power in this configuration is dynamic and varies according to the issues at stake.

Conclusion

Sixty years on the Vietnamese court system remains a Party-led institution. The Party veteran officials, who will work in courts, and the Party through its extensive network of bureaucrats retain control over the direction of court decisions and court leadership generally. Salaries remain low and terms of office remain short. However, the courts today are not the same as the courts of the North in pre-unified Vietnam.

This chapter has sought to show that the Party-state envisages a more technically competent judiciary largely appointed by the Supreme People's Court. Indeed, the package of recently introduced reforms does promote, at least in theory, the Supreme Court as the body responsible for managing the courts. For example, the Court will negotiate the number of judges needed and select personnel. In addition, as noted above, the Court has been charged with taking a lead role in introducing and implementing legislation.

Therefore despite the organic relationship between Party and courts, the courts emerge as an institution instructed to take charge of and manage their own affairs. This must not be mistaken for designing or creating an independent court system. Rather, the reforms point to streamlining leadership of courts. The role of the Ministry of Justice is diminished. The Supreme People's Court has been designated as the authority on court management and personnel, which leaves the ultimate leadership of the Party intact. Where this will lead remains an open question.

Notes

1. See Thayer (2002, 8) on the National Assembly numbers and Nicholson and Quang (2005b) on court numbers. John Gillespie has described this as the "nomenklatura" system of the Vietnamese state (2002, 180–1).
2. In particular, see Joint Circular No. 01/2003 TTLT/TANDTC-BOP-BMV/UBTWMTTQVN dated April 1, 2003 Guiding the Implementation of a Number of Provisions of the Ordinance on Judges and Jurors of the Supreme People's Court, Ministry of Defence, Ministry of Justice, Ministry of the Interior, and Vietnam Fatherland Front Central Committee; and Resolution 131/2002/NQ-UBTVQH11 on Judges, People's assessors, and Prosecutors, November 3, 2002.
3. On constitutional reforms see Sidel (2002, 74). In relation to legal institutions generally see Resolution 8, and in relation to courts in particular, see Resolution 8 Part II B (1) (c). For a more detailed critique of Resolution 8 see Nicholson (2005).
4. Resolution 8 is not only concerned with courts. In the Vietnamese context a reference to "judicial work" is a reference to judges and court staff and also the procuracy (*kiem sat*), the police (*cong an*), and investigators (*canh sat*).
5. This chapter does not take up the story of changes to the Procuracy. See Quinn (2003).
6. The 2002 Law on the Organization of the People's Courts, while generally dealing with the issues raised by the analogous law of 1960, does so in a more detailed manner. For example, the 1960 law notes that both civil and criminal judgments must be enforced (Art. 24). The 2002 law not only provides that judgments must be enforced, but lists those agencies that must respect and give effect to judgments of any court (Art. 12).
7. Prosecutors were appointed from within the pool of people appointed as judges. Thus there was no substantive difference in the skills sought of those prosecuting and those determining cases (Nicholson 2000, 92).
8. People's assessors (*hoi tham nhan dan*) are beyond the purview of this article.
9. The Court completed 2 items of legislation in 1985, 2 in 1986, 5 in 1987, 2 in 1988, 7 in 1990, 9 in 1991, 4 in 1992, 7 in 1993, 13 in 1994, 10 in 1995, 10 in 1996, 17 in 1997, 6 in 1998, 2 in 1999, 14 in 2000, 8 in 2001, and 4 in 2003. Not all "official letters" issued by the SPC appear on Lawdata. It appears that letters relating to specific cases have not been included on the database.
10. This has to be balanced against findings by both Per Bergling (1999) and John McMillan and Christopher Woodruff (1999) suggesting that use of the courts is rarely contemplated by those in commercial disputes.
11. Law on Organization of People's Courts, July 14, 1960, Art. 21. Examples of Guidelines issued by the newly established Supreme People's Court include: "On deciding civil suits related to the agricultural collectivisation movement" and "On the condition and procedures for the early release of prisoners." See V. Kolesnikov (1961).

References

Policies and Legislation

Constitution of the Democratic Republic of Vietnam, 1946.
Constitution of the Democratic Republic of Vietnam, 1959.
Constitution of the Democratic Republic of Vietnam, 1980.
Constitution of the Socialist Republic of Vietnam, 1992.
Statute of the Communist Party of Vietnam, 1992.

Statute of the Communist Party of Vietnam, 2001.

Statute of the Vietnam Workers Party, 1960.

Order 13, On the Organization of Courts and the Status of Judges in the DRVN, January 1, 1946.

Law on the Organization of People's Courts, July 14, 1960.

Law Promulgating the Law on the Organization of People's Courts, Order No 19 LCT, July 26, 1960.

Decree Stipulating the Organization of Supreme People's Courts and Organization of Local People's Courts, March 23, 1961.

Law on the Organization of People's Courts, April 2, 2002.

Ordinance on Judges and Jurors of People's Courts, October 11, 2002.

Ordinance on the Organization of the People's Supreme Court and Local Courts, March 23, 1961.

Joint Circular No. 01/2003 TTLT/TANDTC-BOP-BMV/UBTWMTTQVN, dated April 1, 2003 Guiding the Implementation of a Number of Provisions of the Ordinance on Judges and Jurors of the Supreme People's Court, Ministry of Defence, Ministry of Justice, Ministry of the Interior and Vietnam Fatherland Front Central Committee ("Joint Circular 01").

Joint Circular No. 05/TTLN of Ministry of Justice and Supreme People's Court, October 15, 1993 Providing Guidelines on Ordinance on People's Judges and Jurors 1993 ("Joint Circular 05").

Resolution 131/2002/NQ- UBTVQH11 On Judges, People's Assessors and Prosecutors, November 3, 2002 ("Resolution 131").

Resolution No. 37/NQ-TVQH9 dated May 14, 1993.

Resolution No. 8-NQ/TW of the Political Bureau on Forthcoming Principal Judiciary Tasks, January 2, 2002 ("Resolution 8").

Supreme Court Journal

Toa an Nhan dan Toi Cao. 1964. Bao cao Cong tac Nghanh Toa an Nam 1964 va Phuong huong Nhiem vu Cong tac Toa an Nam 1965 (Report of the Supreme People's Court 1964).

———. 1977. Bao cao Cong tac Nghanh Toa an Nam 1977 va Phuong huong Nhiem vu Cong tac Toa an Nam 1977 (Report of the Supreme People's Court 1977).

———. 2000. Bao cao Cong tac Nghanh Toa an Nam 1964 va Phuong huong Nhiem vu Cong tac Toa an Nam 2000 (Report of the Supreme People's Court 2000).

———. 2001. Bao cao Cong tac Nghanh Toa an Nam 2000 va Phuong huong Nhiem vu Cong tac Toa an Nam 2001 (Report of the Supreme People's Court 2001), February 9, 2001.

———. 2002. Bao cao Cong tac Toa an Nam 2001 va Phuong huong Nhiem vu Cong tac Toa an Nam 2002 (Report of the Supreme People's Court 2002), January 28, 2002.

Interviews

Unless otherwise specified interviews were granted on the basis of anonymity:

Interview by author with Vietnamese Barrister A, 1999.

Interview by author with Vietnamese Lawyer W, 2001.

Interview by author with Vietnamese State-employed Lawyer Y, 2001.

Interview by author with Vietnamese Barrister B, October 6, 2003.

Secondary Sources

Agence France Presse. 2001. Vietnam MPs vote down bill boosting powers of district courts, June 12.

Anonymous. 1961. Election of justices and people's jurymen. Nhan Dan, May 18, Foreign Broadcast Information Service (FBIS).

Fforde, Adam. 1986. The unimplementability of policy and the notion of law in Vietnamese Communist thought. *Southeast Asian Journal of Social Science* 62.

Gillespie, John. 2002. The political-legal culture of anti-corruption reforms in Vietnam. In *Corruption in Asia: Rethinking the governance paradigm.* Edited by Timothy Lindsey. Sydney: The Federation Press, 60–70.

———. 2003. Extra-Constitutional law-making: Vietnam's unacknowledged legislators. Conference paper presented at Mapping Vietnam's Legal Culture at University of Victoria, Canada (forthcoming).

———. 2004. Concept of law in Vietnam: Transforming statist socialism. In *Asian discourses of rule of law.* Edited by Randall Peerenboom. New York: Routledge, 146–82.

———. 2005. Continuity and change in "socialist" legal thinking. In *Asian socialism and legal change.* Edited by John Gillespie and Pip Nicholson. Canberra: Asia Pacific Press, 45–75.

Heng, Russell Hiang-Khng. 2001. Media negotiating the state: In the name of the law in anticipating. *Sojourn* 16(2): 213–37.

Kolesnikov, V. 1961. The Supreme People's Court—Highest judicial organ in the Democratic Republic of Vietnam. *Byulletan Verkhognogo SSSR* No. 3 (Moscow).

Le Kim Que. 1961. Some problems organising the election of judges to the real people's courts. *Justice Journal* 6: 13–17.

Mai Bo. 2000. Can sua doi Phap lenh Tham phan va Hoi tham nhan dan (The Ordinance on Judges and People's Assessors must be amended). *People's Court Journal* 2: 3.

McMillan, John and Christopher Woodruff. 1999. Dispute prevention without courts in Vietnam. *Journal of Law and Economic Organization* 15(3): 637–58.

Nguyen Nhu Phat. 1997. The role of law during the formation of a market-driven mechanism in Vietnam. In *Commercial legal development in Vietnam: Vietnamese and foreign commentaries.* Edited by John Gillespie. Sydney: Butterworths, 307–412.

Nguyen Van Hien. 2001. Tieu chuan tham phan-thuc trang an hung yeu cau dat ra trong thoi ky moi (Judicial criteria—Current situation and requirements for new era). *People's Court Journal* 4: 2.

Nicholson, Penelope (Pip). 1999. Vietnamese legal institutions in comparative perspective: Contemporary Constitutions and courts considered. In *Law, capitalism and power in Asia.* Edited by Jayasuriya Kanishka. London: Routledge, 300–29.

———. 2000. Borrowing court systems: The experience of the DRVN 1945–1976, Doctoral Thesis, University of Melbourne.

———. 2002. The Vietnamese court and corruption. In *Corruption in Asia.* Edited by Timothy Lindsey and H. Dick. Sydney: The Federation Press, 201–18.

———. 2003. Bibliography of Vietnamese law related materials. *Legal Reference Services Quarterly* 22(2/3): 139–200.

———. 2005. Vietnamese jurisprudence: Informing court reform. In *Asian socialism and legal change.* Edited by John Gillespie and Pip Nicholson. Canberra: Asia Pacific Press, 159–90.

Nicholson, Penelope (Pip) and Nguyen Hung Quang. 2005. The Vietnamese judiciary: The politics of appointment and promotion. *Pacific Rim Law and Policy Journal* 14(1): 1–34.

Nicholson, Penelope (Pip) and Nguyen Thi Minh. 2000. Commercial disputes and arbitration in Vietnam. *Journal of International Arbitration* 17(5): 1–18.

Phillips Fox, *Vietnam Legal Update*, September, 2005.

Quinn, Brian J. M. 2002. Legal reform and its context in Vietnam. *Columbia Journal of Asian Law* 15: 221.

———. 2003. Vietnam's continuing legal reforms: Gaining control over the courts. *Asian-Pacific Law and Policy Journal* 4(2): 432–68.

Sidel, Mark. 1998. Law, the press and police murder in Vietnam: The Vietnamese press and the trial of Nguyen Tung Duong. In *The Mass media in Vietnam*. Edited by David Marr. Canberra: Australian National University, 97–119.

———. 2002. Analytical models for understanding Constitutions and Constitutional dialogue in socialist transitional states: Re-interpreting Constitutional dialogue in Vietnam. *Singapore Journal of International & Comparative Law* 6: 42.

Thayer, Carlyle A. 2002. Recent political developments: Vietnam in 2002. Conference paper presented at Vietnam Update, Australian National University, Canberra.

Tran Van Tu. 2003. Doi moi to chuc va hoat dong cua toa an Nhan dan (Reforming the organization and operation of people's courts). *Legislative Studies Magazine* 1: 34–9.

Power and Representation at the Vietnamese National Assembly

The Scope and Limits of Political Doi Moi

M ATTHIEU S ALOMON

Through the different experiences of the twentieth century that gave shape to the Communist political formula, the first image of this regime is without a doubt that of the "Party-State." The Party structure, holding unique political legitimacy thanks to its role in history, was thought to have absorbed state legitimacy. The state, legislature, government, and administration were only smokescreens. This does not mean that these institutions had no function: they fulfilled symbolic, technical, and other roles. But they rarely had any real political power. Modern-day Vietnam has been no exception to this conception of Communist power.

But Communist Parties have also shown that they are able to adapt to new situations and introduce reforms in certain periods. This appears obvious on the economic level, but can it be denied on the political level? How is it possible to consider Chinese and Vietnamese changes and the post-Stalin years in the USSR otherwise? A comparative approach here is fundamental. Political reform in Communist regimes seems to take place on three levels: the internal reform of the Party, the building of a legitimate, autonomous, and efficient state apparatus, and new legislation. At the crossroads of processes is the role played by the system of people's assemblies (People's Councils, *Hoi dong Nhan dan*) and by the National Assembly (*Quoc hoi*) in particular. The People's Council system has three levels: provincial (*tinh*), district (*huyen*), and commune (*xa*). For the five province-level municipalities, the three levels are city (*thanh pho*), district (*quan*), and quarter (*phuong*). These legislative bodies, which are "freely" elected, benefit from a source of revalued legitimacy, based upon a renewed sense of popular legitimacy. The National Assembly is also the supreme legislative body. Its reforms can be seen as a key barometer of *doi moi* in the political arena. The process of reform of these legislative bodies and assemblies at the national and local level truly began with the 1992 Constitution, and the National Assembly's role was strengthened during its last three terms.

In this chapter, focusing on the National Assembly, I consider these issues by analyzing how the pre–*doi moi* vision of these institutions was placed in doubt, and then the reform program affecting these institutions, as well as the limits of these changes.

Renovation of the Communist Model and Political Principles

Characteristics of Marxist-Leninist Political Systems

From the viewpoint of the overall organization of the "classical" Communist political system, a fundamental principle of such regimes is the unification of power that guarantees "good representation." The three powers (executive, legislative, and judicial) are inseparable, even if there is a division of labor between them (as recognized in the 2001 Constitutional amendments). The Vietnamese Communist Party incorporates this unification of power and so is always above the state apparatus. Institutions operate on the principle of democratic centralism. In theory, the National Assembly is the supreme body holding state power; the National Assembly and the People's Councils are "representing the will and hopes of the people, elected by the people and accountable to the people" (1992 Constitution, Art. 6).

Behind these principles, however, are different realities. Experience shows us that of the various political experiments and structures under Communist Party regimes, it is almost impossible, until very recently, to find an example of an elected people's assembly wielding real political power. In Vietnam, these formal popular institutions have traditionally been symbols or props. At the local level, power was in the hands of People's Committees *(Uy ban nhan dan)*, the executive structures "elected" by People's Councils, and even more so within Party cells. At the central level, real decisions were taken by the Political Bureau and the Central Committee of the Party and, eventually, the government (Beresford and Dang 1998).

In the Vietnamese system until the 1990s, legitimation procedures were based on ideology, mass agitation, and propaganda, what Bunner terms heterogeneous-teleological legitimacy, and contrary to autonomous-consensual legitimacy based on pragmatism, fair elections, and legal regulation (Bunner 1982, 27–44). In this sort of system, popular opinion is shaped, not asked for, and it is easy to understand why legitimacy is "with" the Party. Elections, the state apparatus, in general, and the National Assembly, in particular, were only instruments and propaganda tools.

The Official Conception of the National Assembly

Doi moi must be analyzed as a response to a dual crisis: an internal crisis linked to the socioeconomic problems facing the country, and the upheavals in the international political situation. Rethinking the role of the National Assembly (and of the People's Councils) was one of the outcomes of these jolts to the Vietnamese system in the 1980s. And it was due partly to the need to build a legal framework to regulate the rapidly changing socialist market economy under economic reform, and to cope with popular demands for more accountability from political authorities. In this sense, the National Assembly has gradually begun to play a greater role as both legislator and promoter of socialist democracy.

The legislative dimension answers the pressing need for a new and flexible framework for economic and social reform. The second element relates to the changing nature of how the state seeks legitimacy and works with the people. In the reformed Vietnamese system, popular demands and interests flow upward through People's Councils at the local level under a principle of grassroots democracy (*dan chu co so*) and through the National Assembly, which is elected by direct universal suffrage (and which is not the case in China for example). So the people's councils have been reenshrined as a basis of socialist democracy, even though this was always the case on paper.

The future of political *doi moi* is closely related to the goal of "separating the Party from the State." In official terms, since the mid- to late 1980s, the Party has been responsible only for defining general political orientation. The octopus-like behavior of the Party has been criticized because it interfered too much in state management thus reducing the state's efficiency and authority. It was General Secretary Nguyen Van Linh who took this call up first in the context of the National Assembly, saying that the National Assembly must play a real political role in debating and questioning policies (Stern 1993). Since that time, the same basic message has been repeated many times by senior Party officials. National Assembly reforms also help to build a "socialist state ruled by law" (*nha nuoc phap quyen xa hoi chu nghia*). This notion first appeared explicitly in 1991 Party Congress documents and was then integrated into the Constitution in the December 2001 amendments (Art. 2). Even if the idea of a "state ruled by law" is still problematic, as the chapter by John Gillespie in this volume clearly illustrates, the changes in official statements are noteworthy, and discussions on the strengthening of the rule of law are now quite open.

These directions, principles, and concepts point to the three fundamental missions of the National Assembly: to legislate, to make decisions on matters of national importance, and to supervise state activities (Art. 83, 1992 Constitution; Ninth Party Congress 2001). But it is also important to avoid pitfalls in analyzing the changes in the Vietnamese system— pitfalls that can arise from either looking overly cynically at these proclaimed transformations of the system, or naively overinterpreting this new vocabulary through the prism of Western democratic thought. The changes in ideas and principles are real, but the gap between official pronouncements and reality is real too, and immense. The fundamental objective, however, the *sine qua non* condition for these adaptations, is the perpetuation and strengthening of Party power in a new era. And in this context the perspective opposing state and Party cannot be satisfying. The separation of Party and state over many years does not mean opposition between the two.

The Direction of Reforms: Popular Legitimacy, Decision Making, and Creating and Supervising Legal Norms

Listening and Representing

Strengthening National Assembly legitimacy through reforming processes of representation is a key goal of the National Assembly reforms. The Party and the National Assembly seek to improve the Assembly's role in representing public opinion and the views of different elements in the Vietnamese social structure linked to Party-approved reforms and to the implementation principles of grassroots democracy. This assumed additional importance after the rural disturbances of 1997 (February 1998 Directive No. 30-CT/TW the Party Central Committee [February 1998]; Denunciation and Petition Law [November 1998]). The slogan is telling: *dan biet, dan ban, dan lam, dan kiem tra* (the people know, the people discuss, the people act, the people supervise). In this way, the reforms seek to develop "participation" and "consultation" of the people through structured channels in different areas and in different ways.

Structuring Public Consultation Channels

Broadening the Choice of Representatives

One key reform at the level of the National Assembly has been the partial and gradual opening of electoral processes since 1992 through the authorization of independent candidates, broadening the choice of deputies, and submitting candidates to a fairer public vote. Beginning in 1997, independent candidates were also officially permitted to run their own campaigns. Other candidates (the great majority) are proposed by central and local authorities. The same system has gradually been adopted for elections to the People's Councils as well. Official policy is to allow more non-Communists to be elected to the National Assembly (1992 Election Law, Art. 46, repeated in the 1997 and 2001 laws). Before the 1997 elections for example, the senior National Assembly official Vu Mao stated that 20% would be a good number for non-Communist deputies in the future (Balfour 1997). The often evoked official objective is to have two candidates more than the number of seats in each electoral jurisdiction. The ratio since 1992 has been about 1.5 candidates per seat.

The list of candidates is defined through three rounds of negotiations between different political and social groups and popular consultations organized under the aegis of the Fatherland Front. During this process— and as in state administration, where promotion processes work on similar lines of subordinate workers consulting and agreeing on nomination of a colleague to a higher post (Fontanel 2001, 55–65)—reports indicate that the Party does seek to do some listening, even if this listening may be limited because the citizens participating in these meetings are carefully chosen (Salomon 2004a, 41–71). Nevertheless, a candidate who is clearly rejected by people can be excluded from the electoral list. The rounds of public consultation organized before the legislative elections cannot be considered entirely unimportant. This system, which seeks to build legitimacy by excluding what the Party and local authorities regard as undesirables and those who "stir things up," is also used to reject candidates who are too unpopular or corrupt.

There are a number of examples of this process at work. For example, in the spring of 2002, a few days before the election of the Eleventh National Assembly, the Central Election Council struck off the names of three important candidates (Tran Mai Hanh, Le Cong Minh, and Tran Trung Am) from the candidate lists as each became the subject of legal action or corruption investigation. A similar process of consultation is being followed in the local People's Councils, especially since the 1997 disturbances that were primarily caused by the corrupt and authoritarian behavior of local officials. Nevertheless, there is clearly a gap between urban and rural in the freedom of expression of citizens and in the determination of the acceptability level of candidates.

Elections have also now become a sort of popularity test for Party members. In many jurisdictions there are "electoral battles," often among candidates who are Party members. And, in many other constituencies, even if winning an election is not a challenge to a high-ranking candidate, the size of his or her victory is closely watched and important. An internal Party rule, mentioned by then National Assembly Chairman Nguyen Van An before the last elections, provides that any Party Central Committee member who obtains less than 60% of the electorate vote for the National Assembly in his or her constituency must submit to self-criticism and have the matter discussed within the Party. If in the rare event he or she is not elected to the National Assembly, he or she would be excluded from the Central Committee (Interview, Hanoi, August 2003). Such cases are very rare. In 2002, for example, it appears that only Central Committee member Ta Huu Thanh, in Vinh Long Province, was elected to the National Assembly with less than 60% of the available votes (he received 57%). But the contest is not without risks. The same holds true at local levels where elections for People's Councils can serve as tests, trampolines, or sometimes traps. For example the Party Secretary of Quang Binh Province, Dinh Huu Cuong, was not elected to the local People's Council in the 2004 elections despite standing as a candidate (*Tuoi Tre Newspaper*, April 30, 2004).

Evaluation and Control of Representatives

The reforms of people's assemblies at the national and local levels
are moving gradually toward reforms in which the work of their
members—people's representatives—is intended to be at least somewhat
"accountable" to the citizens. Official regulations maintain that once a
candidate is elected, he or she must keep in frequent contact with the
constituency and must receive and listen to citizens during scheduled
meetings (Arts. 51, 52, Organization Law of the National Assembly
[2001]; Do Tien Dung 2003). The issue of "proximity to the people"
(*gan nhan dan*) is also one of the clearly stated selection criteria
announced during the last elections, because the distance between
deputies and their constituencies has been the source of frequent and
serious complaints. The accountability of National Assembly deputies
(particularly for those who are also government ministers and who must
report on the activities of their ministry or agency) can now also take
place during the much-awaited live broadcast of question time (*chat van*)
at each National Assembly session. Media plays a very significant role in
this process.

Opening Up the Legislative Process

Consultation also takes place through arrangements aimed at "having the
people participate" more in the drafting of laws. The first such consultation was in 1979 in the redrafting of the Constitution. These activities
have become more frequent and have been widely publicized. Today,
many means are used, including consultations carried out by deputies,
political institutions, mass organizations, and above all, the mass media.
During the summer of 2003, for example, newspapers actively called on
their readers to provide opinions on the drafts of the new Land Law and
Civil Procedure Code. At the same time, the popular online new service
VnExpress organized an opinion forum on bills relating to the organization of people's councils and committees and to the elections of their
members. These participation campaigns are becoming increasingly
frequent and widespread, and they have been supported by several
international organizations working on the reform of legislative and
representative institutions.

It is difficult to evaluate the importance of citizens' opinions on these
draft laws with any precision. Many of the ideas transmitted during public consultations do not contradict the bills, but there have been cases in
which public consultation did substantially change the original text, as in

the Civil Code adopted in 1995 that grew more than a hundred articles after public consultation (interview with Tran Quoc Thuan, *VnExpress*, July 30, 2003). And making this evaluation even more difficult is the possibility that some changes that were already planned or under discussion may be attributed to public comments. It is clear that here a real political filter is in place, raising the issue of the reality and importance of citizens' participation in these processes.

Petitions and Corporatism

This willingness to build channels for public participation has led to the possibility of petitioning through official channels. The petition field of action remains circumscribed, and most political subjects are outside it, but it does exist and functions in certain areas, reflecting the fact that the Party and state and National Assembly are forced to take public reactions and requests into account. The objective of the petition process is to structure and control debate in public fora, primarily in the National Assembly chamber. In these new spaces, differing sides on particular issues can engage in debates that will become public if they do not veer into taboo subjects (*cam ky*). Specialized institutions have been formed to handle such complaints and denunciations, such as the Department of Public Complaints (*Vu Dan nguyen*) in the Office of the National Assembly (*Van phong Quoc hoi*). Since September 2003 a supposedly independent Public Complaints Commission (*Ban Dan nguyen*, Resolution 370/2003/NQ-UBTVQH 11 of the National Assembly Standing Committee) has been added, and there is little data thus far on the real effectiveness of these mechanisms.

These developments are closely connected and help illustrate the corporatist nature of the Vietnamese political system. Vietnam today is fascinated with the notions of interest groups and lobbies. In Vietnam, these are linked to a traditional political concept that gives intermediary bodies—as opposed to individuals—significant power. Thus we can interpret the Party and state's willingness to strengthen the National Assembly as a way of expressing corporatist interests and demands in a depoliticized manner; a place where decisions can be taken consensually, in a "managerial" and "administrative" way. The 25 senior business managers elected to the National Assembly in 2002 epitomize this process. They are clearly intended to represent the voice of entrepreneurs (Minh Duc 2002, 14–16). Outside the Assembly, this group is also making its voice heard through petitions, as the petition signed by firms to put a 25% ceiling on corporate taxes (*Vietnam Economic Times*, June 2003). While it is true that business leaders have considerably more flexibility in petitioning due to economic power as well as political and family ties and the interests they share with the political elite, this process does represent a form of Vietnamese "state corporatism" (Jeong 1997).

Embodying the National Assembly Community:
The Nation in Miniature

Since reforms began, the idea of representation has held a fundamental place in the official position on the composition of the National Assembly and local bodies: these institutions must "correctly" represent the population. The idea of a "natural link" is fundamental: the legislature must be the nation in miniature in order to make the right decisions. The method used is similar to quotas. A representative number for each social category is determined before elections as the result to be reached. This idea is also linked to state corporatism: different social and institutional sectors lobby and jostle in the negotiations leading up to the definition of "correct representation." To take only two examples: the percentage of women in the National Assembly has been fixed over the past decade at around 25%, while ethnic minorities hold 17% of the seats. It is now generally the same for the local People's Councils.

The representative character of the National Assembly is also based on visual aids: during opening and closing sessions of the Assembly, which are broadcast live on national television and pictured on the front pages of newspapers, female deputies are dressed in *ao dai*, deputies from the ethnic minorities wear their traditional attire, soldiers wear their uniforms, and so on. This representation has an undeniably "dressed up folklore" dimension to it—and it is not new, having occurred throughout the prereform eras in Vietnam, China, and the Soviet Union as well—but it indicates the persistence of these issues in times of reform.

Structural Change Within the National Assembly

In order to introduce greater democracy and more directly represent popular views, the powers of National Assembly deputies (as opposed to the members of the Standing Committee of the National Assembly, a far smaller group) have been revised. Until the end of the 1990s, nearly all the powers of the National Assembly were in the hands of the Standing Committee, and the Standing Committee legislated much more than the National Assembly itself (Vasavakul 2002). The debates on the revision of the Constitution in 1991 and the amendments to the Organization Law of the National Assembly in late 2001 reflect the increasing role of the Assembly itself. The Assembly may now hold no-confidence votes against government ministers or other elected officials. This development goes hand in hand with that of deputy powers, an issue illustrated in the June 2003 session of the National Assembly. Some deputies proposed—in the name of efficiency—that the Standing Committee of the National Assembly be reempowered to amend bills and lists of concerned products. The proposal was opposed by other deputies, who were in turn supported by National Assembly Chairman Nguyen Van An. In their view this arrangement would contravene the principle of democracy in the operations of the National Assembly and would deprive the Assembly of its power to make fiscal decisions—which is one of its key prerogatives (*Vietnam Economic Times*, June 2003).

There is indeed a structural tension between the dual needs for representation and efficiency in a National Assembly that is facing ever more and complex tasks. The definition of powers and prerogatives of the Standing Committee, the internal National Assembly committees, and full-time deputies on one side (especially now that since the Eleventh National Assembly full-time deputies sessions are being organized between plenary sessions)—and the Assembly in plenary session on the other hand, is quite complicated. A battle of wills is going on while the system is working on institutionalizing and defining the missions of its different actors.

The Role of the National Assembly in Drafting and Modernizing Laws

Organizing a Modern and Capable Structure

In the Vietnamese view, a key step in improving the efficiency of the National Assembly is to improve the "quality" of the people in it. Official policy has long emphasized this point and provides a list of certain criteria of what makes a good deputy: honesty and devotion, a good education, competence, adaptation to the new era as shown by their sound knowledge in economics, management, or other subjects (Salomon 2004b, 103–24). During the 2002 Assembly elections, professional experience and (for civil servants) previous level of responsibility were also raised according to the criteria. Some Assembly officials note that the current pay of deputies obstructs the process of attracting competent people to the job, and that higher salaries and other perquisites are needed (interview, Hanoi, June 2003). The nature of deputies is already changing, according to official statistics, though official expectations remain far ahead of the pace of change. I return to this topic at the end of the chapter.

For a modern structure in the spirit of the reforms, the Vietnamese view is that "professional" people are needed. The modernization of the National Assembly means the institutionalization of a permanent organization, composed of a large number of full-time deputies (*dai bieu chuyen trach*). Before *doi moi*, virtually all deputies worked part-time (*dai bieu kiem nhiem*). Only at the end of the eighth term of the National Assembly (1986–92) and in order to meet the National Assembly's rapidly developing needs, did certain deputies—especially members of the Law Committee and the Committee on Economy and Budget—begin to undertake their positions on a full-time basis. The orientation of reforms along with the National Assembly's expanding jurisdiction pushes toward an increase in the proportion of full-time, professional deputies and a more important role for them. And there is a strong sense that deputies are only truly efficient after their second or third year, and that their functions should in some sense be "stable." The part-time deputies act as a link with the voters and ensure ties to the real world. According to the 2001 Law on the Organization of the National Assembly, one quarter of the deputies, or about 125 individuals, will work full-time in National Assembly committees or in local delegations. There were only about 20 full-time deputies during the Tenth Legislature (1997–2002). Meetings bringing full-time deputies together are presently organized between plenary Assembly sessions in order to prepare files, discuss projects and allow an improvement in the efficiency of the National Assembly.

Along with a willingness to broaden the jurisdiction of the Assembly and increase the availability of deputies, officials are working on improving structures and working conditions. The main administrative and management core of the National Assembly is the Office of the National Assembly (ONA), and the Office has undergone substantial expansion, reorganization, and "rationalization" with extensive foreign donor support. The Office of the National Assembly now has eight departments that correspond to the Assembly's eight specialized committees, as well as a Center for Information, Library and Research Services and other entities. This Center, created in 1993, serves as a documentation center and a core point for the flow of information. It has grown steadily, now employing more than 50 staff, many of whom were educated abroad.

In the domain of informing the public, significant change has occurred as well since the 1990s, symbolized by Resolution 2 of the National Assembly Standing Committee (1992). The National Assembly is functioning more transparently and its activities are now being considerably more widely publicized. The best example of this is without doubt the live national broadcasts on Vietnamese television of question time with government ministers since at least 1997. Press conferences have also increased. Newspaper stories and discussions of proceedings in the Assembly now frequently appear on the front pages of the press. These changes have allowed the Assembly to become a sort of national forum and sounding board by the authorities on certain debates. The Assembly also publishes its own periodicals: *Nguoi Dai bieu Nhan Dan (The People's Representatives)*, established as a bimonthly in October 1988 and considerably more extensively read now, and the professional review *Nghien cuu Lap phap (Legislative Studies)* founded in December 2000 and its active website. This willingness to improve the flow of quantitative and qualitative on the activities of the National Assembly and local legislative and representative bodies is lauded as a component of the "democratization" (*dan chu hoa*) of the people's assemblies, particularly with respect to the publicity given to elections (Do Van Tri 2003). And, outside the domestic scene, the National Assembly is beginning to consider itself as a careful foreign policy actor, though it is cautious not to move ahead of or be perceived as differing in any way from party and state foreign affairs institutions (Salomon and Vu, forthcoming).

Legislating to Reinforce Social Regulation

The first mission of the National Assembly is to strengthen its legislative functions. The need to legislate is intrinsic to Vietnam's economic and social reforms: between 1945 and 1984, the National Assembly adopted several dozen laws and several dozen decrees. Since the 1990s, there has been a real legislative plan, adopted by the Standing Committee of the National Assembly, for each five-year term of the National Assembly. Between 1985 and 2000 (but mostly since the early 1990s), 87 laws were passed by the National Assembly and 29 were amended. The Assembly also passed 111 decrees during this 15-year period. The economic field took about 40% of these new laws (68% of the amended ones), and 52% of the decrees (Nguyen Chi Dung 2001, 56–60). Even though bills are generally prepared by government ministries or agencies, the committees of the National Assembly, and later the deputies themselves, play an increasingly important role in the legislative deliberations. The capacity to "produce laws and decrees" is without doubt the greatest success of the National Assembly since the reform era began. Legislation in a sometimes disunified legal system (one in which the public often has little confidence and a system in which enforcement can be exceptionally spotty) provides obstacles to the success of the National Assembly in its legislative functions.

Deciding and Controlling

Deciding on the Important Questions Facing the Country

Among the three official tasks of the National Assembly is discussing and making decisions on the important issues facing the country. The expansion of this role is a certain reinforcement of the Assembly's power and that of its deputies. For example, in 1997, deputies rejected the Prime Minister's proposal to extend the term of the governor of the Central Bank, and the Prime Minister's nominee for the minister of transport (Interview, Hanoi, September 2003). Many observers noted the intense discussions that took place during the 2001 revision of the 1992 Constitution. But this aspect of the National Assembly's role is also very difficult to assess. Decision-making capacities are always subject to dual control by the Party: constraints on official texts, and constraints on individuals who are Party members and who hold all—or virtually all—important positions in the National Assembly.

In some cases, National Assembly decisions are made on what we might call technical questions rather than major issues of national policy. And it is true that important questions are more often than not debated within other walls. Sensitive legal issues are submitted to the Political Bureau or other Party offices for their decision or views. But the political actors who are most discontent with the growing power of the National Assembly are almost always found in government organizations. Here the battle of political and legislative powers often occurs, despite the fact that most of the major individual actors are Party members.

Developing the Power to Supervise

During the reform era, the authorities also wanted to develop the Assembly's power to supervise the government. Deputies are perceived as a check on government mismanagement and as guarantors of Assembly authority. Supervision by the National Assembly was always written into the various Vietnamese Constitutions, but has been exercised far more actively in recent years. Yet there remain different views or tendencies among Assembly staff and deputies. For some, the Assembly should limit itself to Constitutional and legislative control. For others, the Assembly should actively exercise its supervision over the full range of state activities—and in the past decade or more the second view has held sway. The Law on the Supervision Activities of the National Assembly (No. 05/2003/QH11) reaffirms the supervision of all state activities. Five different supervision activities are defined (Art. 7). Deputies supervise state activities by examining bills and activity reports from state agencies, by questioning government officials, and in other ways. The Assembly's committees also have a broad mandate and widespread powers of control. But their efficiency has not yet been proven. Supervision missions by committees in the provinces are often merely formal, though that problem is susceptible to gradual correction.

In this context of supervision, the question time of senior government officials deserves attention. Since its introduction in 1992, these sessions have drawn considerable attention. Initially purely formal, they have become tumultuous occasions for ministers and other senior cadres. Ministers now ask deputies' forgiveness for shoddy job performances and ask them to take responsibility for serious mistakes. Important subjects are discussed, ranging from taxation to corruption to university entrance examinations, although many questions are still not in the spirit of the exercise: too long, or unworthy of being asked during a session (*Tien Phong Newspaper*, November 27, 2002). Question time is being broadcasted live on television since 1997 thus becoming a rare "political minute" of possible truth that attracts mass attention. The press also publishes the often harsh reactions of deputies and citizens to the sessions themselves and to the behavior of ministers or deputies. Since December 2001, deputies can call for a no-confidence vote against senior officials, and that has occasionally occurred when question time has gone particularly poorly. In 2003, for example, Deputy Nguyen Duc Dung asked for a no-confidence vote against the Minister of Education, and then in 2004 he suggested forming a special committee to investigate education issues. Government officials are "afraid of the sessions," though they can also be used to improve their image and showcase their qualities (interview, Hanoi, September 2003). Public opinion polls now judge which officials have performed best during question time (*Vietnamnet*, November 28, 2005).

Evaluation of the Evolution of the National Assembly and the Local People's Assemblies

Limits to Opening the Electoral Process in Vietnam

The somewhat more democratic nature of National Assembly elections in Vietnam is still a far cry from that of Western democracies: the power to decide who has the right to run for office is still in the hands of the Party (Salomon 2004a, 41–71). Independents continue to face significant difficulties in the nomination and selection process, and official organizations are often unwilling to present non-Party members. In 2002, only two independent candidates and about 50 non-Party members (about 10% of the National Assembly) were elected. It should be emphasized that, according to the principle of "cadres recommendations," even Party members cannot run for office entirely on their own initiative. Whether they wish to run for office or not—and some high-ranking officials are not necessarily fond of the idea of sitting for and in the increasingly contentious National Assembly—their candidature comes from on high. According to the Party Statute (Art. 41) and the Interdictions for Party Members (*Nhung dieu Dang vien khong duoc lam*, adopted by the Political Bureau in May 1999), Party members may not run for office without the agreement of their superiors (Art. 7). A Party member who wishes to run for office has no choice, if not chosen to do so by his Party organization, but to turn in his Party membership card and run as an independent. This issue was raised before the 2004 elections for the People's Councils, but this fundamental rule has not been modified.

Therefore selection of candidates is often political and bureaucratic and often depends on avoiding political trouble, avoiding making enemies in the bureaucratic machine, and finding a "powerful protector" (*o du*). This is one reason why the capacity of deputies has not yet matched the formal objectives set by the Party and the National Assembly. This situation is as much a subject for popular jokes as it is for official complaint or self-criticism, particularly when deputies display a low level of education, and poor legal and economic knowledge (Bui Quoc Thanh 2002).

The problem of the allocation of responsibilities within the National Assembly goes hand in hand with the problem of elections. A concentric power circles diagram analysis shows that the more the elements come from outside the system, the more they stay at the outskirts of the National Assembly's working mechanisms (Salomon 2004b, 103–24).

Realities of Participation and Public Consultation

On the other side of the official mirror, public meetings between citizens and deputies are generally organized by the authorities, and usually touch only a small segment of the population, often Party members and other "good citizens." Based on interviews conducted in Vietnam it appears that many people do not believe in these consultations and do not have any interest in participating in them. Public comments about these popular participation meetings are often quite cynical. Participation is highly structured. Caution is often the order of the day in these meetings, as it has long been for Party and state officials. Citizens who do participate in public meetings generally stay "within the line." The common wisdom for public appearances can be expressed thus: "how not to make one's superiors angry" (Nguyen Si Dung 2002, 3–4). Participation is then highly structured, volunteered, and most of the time seems to become a sort of self-fulfilling prophecy.

However when these meetings do take place, they tend to be useful for leaders by supplying them with discussion points and arguments for use during negotiations and other events. Where the leadership cannot reach a consensus, seeking and obtaining public opinion may be useful. These institutionalized upward channels for the hearing of grassroots opinions are important for legislative reform and broader political legitimacy.

Problems of Organization and Competence

The steady increase in deputies' responsibilities involving both central and local meetings, missions to constituencies, and other events has made participation by the part-time deputies—who often do not have any staff and budget—very complicated. The part-time deputies who sit on Assembly committees rarely participate in those meetings. For example, the Law Committee of the Tenth National Assembly term consisted of 31 deputies, of whom 29 were part-time and only 2 full-time. As a result, most of its meetings were attended by about fifteen participants on an average (*Vietnam Economic Times*, May 2002). And this problem of part-time availability is further aggravated by the problem of competence.

Above and beyond these realities is the problem of internal Assembly functioning. Improving the efficiency of the National Assembly depends upon a clearly stated institutionalization of the jurisdiction and prerogatives of each player in the system: the Assembly's Standing Committee, the specialist committees, the provincial and municipal delegations, and others. Clarification is also needed "outside," with other players in the

Vietnamese political system. To cite only one unresolved example: How can part-time deputies who also work within such executive and judiciary bodies as the Supreme People's Court, the Supreme People's Procuracy, or the Ministry of Justice (or other institutions) simultaneously fulfill a supervisory role in the Assembly?

Questioning the National Assembly's Credibility

Party leaders and historical figures are at the opening and closing of important Assembly sessions, an indication of the relationship between the Party and the National Assembly. Sometimes these symbols go further: In June 2003, National Assembly Chairman Nguyen Van An (who is also a member of the Political Bureau of the Communist Party) left a parliamentary session in order to attend an important Party meeting with other Party leaders in Nghe An.

The close relationship with the Party may—or may not—be one reason why, despite significant reforms, many Vietnamese still doubt the credibility of the National Assembly. Public opinion polls conducted by the Office of the National Assembly seem to confirm this impression: the National Assembly's legislative activities are evaluated positively, but people are skeptical when it comes to the Assembly's decision-making capacities on important matters as well as its supervisory activities (Interview, Hanoi, June 2003). The credibility of official statements on the representatives' powers must go hand in hand with a demonstration of their strength. How can the population believe in the possibility of holding a no-confidence vote if that right is never exercised? Without concrete proof, these new arrangements, jurisdictions, and prerogatives are only words. The challenge is significant: reconciling the traditional organization of politics and functioning based on apparent consensus, the hiding of conflicting interests with the affirmation of an institution now based on debate and conflict and real supervision. How to introduce some discord into controlled political life is the most important long-term challenge for the National Assembly.

Conclusion

According to an official who has worked in the National Assembly for many years, the Assembly is "not yet powerful, but troublesome" (Interview, Hanoi, September 2003). The twelfth term of the National Assembly will be decisive in affirming the trends toward increased authority and capacity. The changes in the Assembly reflect Party policy, interests within the Assembly and its leadership, the evolution of the Vietnamese political system, and increasing demands from below. For many Vietnamese, the credibility of the political aspects of *doi moi* is to be found in the transformation of the National Assembly and the local assemblies. They also have a significant symbolic place in the demands of the regime's opponents (Abuza 2001, 95–103).

Despite this course of reform, the National Assembly and the Party must not be considered in terms of opposition or confrontation, but in terms of cooperation, a cooperation that is now signaled by the increasing political and protocol importance of the Chairman of the National Assembly, joining the General Secretary of the Party, the President, and the Prime Minister as the key Party and state officials. As considered by the Party and state, the National Assembly may be envisioned as a major economic and social forum, open to real debate, but generally limited to more technical problems. It is here that the political logic of the National Assembly reforms may rest.

References

Abuza, Zachary. 2001. *Renovating politics in contemporary Vietnam.* London: Boulder.

Beresford, Mélanie and Dang Phong. 1998. *Authority relations and economic decision-making in Vietnam: An historical perspective.* Copenhagen: Nordic Institute of Asian Studies.

Balfour, Frederick. 1997. *Slouching towards Democracy: Vietnam Elections Promise Few Surprises.* Agence France Press, July 16, 1997.

Bui Quoc Thanh. 2002. Ve hoan thien to chuc va doi moi noi dung hoat dong cua cac co quan chuyen mon cua Quoc hoi (On perfecting the organization and renewing the contents of activities by specialized organizations in the National Assembly). *Tap chi Cong san (Communist Review)* (August): 36–40.

Bunner, Georg. 1982. Legitimacy doctrines and legitimation procedures in East European systems. In *Political legitimation in Communist states.* Edited by T.H. Rigby and F. Feher. New York: St. Martin's Press, 27–44.

Do Tien Dung. 2004. 5 nam thuc hien cong tac tiep dan dinh ky (Five years of implementing the task of receiving the people). *Nguoi Dai bieu Nhan dan (The People's Representatives)* 159(80) (September): 4.

Do Van Tri. 2003. Thong tin cong chung cua Quoc hoi trong thoi ky doi moi (The National Assembly's public information in the period of renovation). *Nguoi Dai bieu Nhan dan (The People's Representatives)* 158 (79) (September 1): 5.

Fontanel, Alain. 2001. Les fonctionnaires au Viêt-Nam: une classe sociale en transition. Raisons politiques, (3) (August): 55–65.

Jeong Yeonsik. 1997. The rise of state corporatism in Vietnam. *Contemporary Southeast Asia* 19(2): 152–72.

Minh Duc. 2002. Tieng noi doanh nhan trong Quoc hoi (The managers' voice in the National Assembly). *Nghien cuu Lap phap (Legislative Studies)* 12: 14–16.

Nguyen Chi Dung. 2001. Tinh hinh xay dung phap luat hon 15 nam qua (The law building situation over the last 15 years). *Nghien cuu Lap phap (Legislative Studies)* 4–5: 56–60.

Nguyen Si Dung. 2002. "Quyet" o Quoc hoi (Decision making in the National Assembly). *Nghien cuu Lap phap (Legislative Studies)* 12: 3–4.

Salomon, Matthieu. 2004a. Les élections du 19 mai 2002 (XIème Assemblée Nationale): Processus de sélection et vote populaire dans le Vietnam contemporain. In *Le Vietnam à l'aube du XXIeme siècle. Bilan et perspectives politiques, économiques et socials*. Edited by C. Gironde and J.-L. Maurer. Paris: Khartala, 41–71.

———. 2004b. L'Assemblée Nationale dans la période du Doi Moi: lieu de renouvellement des élites politiques du régime communiste vietnammien? *Aséanie* 13: 103–24.

Salomon, Matthieu and Vu Doan Ket. 2007, forthcoming. Strategic and foreign relations: The case of the National Assembly: Modernization for normalization? In *Vietnam's strategic and foreign relations*. Edited by Carlyle A. Thayer. Singapore: Institute of Southeast Asian Studies.

Stern, Lewis. 1993. *Renovating the Vietnamese Communist Party: Nguyen Van Linh and the programme for organizational reform, 1987–1991*. Singapore: Institute of Southeast Asian Studies.

Vasavakul, Thaveeporn. 2002. *Rebuilding authority relations: Public administration in the era of Doi Moi*. Manila: Asian Development Bank.

Vietnam Economic Times. 2003. Power struggle, June 2003, 19.

Vietnamnet. 2005. Di la nguoi tra loi chat yan thuget phunchat? (Who Answers Question Time the Best?), www.vnn.vn, November 25.

C H A P T E R   T W E L V E

Modern Law, Traditional Ethics, and Contemporary Political Legitimacy in Vietnam

D AVID K OH

Introduction

I will start with an anecdote. On April 30, 1997, the day commemorating the twenty-second anniversary of the liberation of Saigon, I accidentally knocked down a lady while rushing on my motorbike. It was in front of the market that was commonly known as the Market of Hades (Chợ Âm phủ or the 19–12 Market)—quite an ominous sign. She fell and held her right ankle in agony, I braked and, leaving the motorbike engine roaring, tended to her immediately. Soon, a small crowd gathered in the middle of this four-lane road, and a few of them helped the lady back to her home, which somebody said was nearby.

Some people said I should wheel the motorbike to the lady's house, so that the traffic police (the state, here defined as the regime or rule of government) did not know about it and got no chance to make things difficult so as to extract bribes. I hesitated, for I had also read frequently in local newspapers that getting the owner to wheel the motorbike to the victim's home was only to subject him or her to endless demands from the victim's family. My motorbike could become hostage. But I was prepared to stand before the law for an act done without a driver's license and without proper vehicle registration.

Soon enough, the Hanoi city traffic police came. I was relieved of my motorbike and was asked to come back to their office in a few days for a statement. I went home and sought advice from neighbors; they told me I should go visit the victim immediately so as to take care of her ego, showing that I cared. I visited her daily with bags of fruits and bunches of flowers, and built much goodwill. My Vietnamese neighbors counseled me to persuade my victim to write some "advice" to the traffic police to say that I had looked after her well-being after the accident, by visiting and offering to pay for medical fees. She agreed; in addition, she also wrote that I should not be blamed for the accident and that the traffic police should return the motorbike to me. Further, she added that she would forgo all rights to make a claim for damages from either me or from the traffic police. Two days later, I claimed my motorbike from the traffic police. I suffered no fines for driving a motorbike without a license. It helped that the family of the lady was well known to the traffic police because she was the daughter-in-law of a senior Party official, and they lived on the same street.

This experience is personal but not singular. I have had similar accidents in Thai Nguyen province, in Ha Tay province, in Ho Chi Minh City, and in Hai Duong province. I have no doubt that the ways both people and agents of the state deal with each other on traffic matters, as I experienced, are widely practiced. The state quite paradoxically has a role and has no role, both at the same time. The state could have interfered and flexed its muscles. Its agents did so initially by retaining my motorbike, but later the state withdrew, seeing little social and public consequences. What I did was no doubt an offence against the state but in the end no untoward consequences befell me. I had also played my cards well vis-à-vis my victim. In the end, an offender such as me went unpunished. And such experiences appear to be spread across social and economic strata.

How can one make sense of the reality of the lack of maximum power in Vietnam—or the reticence in its use by the state? It seems no state will exert maximum power at every available opportunity. Even in a strong state such as Singapore, where every inch of the road is marked to keep it within a regime of rules and manifest state power, the government sees it fit to overlook some rules during religious and civic ceremonies. For example, parking offenses around mosques and churches on prayer days are deliberately ignored. In Vietnam, one of the reasons for the lack of maximum state power or the lack of its implementation is the disaggregation of the state. People in society are fully aware that the state—or each of the different parts of the state—acts in disaggregated and uncoordinated ways, with an overlay of traditional societal values about what is right, values that may not coincide with those of the state. If the state is analyzed bearing this in mind, behavior by state agents that openly contradicts declared state objectives may perhaps be meaningfully understood (Migdal 1994; Koh 2006). Disaggregation will show a variety of motivations that operate in different contexts, and therefore different results are to be expected. Yet it was not too long ago that Vietnam could lay claim to be a fairly tightly controlled society by the state. In a number of aspects it remains so, but these are less prominent, and political, aspects. In general, the daily routine in Vietnamese society is relatively free from constant, strict state control. Vietnamese state-society relations as a result are fairly complex, producing contradictory observations and conclusions on when, where, and how the state exercises its power.

Returning to my story, state capacity in Vietnam is a function not only of legality, power, and authority. It is also a function of ethics— norms that speak of the basis of interpersonal relations and society- individual relations, how they should be interpreted, and how those relations should be acted out. The ethical ethos that one comes to understand from my anecdote may be seen as akin to that of a small town, where much is done on trust and on goodwill, rather than enforced on a legal basis. The traffic police officers felt there was no need to create more work for themselves; and they felt it was troublesome to deal with foreigners who have offended the law. My concern touched the lady's heart, and she was willing to release me from any obligations because her injury, a swollen ankle, was slight and was neither permanent nor debilitating. I also did what a decent human being should have done. Elsewhere, such as in Singapore, I doubt that a similar accident would be treated in the same way. There would be insurance claims, state records, and punishment, and perhaps even civil suits. But Singaporean culture is not Vietnamese culture. Singapore, especially its legal culture, is heavily influenced by the British colonial legacy, while in Vietnam a strong rural tradition still informs many current practices and customs. The two imbue different sets of values and ethics and this is at least one significant reason why state-society relations are also different in the two countries.

The key question in this chapter, however, is the tension or synergy arising from the interaction between what the state wants and what society desires. In the case of Vietnam, integration with the world, as part of the globalization process, is an important driving force. To shed light on how globalization impacts on the state's ability to govern society, this chapter makes three points. First, there are interpersonal and social ethics that underlie state-society relations. Second, these ethics or values will change as global integration makes an impact on individuals, society, and the state. Third, as ethics change, so will state-society relations. The aim of this chapter is to discuss the ethics and visions of state-society relations in Vietnam. I will highlight how they have changed as the country opened up, and the likely changes as Vietnam's integration with the world intensifies.

The next section discusses the ethics of state power and state-society relations in Vietnamese history. The third section examines the imperatives for integration, and its initial impacts over the last twenty years. The final section discusses the implications for the state in its task of governance.

Ethics of Vietnamese State Power and State–Society Relations in History

Ethics and Visions in Vietnamese State-Society Relations

In the precolonial and premodern period, Vietnam had a monarchy that was both Confucianist and traditional in its basic ideas about how to organize state-society relations. Vietnam's kings had power and rights that were absolute; they had the "mandate of heaven." But they left local governance to locals and made alliances with influential families. A nexus between these families and local authority, provided that local authority was morally upright to an acceptable degree, held the peace and delivered the goals of feudal governance to central authorities. How local officials interpreted and acted on court instructions as well as on their own interests was an important feature of central-local relations. Taxes, for instance, were left to negotiations between the court and local officials. There was no doubt that the extent of central government control varied over time, but state power during this period stopped outside the fences of the village (*Phép vua thua lệ làng*). Under this Confucianist vision, the king undertook to protect the realm and its people in exchange for obedience and contributions from his subjects. Local authorities and other influential individuals mediated conflicts of interests between the central authority and the people (Marr 2004).

When the French colonized Vietnam they attempted at first to work with the system rather than against it, in Annam (Central Vietnam) and Tonkin (Northern Vietnam). In Cochin China (Southern Vietnam), the colonizers took a more direct approach to governance when it appointed colonial officials to oversee specialized areas and public administration at levels as low as the district. And precolonial state-society relations and ethics collapsed: the king lost power and authority in the eyes of his subjects when he could no longer protect them from the French. Gone was the vision of a stable cosmos; contrary opinions were heard about how the court had sold the people out in order to retain its position under French—and later under Japanese—rule. A whole discourse dwelt on how the Confucian order had set the nation backward and was thus unable to deal with the colonial onslaught. The Confucian social contract that underlay state-society relations was turned upside down. Similarly, the French colonialists had no legitimacy. In Cochin China, direct taxes heralded a new era of state-society relations that was not just oppressive; it was also seen to be unjust when compared to the Nguyen dynasty (Long 1973). It was unfamiliar to most Vietnamese used to dealing only with local officials. Adding to the trauma, the state now wanted to have a significant say in determining how much people paid in taxes, and it significantly reduced the role of local officials in mediating between the court and the people. The French had this modernizing vision that was contested from the time they set foot in Vietnam until long after they left. The old ethics in state-society relations had completely broken down.

In discussing the postindependence period, I concentrate on the North. The socialist period introduced, for the second time in a century, what may be termed a new set of ethics and vision in state-society relations. Class was crucially important. How one was treated depended on one's class. The state provided goods and services and in return demanded obedience from its people. The state had control of resources and determined who could consume those resources, and at what rate. But this vision or ethics of state-society relations stifled enthusiasm and discouraged excellence. Production became stymied and could not supply enough as other challenges to the country, including war and economic competition, further worsened the burdens. Citizens found ways to negotiate and circumvent the socialist production and distribution system, a system that was strict only in principle and tenuous in implementation. The proverb *the state has policies and the people have ways* (*Nước có sách, dân có cách*) epitomized the postindependence period (Tran Do 2000). People soon found ways: in general, the more resourceful ones enriched themselves, and those below them either enjoyed a spillover effect or continued to wait for handouts from the state. And thus the socialist vision of state-society relations broke down, the third time in less than two centuries that a vision of state-society relations had collapsed.

With *doi moi* came some fundamental change, although by no means was this new vision as articulated by the state accepted by society without suspicion. Note, for instance, that former Communist Party general secretary, Le Kha Phieu, lamenting the lack of vision, spoke of the progress that could be made if only the three billion dollars of "pillow" savings would be put into the formal banking system. But on what basis should the society trust primarily state-owned banks? Why should society believe the state's promise that it will not later put limits on withdrawals and take other steps that dwindle citizens' savings, as it happened in the late 1980s? State-owned banks had shown that they were willing to lend largely to major companies that could afford to mortgage property to guarantee repayment, and to state companies at the behest of politicians and bureaucrats. From the mid-1990s toward the present such scandals—Tamexco, Minh Phuong, La Thi Kim Oanh are the best known—occurred at regular intervals.

Therefore, it takes much more than a vision for the state to have its ethics accepted by citizens. The basis of the legitimacy of ethics is action, while vision takes a leap of faith. In Vietnam, the vision of a rich nation (where individuals could openly show and declare themselves owners of production resources and wealth) is stunted. That vision is not backed up by guarantees of strong rules and ethical practices in corporate governance as well as in strong government action to make sure that rules are fair between the haves and the have-nots, and between those that set the rules and those that are its subjects. To a certain extent, the motto that many Vietnamese hold, at least with regard to their assets, is to "trust no one, least the state." Nevertheless, from the second stage of *doi moi* (from the early 1990s) the state has tried to move toward a law-based system, though with the continuing and serious problems of a weak and corrupt judicial system and significant conflicts of interest within and among the legislative, executive, and judicial realms.

This broad historical sketch is by no means comprehensive, but it is intended to give a sense of the issues relating to "ethics and visions in state-society relations." Other problems also recur: through what means do people exercise power in their relations with the state, and how much power do they have; to what extent and on what basis do people accept state authority, and what are the specific rights and obligations that state and society owe each other; and what are the codification of rights and obligations and the challenges to them?

What I term ethics in state-society relations play an important part in all these considerations. Ethics also do not remain stagnant; they evolve over time and often the gap between the state's vision and what society can accept help produce dynamics that lead up to change in state-society relations. Many governments understand this and have tried to regulate or control information and cultural influences that their subjects receive from overseas.

The Imperatives for Integration and Their Initial Impact

Vietnamese integration with the outside world had, of course, begun earlier than the influences of globalization in the 1990s. But globalizing influences have been faster and more intense than in earlier history. In Vietnam, precolonial era contact with the outside world rarely took place on terms of equality: it was either with the Chinese, whom the Vietnamese saw as stronger, or other ethnicities and nations on the Indo-China peninsula, such as the Cham, the Thai, and the Cambodians, whom the Vietnamese saw as less than equals. The West came, but the Nguyen dynasty looked down on westerners as barbarians and sought to close Vietnam's doors to them, following China's example. With colonialism came many compelling influences from the West. During the French colonial period and the American War, the urban areas of the south, especially Saigon, may have been the most globalized regions of Vietnam, taking in Western values and ways of life. In the 1950s and beyond, the north was the epitome of socialization by socialism that was sourced from China, Russia, and Eastern Europe. Was this not a form of globalization as well? As the war with Cambodia started to wind down in the late 1980s, Vietnam began to attract foreign investment, especially from East Asia. With the normalization of relations between Vietnam and the United States in the mid-1990s and the growth of American, western European, and other investment, globalization is truly a thing of the past for Vietnam.

These stages of history have given Vietnam's globalization a layered texture. In the North during the wars against the French and the Americans, there was a strong influence of things Chinese, from food to fashion. After Vietnam joined CMEA and received huge amounts of Soviet aid, the Russian and Eastern European layer grew stronger. When the Japanese, Taiwanese, and Koreans arrived in Vietnam with investments, they too brought cultural and social influences. The growth in marriages of Taiwanese to Vietnamese, and the picture of Saigon's Korea town on Pham Van Hai Street are but two examples of these currents. The imperatives for integration are urgent and the calculations are economic in nature. Globalization involves a reasonably open door to investment, flows of capital and technology, flow of goods without tax impediments, social reforms of various kinds, and other changes. The way Vietnamese do business with the outside world must also adapt to existing international practices and adhere to international rules and standards.

Awareness of these needs in Vietnam became even more acute when China became a major source for international funds and investments. In the 1980s, Vietnam competed with China for foreign direct investment. By the late 1990s, Vietnam had lagged behind, even as it enjoyed years of strong growth during the intervening years, joining other countries in seeking to resolve issues relating to economic competition from China.

More than a decade after the Internet came to Vietnam, Western ideas today are creeping into the minds of the young. Given this age of satellite television, Internet, instantaneous relay of information to places all over the world, no system of interpersonal and social ethics can be fenced in and expected to remain unaltered. This is also the case for the values underpinning state–society relations.

Immediate Impact on State-Society Relations

From a Communist Ideal to the Developmental State could be the heading of a study devoted to studying how the state in Vietnam has altered the basis of its claim to rule in an uncompetitive political environment (Vasavakul 1995). How legitimacy is justified affects the way the state plays its part in state–society relations. As the country continues its global integration, the Vietnamese Communist Party has had to face an essential challenge. Although its ideological rhetoric continues to be based on Marxist-Leninism, in reality what it *must* do over time, because globalization requires increasing conformity with international practice, will have less and less to do with Marxism-Leninism. In present-day Vietnam a concern with what works for Vietnam often conflicts with ideological visions about its future, and there is little doubt that integration now takes priority over ideology.

Governability

One initial impact is the governability of Vietnamese society. The dominant value before the open-door era was national commitment to victory in an era of war. Personal interest gave way to collective interest. That made the job of governance much easier and state–society relations a more sedate affair. However, some individuals did not give up rights without a fight. The most famous such struggle was the Nhân Văn Giai Phẩm affair. A group of elite literary writers and publishers struggled with the state for the right to publish independently and to write without having to place the values of revolutionary struggle at the center of their work. The state clearly triumphed in that struggle (Heng 2000). In the late 1960s, the Kim Ngoc affair caused ripples of a different sort in state-society relations. Kim Ngọc, Party Secretary of Vĩnh Phú province, experimented with an agriculture contract system that would have given individual farmers incentive to produce more by promising higher returns. This was a heresy to the orthodoxy of collective farming of the time; Kim Ngoc was censured and the experiment stopped. These were the two examples of defiance, at the elite level, that occurred before the current era of integration.

In the early 1980s, the state tried to impose a collective farming system in the south but failed. This failure came, of course, after the war, and after a period of three decades in which southern society had experienced a different set of relations with another state. In the south it was virtually impossible to persuade individuals to follow the socialist state's visions and abide by the ethics of that vision.

In fact, as Tran Do, the retired general turned strong critic of the Vietnamese Communist Party, indicated in his memoirs, during his travels across the country after the Vietnam War, he sensed a desire for the relaxation of state controls, and a frustration on the part of individuals who sought a restructuring of state-society relations so that individuals could do what they wanted, at least where livelihood matters were concerned. The Vietnam War had ended, national unification had been achieved, and people saw no need to sacrifice their entire selves, their private goals and aspirations, for the revolution.

The Fourth Party National Congress of 1976 issued a call to continue to work collectively for the goal of building socialism, but the response was much less enthusiastic than the response to work for national liberation and unification. These calls were idealistic and ideological, but values are useful only if they can provide a guide to practical action. Coming as they did in the forms that took away private rights, diminished incentive to work, and distributed misery rather than happiness, they were not sustainable. Fence-breaking offences from the late 1970s onward showed that clearly. In time, the Party was forced to recognize that not only was the state's vision of socialist production and distribution flawed, unrealistic, and therefore unpopular, but that the ethics of a majority of its own employees, from top to bottom, have also been acting in ways contrary to that vision. In late 2005, the newspaper *Tuoi Tre* carried a series of articles by local administrators and policymakers of the late 1970s and early 1980s reminiscing—*taking pride*—in their successful attempts in avoiding man-made disasters by acting against cardinal rules of the socialist system. The former Prime Minister, Vo Van Kiet, for example, described how, when he was Party Secretary in Ho Chi Minh City, people would have died of starvation if he had not ordered Saigon's state banks to loan funds to the city's food supply office to purchase rice from Mekong Delta provinces at rates much higher than state-set prices. The decision to act against the central state's ethics meant standing on the side of society. By any standard, it was daring and heroic.

After 1986, when Vietnam consciously decided to open its door to the outside world, the state found the nation much more difficult to govern than in the past. The *doi moi* years saw the upholding of individual values; persons were allowed more freedom in virtually all spheres of life, although the exact nature of the freedom—a paper concession or a hard, long-term fact—was often up for negotiation. Individuals' rights were predominant, and in some instances they may have been unduly emphasized at the expense of the interests of the collective, with the pendulum perhaps swinging too far toward the individual. Note, for example, the popular demands in 2005 for the recognition of the widest possible interpretation of the Constitutional right of individuals to own property over the policy of restricting motor vehicle registration in Hanoi. In the end, ownership rights were considered more important than other public demands to reduce air pollution and traffic congestion. Political rights have been returned to the individual, but not fully resembling what one would find in Western countries, or Singapore, which arguably has a model of politics closer to that of Vietnam than of the West.

In the late 1980s, some state obligations (such as rations) to individuals were cut this also reduced the need for individuals to glance over their shoulders. These moves instead forced individuals to look to market and nonstate factors for signals on personal economic decisions. With this return, after many years, of same rights and responsibilities to individuals, the state has found it more difficult to impose and direct its own will. Governance, more than ever, would have to rely on incentives and punishments based on law.

Private Sector Growth

A second impact of integration has been the rise of the private sector. In 2003, a consultant from Singapore belatedly wanted to start a research project on planting the seeds of the idea of private sector development in Indochina countries, including Vietnam. In Vietnam the idea and reality of the private sector (often conflated with the household sector) had been very much alive but suppressed in the early *doi moi* years. But in the last five years or more, the private sector has flourished, with economic contributions coming mainly through small scale, low capital, labor intensive, and easily-started retail and small-time production businesses. In the rural areas, the combination of individual and private sector rights has triggered a boom in the agriculture sector and a decline, probably the eventual death, of the agricultural cooperatives sector. And in the context of the Asian financial crisis, other dynamics have pushed the Vietnamese leadership to seek to transform the domestic private sector into an engine of growth. These dynamics include competition with other economies at the international level, as well as obligations under multilateral trade and investment agreements. The government's revision of the Enterprise Law in 2000, which combined the prior domestic investment law and company law, gave increased legitimacy and importance to the private sector. Above all, the Tenth Party National Congress of 2006 ushered in important changes in the forms of ownership protected by law. It further extended individual rights by expanding the categories of ownership beyond the whole people and collective to include individual and private business. The private sector will continue to grow as an important pillar of the Vietnamese economy, with its contribution to state revenues at 7% in 2004 and growing at 13% annually. Between 2000 and 2004, the amount of registered capital for new private enterprises reached nearly US$10 billion, which surpassed the level of foreign direct investment in the same period. The private sector also captured 48% of the country's non-oil exports (Le Dang Doanh 2004).

The impact of the rise of private sector on state-society relations may be smaller than that of returning rights to individuals. State companies still hold a dominant share of the economy; major companies are still in government control, although there is a plan to privatize some of the large state monopolies in order to mobilize funds and kick the sluggish stock market into action (Le Xuan Sang 2004). Government policies regarding private sector in this era are not just about liberalization, but also about helping the state by playing a role in achieving national goals (*Tuoi Tre* 2004).

The chief aims of allowing the private sector is for the state to recognize private property rights and to allow individuals (including Party members) to form companies and other entities, and to invest in any kind of property or economic activity without fear of nationalization. The longer the private sector is able to operate, the stronger the society's trust will be in the state's continued adherence to its own rules. The underlying issue is the extent to which society can trust the state, given a history of nationalization, betrayal of promises, and sudden reversals in important economic policies until the early 1990s. Here, globalization has a role to play. The more the foreign investors trust the Vietnamese state (as measured by flow), the more likely the state will be to consider not just domestic unrest and even revolt, but also the international dimensions and adverse responses, in how it views private property.

Rule of Law and the Emphasis on Rules

Many observers of socialist Vietnam have commented on lawlessness, which has several meanings. The first is lack of respect for the rule of law. Law, where it existed had been superseded by government directives or by prevailing ethics and norms that may have conflicted with the text of statutes and regulations. The lack of rule of law in Vietnam also reflects the state's lack of respect for the sanctity and permanence of law; the Party and government viewed the law as an instrument of politics to be altered or reversed by the same cowed parliamentary process that established the original law without giving it powers of review or challenge in the invariably Party- and government-controlled courts. Under such a politico-legal system, the centre of gravity in state-society relations was certainly on the side of the state. The lack of rule of law in Vietnam has also been spoken of in a third sense: individuals readily ignoring written rules to do what they want instead of obeying the state's visions and view of ethics. Informal contracts and understandings in lieu of written contracts have often been, in fact, the predominant forms of business transactions.

Doi moi saw important changes in the Vietnamese legal system, although they cannot be detailed in this chapter. But the spirit of the changing role of law in state-society relations has been important. In the early 1990s came a push not only to legislate more, but also better. From better legislation came the question of state accountability to the law and the legal reordering of state-society relations. This has required adjustment on the part of the state. For instance, over the last ten years we have seen more and more cases of illegal electoral practices, instances of which have been documented by the mass media. The Party and state have generally allowed the law to run its course and to prescribe remedial action. Abuses of the legal system by state officers—including framing innocents and faking evidence—were covered up in the past. But by 2004, the media and defense lawyers had exposed many such practices, and public prosecutors and police had apologized for these misdeeds. Whether those wrongly convicted will be able to sue the state is the next key question in this development.

One of the most significant of the rule of law issues involves the reclamation of dwellings wrongly confiscated from citizens during the socialist period. The confiscations were wrong because they had no legal basis. The state has admitted that these actions were wrong and agreed either to return the dwellings or to compensate the victims. Legal reform issues are complex, but this arena seems to have witnessed some far-reaching changes in state-society relations. Increasingly, within the main legislative body, the National Assembly, discussions of the constitutionality of legislative or state acts are held. In 2004, for example, the National Assembly debated the legitimacy of the Ministry of Finance in deciding to impose taxation on higher-income brackets and on profits derived from the sale of land use rights without prior approval from the National Assembly—in essence a debate on Constitutional ordering, not on the authority of the government to levy taxes (Nghia Nhan 2004).

The increased emphasis on rule of the law has affected implementation of government policies and relations in society. More law is often thought to mean more rationality, and less sentimentality. Although socialist Vietnam has always had laws, implementation has often been weak, especially if the situation seemed to have a strong humanistic angle that warranted considerations beyond legality. Such exceptions usually strike a harmonious chord with prevailing values of state-society relations. But in recent years, there has been a greater readiness to resort to judicial process, even though prevailing values would suggest that disputes are best settled outside the courtroom. A specific case may illustrate these conflicting issues, including the difficult path of the rule of law and the complex relationship between values, ethics, and the legal system, along with the diffidence of local authorities in private matters.

The B family lives on a large plot of land of several hundred square meters in what was considered the outskirts of Hanoi more than a century ago. In those years, the city's dead were buried in the vicinity of where the B family home is located today, and few living souls wanted to reside there. The children of the main branch of this family had gone away for many years, and in the years after 1945 hardly any young members of the main branch of the family stayed in Hanoi to look after the old and feeble. B.K., a nephew of the B family, married in the 1950s and needed a place to stay. As a familial gesture the family patriarch asked this couple to stay with them and asked the young bride to help look after the ailing matriarch. According to B.K. and his wife, the patriarch promised them that in return for this kind deed, they would have the right to live in the family house forever. But nothing was said about ownership, and there were no papers signed and filed with the state to give recognition and legal status to this agreement. In the days before the revolution, such matters were not given priority in Hanoi. After the war broke out and older people died, the B.K. family became the sole occupiers of this plot of land, while the children of the main lineage continued to live elsewhere and were given housing by the state. So long as it was almost impossible, because informal transactions were still possible, to sell land and houses in the socialist economy, the matter could have stopped there.

But when the market economy boomed under *doi moi*, packaged with the right to buy and sell land and houses and with the right to keep the profits, the direct descendants the B family decided it was time to take back what was rightfully theirs. They petitioned the court for the return of their assets, claiming that B.K. and his descendants were relatives who had merely been lodging temporarily and should now leave. The B.K. family did not challenge the claim that they did not own the house, but they insisted they had the promise of the late patriarch and that they would not move. After the case went from district court to a higher municipal court, the B.K. family lost. A meager compensation of about 10% of the cost of an old flat elsewhere was given to B.K. It was a disheartening result for B.K. and his wife because they had lived in the neighborhood for over half a century; the house was as good as theirs in their hearts, if not on paper.

B.K. and his family refused to move out. At the request of the other side, the municipal court issued an eviction order, and this eviction order was given to the ward authority (a level of urban local administration beneath the district) to execute. The ward authority objected to the court order, telling the court and the petitioners that it knew the B.K. family very well and that the family had contributed tremendously to the revolution as well as to the grassroots work of the ward authority, and that their presence had been very important to the well-being of the departed elders in their last years. But the most effective argument provided by the ward, citing the Constitution and a housing ordinance, was that the old B.K. couple would have no place to stay if they were evicted, requiring that at least some rights be safeguarded. And, of course, the petitioners did have a place to live. The ward's position was that the petitioners should buy equivalent homes for B.K. and his wife and one each for their four children before the ward authority could agree to executive eviction. (The four children were living elsewhere but their residential registration was still with their parents.) With such an enormous obstacle to enforcement—the cost of five homes in Hanoi in 2006 was about half a million U.S. dollars—the petitioners had to suspend their plans to re-acquire what was originally, and legally, their property. But the B.K. family was also put on notice that they did not have the right to sell the house.

Role of Family

As Vietnam integrates with the world, the Vietnamese state has found that using the family as the primary unit of accountability in state-society relations is no longer as effective a method for social management as it was in earlier eras. In the socialist period, each family was one household (hộ); every household had a booklet that recorded the personal details of its members, details that could be altered only with the permission of the state. Every household received from the state social welfare (other than consumption necessities), including housing, based on the number of people recorded in the book. Linked to the household registration booklet was the sổ gạo or rice booklet that stipulated how much rice the family was entitled to buy within a period of time. To add or delete a member from the registration booklet was a major decision that had to take into consideration benefits and costs, especially with regards to what people could claim from the state's provision of goods and services. Changes to the booklet had to be certified and approved by the local authority. If the book was lost, the household theoretically ceased to exist in the eyes of the distributors of goods and services from the state.

The idea of household now has decreasing relevance in state-society relations, because today the family in Vietnam is arguably not as closely knit as in earlier eras. In the past, in the face of difficulties posed by the economy as well as the state, family members had to band together against common difficulties. *Doi moi*'s economic and social milieu offers more opportunities for everyone as individuals. Although family connections certainly do help, opportunities are also more diverse as new sectors of the economy open and new jobs are created. A growing number of individuals who work for nonfamily economic units are expected to perform as individuals; and many more individuals than before qualify for jobs on their credentials rather than due to their blood. Many more families now live at greater distances from each other as cities expand; the crossing of economic space within the country and overseas has become easier.

It is increasingly difficult for the state to sanction what it wishes through the household or its head. Individuals in the family have been freed from notions of absolute security (via strong support for the state in the face of external aggression) that inflicted earlier families, and it is more difficult for the head of a household to control household members if he does not any longer control all the basic resources within that entity. State attempts to do so continue. When the state wants to implement a policy with wide public implications, ward officials and police usually approach the head of the household, as was the case in the prereform era. The household head, informed of state policy, is expected to propagate that policy to his family members. In the past, according to families in Hanoi and elsewhere in Vietnam, household heads would usually have made some effort to have the family comply because necessary supplies were at stake. But with reforms and the arrival and growth of markets, regularity of supplies depends primarily on disposable income and not on obedience to the state.

Demonstration Effects: The Demand for Accountability

Finally, integration also brings important demonstration effects in matters of governance. As globalization proceeds rapidly, these effects can be deeply felt. Such effects were important in earlier times, to be sure: National liberation, independence, and democracy were ideas that shaped the world and spread to almost all countries, including Vietnam, in the last 150 years. Their success elsewhere demonstrated to Vietnamese that it should be their right to demand that those ideals be realized in Vietnam as well.

In more recent times, the idea of accountability in governance has found currency and support. In the Third World, especially in countries in transition, accountability has, at least rhetorically, proven popular for regimes, donors, and international organizations alike. Vietnam renewed the process of building accountability in governance, a process that began in the early 1980s, with public administrative reforms and the strengthening of bureaucratic capacity and ethics. These reforms will require many years to be successful. And while public administration reform may fail to achieve some or all of its objectives, they can succeed in raising awareness on the part of *both* bureaucrats and the people they serve. This awareness in turn raises expected standards of service and the acceptability level of public policy outcomes.

This rise in expectations is also a result of the demonstration effect. More and more Vietnamese have, during their overseas experience, seen patterns and quality of public service and governance that are a world apart from their experience in Vietnam. Reactions to such influences can of course vary, ranging from promoting reforms at home to discouragement, frustration, or even despair. But for those who seek to improve conditions in Vietnam, demonstrations abroad can become reference points or "best practices" to serve as markers of desired goals. Donors, businesses, and international organizations also demand change, backed up by aid and investment funds, and the Party and state have shown a capacity to listen through meetings and exchanges, often conducted at a very high level.

The impact on state-society relations is clear: Society has different and growing expectations of the state. And in this, the media has an important role to play. Theoretically the Vietnamese media is fully controlled by the Party and state, but the media regularly (and either subtly or not so subtly) turns up its nose at the state. The Vietnamese press gives air to the lungs of a society dissatisfied for many years with the state and its bureaucratic actors. And as the state supports accountability in governance and public administration reform, individuals have gradually also gained greater confidence in their views and rights.

The most obvious example of this point is the assertiveness of the National Assembly, a process that is ironically but decidedly state-engineered. Another example is the greater tendency for individuals to air their grievances and complaints in the mass media, directly expecting particular political authorities to address them. There is thus greater attention being paid to strengthening laws on denunciations and registering complaints (*Lao Dong Dien Tu* 2004). When wrongs to individuals are addressed, when the National Assembly embarrasses government ministers into apology or resignation, ripples can occur around the country—especially when these events are reported in the mass media, sometimes live on television.

Some Implications for the Vietnamese
State in Its Governance Tasks

These changes in policy, and perhaps values, also impact on governance. First, tensions cluster—between ideology and reality, between vision and practice, and between the collective and individuals. These tensions make the task of governance much more difficult, for a dominating state and its dominating vision are no longer present, and contending social forces and visions have emerged. These tensions also require the state to weigh policies and seek to strike a balance between its own interests and society's desires, in the absences of a dominating ideology that provides an operational context for both state and individuals. There is an increasing divergence among policy options that puts the Party and state in a spot—should it go with what works, or with what its ideology dictates?

In addition, a broader range of individual rights is coming under legal protection, and government policies are being drafted and implemented. One issue at the core of these problems is the right guaranteed to Communist Party members to engage in free markets and business enterprises. Communist Party documents may not have as yet stated this clearly or loudly, but the Prime Minister has declared that "The [Tenth] Party Congress will allow Party members to engage in business irrespective of the size of the business" ("*Dai hoi Dang se cho phep Dang vien lam kinh te khong phan biet quy mo lon nho*") (*Lao Dong Dien Tu* 2006).

To avoid increasing tension, the nature of governance in Vietnam has become much more tolerant of diversity in its views and action. The road to reduced conflict and lesser tensions should mean greater governability, and greater diversity and flexibility through increasing the range of lawful activities, rather than a disapproving state. This requires stronger law and an ever more strengthened rule of law in society, including working assiduously on the serious problems of implementation. While it may not be in the nature of Vietnamese society to challenge existing paradigms every day, the wiliness of the people honed from decades of experience in dealing with the state continues to engage and pressure the state in its governance roles, every day and at every level. Individuals generally know enough not to challenge the Party and state directly on political and security issues, where older paradigms and measures still prevail. In other arenas, however, it is fair game.

How the state earns society's trust is a second, related issue. A continued emphasis on the rule of law, perhaps holding even the highest office holders to account, may help in building that trust. Opening this accountability to public scrutiny—and undertaking it through legal mechanisms, rather than only through murky, often hidden, Party disciplinary policy and rules—would certainly also help. Key cases of discipline resolved on the basis of written law applicable to all would be important, though such processes are difficult in the Vietnamese political environment, where the decision to proceed with public use of law to punish errant senior officials can be fraught with political conflict and danger. Beyond the political arena, a more equal economic playing field may help engender a spirit of trust in the state's actions in the economic sphere. Inflexible policy, corruption, and other impediments make the realization of new policies and values more difficult, but a start has been made.

Globalization and markets have also had a substantial effect on the revolutionary spirit that drove governance in the past. A call to work and sacrifice in the revolutionary spirit certainly no longer motivates society or attracts talent in an era of different values, porous borders, and multiple external influences. Those whose work and whose families' lives have been dramatically and positively influenced by and benefited from Vietnam's integration with the broader world—a skin grafting specialist in Singapore, a demographer in Seattle, an economist in Australia, a trader in Angola, a businesswoman in Moscow—cannot be faulted for making choices that may seem less nationalistic at a time when a revolutionary spirit provides less of a guide to Vietnamese action. The broader and more difficult challenge for the state is how to foster and harness such talents now that individuals, within or outside the country, are influenced by a broader range of values and options than those of the state.

Conclusion

The Vietnamese state has now seized the globalization and integration agenda and has made its political longevity dependent on it. The Vietnamese state has long existed in a complex relationship with society. But the state has conceded more ground to society by relaxing a wide range of social controls. This is, perhaps ironically, how the one party regime may survive, as globalization helps (it is hoped) build prosperity and burnishes the credentials of the Communist Party as the political force most able to deliver the goods to the people of Vietnam. But since legitimacy through economic performance may not be sufficient to sustain an uncompetitive political environment, there have also been simultaneous moves to order state-society relations on a strong legal footing. This is a significant but very difficult and conflict-fraught step, from the political to the legal, to retool the state's basis to claim obedience from its subjects. But it is important, however, to note that in the prereform days the Vietnamese state was not always able to get its way through society, and the current means of seeking legitimacy may encounter ongoing difficulties as well.

References

Heng, Russell. 2000. *Of the state, for the state, yet against the state: The struggle paradigm in Vietnam's media politics*. Doctoral dissertation. Department of Political & Social Change, The Australian National University.

Koh, David. 2006. *Wards of Hanoi*. Singapore: Institute of Southeast Asian Studies.

Lao Dong Dien Tu. 2004. Thong qua Luat sua doi, bo sung mot so dieu cua Luat khieu nai to cao va 2 quy che hoat dong cua Quoc hoi (Adoption of the amended Law on Complaints and Denunciations and two National Assembly regulations), *Lao Dong Dien Tu*, June 1, 2004. Online at www.laodong.com.vn, accessed August 16, 2006.

———. 2006. Phai xay dung tieu chuan dac thu chu DN o mot dat nuoc di theo con duong XHCN. *Lao Dong Dien Tu*, January 27, 2006. Online at www.laodong.com.vn, accessed August 16, 2006.

Le Dang Doanh. 2004. The Enterprise Law and the development of the domestic private business sector in Vietnam. Hanoi: International Policy Conference on Transition Economics.

Le Xuan Sang. 2004. Developing the stock market in China: Are there any lessons to be learnt for Vietnam? Unpublished paper, January 19, 2004, Institute of Southeast Asian Studies, Singapore.

Marr, David G. 2004. A brief history of local government. In *Beyond Hanoi: Local government in Vietnam*. Edited by Benedict J. Tria Kerkvliet and David G. Marr. Singapore: Institute of Southeast Asian Studies, 28–53.

Migdal, Joel S. 1994. The state in society: An approach to struggles for domination. In *State power and social forces: Domination and transformation in the Third World*. Edited by Joel S. Migdal, Atul Kohli and Vivienne Shue. Cambridge: Cambridge University Press, 9–29.

Nghia Nhan. 2004. Chua danh thue thu nhap cao voi viec mua ban dat. *VNExpress*, March 3, 2004. Online at vnexpress.net/Vietnam/Kinh-doanh/2004/03/3B9D042F, accessed August 16, 2006.

Ngo Vinh Long. 1973. *Before the revolution: Vietnamese peasants under the French*. Cambridge: MIT Press.

Tran Do. 2000. *Doi moi, niem vui chua tron*. California: Van Nghe.

Tuoi Tre. 2004. Thuc hien triet de viec ke khai tai san, thu nhap can bo. *VNExpress*, 5 April 2004. Online at vnexpress.net/Vietnam/Xa-hoi/2004/04/3B9D14FC accessed August 16, 2006.

Vasavakul, Thaveeporn. 1995. Vietnam: The changing models of legitimation. In *Political legitimacy in Southeast Asia*. Edited by Muthiah Alagappa. Stanford: Stanford University Press, 257–89.

CHAPTER THIRTEEN

Building Blocks for the Rule of Law?

Legal Reforms and Public Administration in Vietnam

KARIN BUHMANN

Introduction

As part of the general reform process since the introduction of *doi moi*, Vietnam has undertaken a number of changes of its legal system and legislation in its transition from a socialist planned economy to a market-based economic system. Reforms of the organizational and substantive legislation relating to the public administration, procedures, and complaints have formed part of the overall public administration reforms. Public administration reforms focusing on streamlining and increasing efficiency of administrative governance systems and procedures have involved not only a decentralization and delegation of certain powers to local authorities, but also a range of measures to provide for clearer and simpler administrative procedures, transparency, and remedies against administrative acts.

This chapter discusses some of the legislative measures introduced as part of the post–*doi moi* legal reforms in order to improve governance in the public administration and especially to improve due administrative process and provide for remedies against administrative acts. The reforms and specific measures have been selected for their potential for building rule of law, and they are discussed from that perspective.

Public Administration Reform, Due
Administrative Process, and the Rule of Law

In public administration reforms, administrative governance is often seen as closely related to strengthening the effective and efficient management of public resources. However, for due administrative process to be in place, effectiveness and efficiency of administrative governance is not sufficient: there must also be accountability and transparency. Legislative reforms and the general existence of legislation providing for remedies and transparency of administrative acts form an important element in establishing due administrative process and may at the same time contribute to building the rule of law.

There is no universally accepted definition of the term "rule of law," nor of the related but substantively different term "rule by law" (e.g., Peerenboom 1999, 2002). However, there appears to be general agreement that rule *by* law is narrower than rule *of* law. It is implicit in the term "rule by law" that it is mainly concerned with legality, that is, procedure, and less with substance, less with the autonomous power of law. The *rule of law* is an important element in the modern accountable state that respects the rights and interests of natural and legal persons, provides for remedies, and uses law for these purposes. The rule of law is also a key concept in the respect and protection of human rights (Buhmann 2001; Peerenboom 1999, 2001). Through its conceptual implications of legality and prevention of arbitrariness in the exercise of state power, the rule of law implies that the individual should enjoy safeguards against exercise of power that arbitrarily and adversely affects his or her integrity, rights and freedom. This means observance of equality, proportionality, and qualitative legality.

The notion of rule of law should be distinguished from *rule by law*. In a continuum going from anarchy to *rule of men* ending with the *rule of law*, rule by law would be placed between a rule of men and the rule of law (Liisberg 1999). Rule by law denotes a rule that is simply exercised according to law, but without the legal guarantees to provide safeguards against abuse of state power and to provide for equality and independent remedies that are implied in the rule of law. The notion of the rule of law implies an assumption that rule is not only in accordance with law but also based in law, and that the law that forms this basis is of a certain quality based on equality before the law and respect of rights and interests of natural and legal persons. Rule by law simply implies that governance is exercised on the basis of law. In its pure form, the notion does not hold any assumption or guarantee that this law is of a particular quality regarding equality before the law and respect for subjects' rights or interests, or that the law is imbued with safeguards or remedies against abuse of state power.

A political expression of a decision to build a state *ruled by* law does not necessarily mean the creation or existence of *rule of* law. It is possible to have a highly detailed legal framework, without observing the rule of law. Weaknesses in the quality of the legislation, in equality before the law and legal certainty, in access to and independence of remedies, and in enforcement mechanisms, all may lead to low levels of the rule of law in a state otherwise formally governed by law. Legality does not necessarily lead to governance in accordance with the rule of law. Law can be discriminatory or made for the purpose of serving the state's ends rather than the protection of rights and interests of the populace. If governance is exercised on the basis of such laws, it may be in contravention of the rule of law, even though a principle of legality (in rule by law) is technically observed.

It is therefore not only possible but also necessary to distinguish rule of law from the notion of rule by law. However, in assessing reforms of law and other legal developments against the notion of rule of law, it is useful and sometimes necessary to keep the notion of rule by law in mind. Rule by law denotes an extent of law and order. Rule by law may apply to authoritarian regimes in partial or extensive contravention of some or all of the principles of rule of law except for technical legality. On the other hand, rule by law may also signify a stepping-stone toward the rule of law. This could be the case for a state in a transitional process from "rule of man" (authoritarianism) toward a more or less clearly defined goal of rule of law (Dang and Beresford 1998). If law is taken as the basis for exercise of governance, but without an aim of protecting subjects against abuse of state power, for example, in the form of corruption, a state and its use of law may be closer to rule by law. Making a distinction between rule of law and rule by law may serve to precisely target the development of rule of law in enabling partners in a reform process, such as the on-going Vietnamese reform process to address rule of law weaknesses.

Increased transparency and accountability in administration, the executive arm of government, potentially helps decrease abuse of administrative power. To be effective, there must not only be accountability to an administrative body responsible for making a decision but also access to information. Accountability must be supplemented by access to administrative review, ideally by a body empowered to make decisions on redress or compensation of damages, and by access to judicial review by an independent court of law (Council of Europe 1996). Due to their inherent—if secondary—functions as measures of control, access to remedies and transparency provided by administrative law potentially contributes to due process in the administrative arena. Simultaneously, reforming administrative law to provide for remedies and transparency provides an avenue for a regime to improve its observance of the rule of law.

Post–*Doi Moi* Reforms of Administrative Law: The Potential for Building the Rule of Law

The Obstacles

The socialist legal system of Vietnam and the arrangements for public administration allow executive bodies at various levels of government considerable legislative and quasi-legislative powers and considerable exercise of discretion in implementing legislation and regulating the work of the state and society. Reports prepared prior to the launch of the current 2001–10 Public Administration Reform (PAR) Master Programme identified a number of obstacles to effective law-based administrative governance and due administrative process. A lack of clear boundaries between the substantive areas of different government agencies, as well as legislative or quasi-legislative powers of local executive and jurisdictional bodies, allow different agencies to make regulations pertaining to the same substantive area. This resulted in overlaps and inconsistencies, nonuniform application of legal provisions, and fragmentation of administrative power (Rose 1998; Dinh et al. 2000; Hoang et al. 2000). Lower level administrative bodies may be subordinate to more than one higher-level body at various government levels. These organizational structures create difficulties for organizations and individuals in identifying the correct higher level body concerning a particular issue under regulation and have been recognized to result in overlapping responsibilities in some areas, gaps in others, duplication of work, and difficulties in deciding which body to be held accountable for a decision or for faulty or deficient implementation (Dinh et al. 2000). Excessive regulation and cumbersome administrative procedures lead to opportunities for abuse of power and corruption by state officials. Faulty and opaque implementation of legislation and inefficient supervision and investigation of violations of law (Dinh et al. 2000; Hoang et al. 2000) negatively affect respect for individuals' lawful rights and their effective exercise of rights to complain and obtain judicial review.

The Vietnamese Party and state have officially recognized that along with increased market reforms, corruption is growing and developing into more sophisticated forms that sometimes involve cooperation between government officials and the private sector (Buhmann 2001). Corruption and other forms of abuse of power, including those committed by high-level officials, have been met with severe penalties, including the death penalty, serving partly as a deterrent measure. The effectiveness of these measures—particularly given the sense of continuing and significant corruption—is debated in Vietnam.

Public Administration Reform

By the mid-1990s, the Vietnamese state had defined public administration reform as a pressing need and central task in Vietnam's development process. The main objectives of Vietnam's public administration reform were defined as the development of a competent, clean, and transparent administration that does not abuse its powers and manages the affairs of the state effectively and efficiently. Administrative routines based on rule of law (or, depending on understanding and translation, perhaps rule by law) should be developed. The current master plan for the 2001–10 public administration reforms is guided, inter alia, by a recognized need to decrease unnecessary bureaucracy ("red-tape") and corruption, make the legal and regulatory framework more effective and efficient, and increase transparency in the operation of state agencies (Asian Development Bank 2003; World Bank 2004; Ministry of Home Affairs 2006). The ethical behavior of civil servants has been identified as an important element to limit corruption, favoritism, and other forms of abuse of executive powers by institutions and individual civil servants (Dinh et al. 2000; Hoang, Uong and Vu 2000; Painter 2003), though appeals to ethical behavior have their doubters in Vietnam.

Thus the key components of public administrative reform fall into three areas:

1 Legal reform, including simplification of administrative procedures, increased legal basis for state activity, and improved legislative process and capacity.
2 Organizational reform, including restructuring of central and local governments and some degree of decentralization of administration.
3 Reform of human resource management, including new legal frameworks for management of the civil service, reform of the remuneration system and of training and upgrading of civil servants.

Reforms of law are often an indispensable part of larger reforms of administrative structures. In Vietnam, legislative reforms seem to be addressed largely technically, part of a lower level of the public administration reform process rather than as independent parts in a process of improving public administration. Maybe this is the reason why legal certainty and a language referring to administrative process do not appear as strong elements in the legislative reforms. This is in seeming contrast to the strong political condemnation of corruption and other forms of abuse of administrative and other government power. The contrast, however, may to some extent be due to the strong influence of foreign donors on the public administration reform process. Donor agencies dominated by economists and political scientists tend to be more concerned with economic efficiency and effectiveness than with observance of rule of law in the legal sense, including administrative process. Legal specialists have an important challenging role in contributing to mainstreaming law into development of the public sector at levels of similar strategic and political importance as economy and political science are awarded.

Legislative Reforms

The government's Resolution No. 38/CP of May 4, 1994 on the Reform of Administrative Procedures in Dealing with People's and Organisations' Affairs was a key step in setting in motion the reforms of administrative law. The resolution called for a review of administrative procedures, fees and charges, in order to abolish excessive procedures and regulations issued by unauthorized bodies, and for a revision of procedures and of internal regulations on the operations of administrative bodies of the state in order to ensure uniformity. The resolution was primarily intended to improve governance and administrative process related to those (numerous) types of business relations and acts that are dependent on permits or other acts by administrative bodies. But these reforms relate more generally to administrative process as well, and it is important to differentiate between the formal wording of the policy objectives and their actual substance. It was stipulated that all social activities were to be governed by laws and by installing order and rules. At the formal or policy level of wording, the resolution indicates a move toward rule of law, through a provision that the protection of human rights and basic civil rights is part of the process.

During the 1990s, initiatives addressing abuse of power included the establishment of an Anti-Corruption Commission and increased auditing and financial inspection of People's Committees and People's Councils. General as well as specific legislations have been enacted providing for administrative remedies or criminal liability for acts of corruption or bribery. The Criminal Code has been amended to add criminal sanctions for financial abuse of power. Less severe violations that do not constitute criminal acts may be handled according to the 2002 Ordinance on Handling of Administrative Violations. This Ordinance functions as a sort of administrative procedures and powers legislation in relation to administrative fines. The severity with which Vietnamese society treats violations pertaining to financial and related matters is indicated by the fact that the normal one-year limit on sanctions is extended to two years for such violations (e.g., those related to finance, securities, intellectual property, construction, housing, land, export, import, and smuggling). Specific sublegislation on such violations has been made in a number of substantive fields. Reforms undertaken in 2004 of legislation in the customs and tax domains include regulation of sanctioning of administrative violations, building on and expanding reforms undertaken in 1998.

A number of overlapping and outdated legal documents have been abolished. New legislation has been promulgated to strengthen the legal basis for activities of the state, including the activities of administrative bodies. Government regulations have provided rules for the organization and operation of public administrative bodies. Administrative procedures have been reformed in order to attempt to reduce opportunities for and risks of corruption and other forms of abuse of power, combining it with simplification of administrative procedures. This includes an expansion of the "one stop shop" mechanism, launched in Ho Chi Minh City in the late 1990s on a pilot basis and as part of the current 2001–10 public administration reform cycle expanded to several provinces (Buhmann 2001; World Bank 2004; Bartholomew et al. 2005). In a process started in the mid-1990s that continues under the 2001–10 public administration reform cycle, the remuneration, training, and personnel management systems for civil servants have been revised to reduce temptations to exhort or accept bribes. This has been done by improving civil servants' salaries, regulation of public servants' receipt of money or other assets in relation to their tasks, introducing merit-based examinations for some categories of civil servants, in-service training to develop capacity and professional norms, and legislation to improve salary structures in order to attract competent candidates and limit temptations to corruption. Modalities for individuals and organizations to lodge complaints and to obtain administrative reconsideration and judicial review of administrative acts and decisions have been introduced and previous ones revised, it is hoped, to make their use simpler. These steps are discussed in the following section.

Remedies and Handling of Administrative Violations

According to Vietnam's 1992 Constitution, infringements of the rights and legitimate interests of individual citizens and of collectives shall be dealt with in accordance with the law (Art. 12), and "every citizen has the right to lodge complaints and denunciations with the competent state authorities against acts of state organs, economic bodies, social organizations, units of the people's armed forces, or of any individual" (Art. 74). Those who are found to have suffered loss or injury due to administrative abuse of power are entitled to damages for material losses, to restoration of their legitimate rights or interests that were infringed upon, and, if relevant, to reparation of their reputation (Art. 74). Similar provisions are found in the Law on Complaints and Denunciations, which is discussed below. The Civil Code prescribes that administrative, judicial, or procuratorial (prosecutorial) bodies shall be held liable for damage caused by civil servants during their tenure.

The most comprehensive legislative documents on remedial rights related to administrative acts are the 1998 Law on Complaints and Denunciations as amended in 2004 and 2005, and the 1996 Ordinance on the Procedures for the Settlement of Administrative Cases as amended in 1998. A relatively detailed overview of these is provided here in order to allow for a discussion of the role these statutes may play in administrative processes and for helping to build the rule of law in Vietnam.

Complaints and Denunciations

The Law on Complaints and Denunciations provides for a complaints modality that may be partially equated to administrative reconsideration as known in many other countries. This statute provides for a right to lodge complaints regarding administrative acts or decisions concerning the complainant himself or herself ("complaints") or third parties ("denunciations") and prescribes procedures for lodging complaints and denunciations and for the authorities' handling of these. According to the Preamble, the objectives of the law include ensuring that complaints and denunciations are settled lawfully, and protecting the legitimate rights and interests of citizens. Modalities for lodging complaints or denunciations are relatively complicated; they involve a number of agencies and do not simply provide for lodging a complaint on an administrative act so that a higher administrative agency could reconsider it. Amendments made in 2004 and 2005 have somewhat streamlined the procedures that the 1998 version of the law gave, though it is unclear whether these amendments helped significantly in the earlier, relatively low-usage rate for these procedures. The 2004 and 2005 revisions have also resulted in increased possibilities for complainants to present their cases at court for judicial review if they do not agree with the findings of the administrative body handling the complaint. Individuals now have the right to hire lawyers to represent their administrative complaints. Other amendments in 2004 and 2005 aim at improving the accountability of heads of administrative bodies and the effectiveness of the complaints handling process. Measures taken toward this include requirements that higher-level administrative bodies improve communication with complainants and respondents (the administrative body complained against), make provisions to prevent bias (e.g., ensuring that those who handle a complaint are independent from those who made the complained-of act or decision), and authorize the Inspector General to resolve some types of complaints that have not been solved in the complaints handling process of the relevant administrative bodies.

Citizens, agencies and organizations are entitled to lodge complaints about administrative decisions or acts, or about staff of administrative bodies. Complaints may be lodged when the plaintiff believes that the administrative decision or act has been made in contravention of law and has infringed upon the legitimate rights and interests of the plaintiff. Officials and public servants may lodge complaints about disciplinary decisions if they believe that the decision contravenes law and infringes upon the legitimate rights and interests of the plaintiff. Denunciations may be made by third parties who observe faulty administration if the pertinent acts of public agencies, organizations, or individuals are believed to cause actual or potential damage to the interests of the state, or to the legitimate rights and interests of citizens or legal persons. A person who lodges a denunciation need not be personally affected by the administrative act.

The Law on Complaints and Denunciations is relatively brief but rich in the range of topics it addresses. Apart from provisions concerning the procedures for the handling of complaints and denunciations, it deals with supervision of the handling: disciplinary or penal measures to be taken against bodies or civil servants who are responsible for dealing with a particular complaint or denunciation or for executing settlements but fail to do so or act irresponsibly, as well as against those who are responsible for the original faulty act or decision that led to the complaint or denunciation. Unlawful acts and other violations of regulations on the tasks and duties of the pertinent administrative body or organization are the key issues to be considered in the handling of a denunciation. The Law on Complaints and Denunciations provides details of the procedures for handling denunciations, these details are more compared to the relatively sparse provisions or information on possible procedural or substantive faults of the original act or decision that should be taken into account in the handling of the complaint or denunciation. The law provides, for example, that denunciations must be handled in an objective, honest, and lawful manner, but it is less clear to what extent objectiveness, honesty, and legality of the making of the original decision or act must be considered. If a severe violation or criminal offence is found to have taken place, the agency handling a denunciation may refer the violation to other competent authorities.

If during the consideration of a complaint the respondent administrative body finds that the execution of the original decision or act would have irremediable consequences, it must issue a decision temporarily suspending the act or decision. If the responding agency's settlement decision has been appealed, the appellate institution may order the agency to suspend the original act or decision. Thus, the general rule is that a complaint or denunciation does not lead to a suspension of the original decision or act. Grounds leading to a finding that the decision or act should be amended or annulled are not specified in detail.

If the complaint or denunciation leads to a finding that the legitimate rights or interests of the plaintiff or denunciator have been violated, compensation must be made for the damage suffered. Rewards are offered to plaintiffs or denunciators if a complaint or denunciation leads to prevention of damage to the state. Discipline or penal sanctions are prescribed for those who demonstrate irresponsibility in the settlement of complaints or denunciations, obstruct the exercise of the right to lodge complaints or denunciations, deliberately delay settlements, falsify complaint or denunciation files, issue settlement decisions in contravention of the law, fail to act promptly to stop unlawful acts, threaten or retaliate against plaintiffs or denunciators, or violate provisions of legislation on complaints and denunciations.

Judicial Review of Administrative Acts

Administrative courts were established in 1995 within the Supreme People's Court and in a number of lower courts. District (local) courts do not have an administrative court, but generally at least one judge at each local People's Court specializes in administrative matters. The jurisdiction of the administrative courts includes the legality of specific administrative decisions and acts.

The 1996 Ordinance on Procedures for the Settlement of Administrative Cases as amended in 1999 (hereafter termed the Ordinance on Administrative Case Procedures) provides the procedural rules for judicial review of administrative cases. The preamble of the Ordinance on Administrative Case Procedures provides that its purpose is to ensure the timely and lawful settlement of administrative cases in order to protect the legitimate rights and interests of individuals, state agencies, and organizations and to contribute to raising the effectiveness of state management. Following a review process of some years' duration, amendments to the Ordinance on Administrative Case Procedures were proposed to the Standing Committee of the National Assembly in June 2005 and are expected to be passed during 2006. Proposed amendments include expanding the courts' jurisdiction of administrative cases and reducing the role of the procuratorate in the prosecution of administrative cases (Vietnam Law and Legal Forum 2005).

The current jurisdiction of administrative courts comprises administrative penalties; administrative decisions or acts on land management; permits and licenses in the fields of production and business; collection of taxes and tax arrears, charges and fees; and forcible requisition, purchase, or confiscation of property. Administrative courts may also review decisions on disciplinary dismissals of certain civil servants. Petitions may be filed by citizens, state bodies, and social organizations, against administrative decisions or acts made by executive bodies of the government and People's Committees at all levels, the People's Courts, and the procuracy (state prosecutors' offices). They may concern a civil servant's alleged abuse of authority, acceptance of bribery, or other instances of noncompliance with procedures. Petitions must concern concrete administrative acts or decisions. The remedy of lodging a complaint with the administrative body of first instance, according to the Law on Complaints and Denunciations, must be tried but need not be exhausted. If the complainant is not satisfied with the outcome of the administrative body's reconsideration, or if the administrative body of first instance has not finalized its consideration of the complaint within a set time limit, the plaintiff may lodge the case with the administrative courts. Administrative review may also be used as an alternative to appealing a settlement made by an administrative body of first instance within the administrative system.

In their examination of the administrative decision or act, administrative courts consider the legality of the decision and act, and whether that decision or act is based on administrative negligence or on delay. The administrative court may order that the original administrative decision or act be amended or annulled. The responding agency may make a similar decision during the proceedings. The administrative court may make a decision on giving compensation to the plaintiff for losses incurred as a result of the faulty administrative act or decision. The parties may also reach a settlement, provided that it is in accordance with law. When the decision or judgment of an administrative court is appealed, the appellate court may overturn the original decision if it does not conform to the facts of the case, or if there have been serious errors in the application of the law.

Role as Building Blocks for Due Administrative Process and the Rule of Law

In relation to administrative reconsideration and, especially since the 2005 amendments, judicial review of administrative acts, the Law on Complaints and Denunciations provides a remedy against unlawful administrative decisions or acts. In this sense it is an element in Vietnam's progress toward building the rule of law, in particular with regard to providing for legality and for reconsideration of administrative acts. The law ensures a type of what may be termed "public interest administrative reconsideration" by allowing for denunciations to be lodged by parties not individually affected by the denounced administrative act. Although the public interest character is limited in the sense that the denunciation relates to a concrete administrative act, its impact may be wider than merely resulting in an amendment or annulment of a specific administrative act. The actual public interest significance may be that a denunciation may draw attention to administrative practices that are detrimental to the quality of administrative process within a specific administrative body or even beyond.

Building a modern public administration with the legal guarantees associated with the rule of law is a comprehensive process that requires a number of institutional and organizational changes, changes of procedures, and often changes of attitudes and approaches to administrative tasks. Given this, it is not surprising that it is possible to point to some weaknesses in the Law on Complaints and Denunciations that can be improved, and that would further contribute toward strengthening the rule of law. Several of these affect the law's role for the implementation of due administrative process and the rule of law.

The Law on Complaints and Denunciations is not always clear and sometimes requires or allows too much interpretation by implementing bodies. For example, provisions on the consequences of an examination of a denunciation are not entirely clear, and provisions on issues and circumstances relating to the original act or decision to be taken into account in the consideration of a complaint or denunciation also leave scope for interpretation. Although the powers and jurisdictions of the various bodies charged with the implementation of the law are specified and have been made more detailed as a result of the 2004 and 2005 amendments, there is still a range of competent bodies. This may lead to uncertainty and inconsistency in the application of the law. In particular, it may be difficult for citizens without much knowledge of law and the hierarchy of administrative and judicial bodies to lodge their complaint with the correct body. Strict time limits for lodging of complaints may prevent complaints or denunciations from being handled. Similar effects may result from a lack of knowledge (and maybe information) as to what bodies are competent to receive and handle complaints and denunciations. This may lead to loss of the opportunity to have an administrative act reconsidered by an administrative body or examined by a court. Such lack of specificity risks undermining the potential of the remedies provided by the law.

The implementation of the Law on Complaints and Denunciations requires substantial exercise of discretion. In view of this, the amendments to prevent bias between the respondent body and the body considering the complaint are important if they are fully implemented, because the need for discretion may well be detrimental to the possibility of independent reconsideration. Regardless of its relative lack of clarity and specificity and the cumbersome nature of the procedures prescribed by the Law on Complaints and Denunciations, this statute indicates that complaints and denunciations may be lodged in cases of perceived illegality or other violations in the course of administrative action, the law sends a message to administrative bodies and their staff that legality is to be observed in their tasks—a message that may become more important as time passes. By instituting a means for reconsideration, the law seeks to provide a certain measure of legal certainty and remedies. This is supplemented by the provision of access to judicial review that may help in reviewing executive power as well.

The substantive and procedural provisions put an emphasis on the observation of legality perhaps a kind of rule by law approach. Future steps would include greater clarity and more comprehensive provisions on the acts or types of cases that may form the subject of a complaint or denunciation, details on procedural or substantive issues that must be examined during the handling of a complaint, and effective and speedy remedial action to annul or remedy an administrative act. An expansion of the scope of the examination beyond the legality of the act and violations of tasks and rules to include specific principles of administrative law that are acknowledged in many legal systems—in particular, principles of equality and proportionality—would help increase the law's role in eventually helping to build the rule of law, and in indicating that equality and proportionality must also be observed by administrative bodies in their making of administrative acts. Pending the possible drafting of general legislation on administrative procedures, such provisions could function as a sort of administrative procedures law. Related Chinese law may serve as a model for inspiration in this case: Until the 2004 adoption of an Administrative Licencing Law in China (a combination of detailed provisions in legislation on administrative reconsideration) judicial review of administrative cases, and procedures relating to administrative penalties, served as a sort of administrative procedures legislation (Buhmann 2001). An extension of the public interest aspect would be another useful element in strengthening the role of Vietnam's Law on Complaints and Denunciations in the protection of the public's rights and interests.

The possibility of access to judicial review of administrative acts that is granted in the Ordinance on Administrative Case Procedures is also important. Judicial review per se is an indispensable element of the rule of law; it provides for accountability and contributes to legal certainty and to transparency of administrative procedures (albeit ex-post facto). Under the current Ordinance on Administrative Case Procedures, the range of cases subject to administrative review is relatively limited. But it is significant that the proposed amendments include an expansion of the types of cases covered by the Ordinance. The proposed additional types include administrative decisions and acts related to foreign investment, granting of business registration certificates, and imposition of taxes (Vietnam Law and Legal Forum 2005). It would also be useful to add to the provisions for judicial review some emphasis on legality, equality, and proportionality to be observed in the making of administrative acts—this would send a substantive and important message to administrative bodies and their staff, and it would serve as yet another building block in the very long transition from "rule by law" to "rule of law." In this way, the Ordinance too could serve as a basic, if reactive, form of "administrative procedures legislation" by indicating the general principles that should be observed by administrative bodies.

The current Ordinance on Administrative Case Procedures provides the respondent with the option to amend or annul the decision or act during the course of administrative review. The possibility to change the decision or act contributes to the plaintiff's possibilities for a reversal or annulment of an illegal or incorrect administrative act, but it also limits the effectiveness of administrative review as a general measure to control administrative bodies and to emphasize legality in the making of an administrative act from the outset. The respondent may halt the court's examination of the legality of its exercise of its administrative powers by simply amending the original decision or act during the course of the dispute. Finally, the effectiveness of administrative review as a remedy in its move toward rule of law would be further strengthened if the court's powers were expanded to examining abstract administrative acts. Regardless of these weaknesses, the institution of judicial review of administrative acts in current legislation is a significant step forward, through the indirect though primarily ex-post facto message it sends to administrative bodies about the significance of legality and administrative procedures.

Conclusion

Since the start of the *doi moi* process, Vietnam has initiated and implemented a number of policy and legal reforms relating to public administration, and these are positive contributions toward the strengthening of the role of law and eventually toward building the rule of law. This process gained speed during the 1990s and continues with the 2001–10 public administration reform master plan. In particular, measures that provide for legality of administrative acts, decreased risks of corruption or other abuse of power by civil servants, complaints against administrative acts that are perceived to be illegal, and administrative review and compensation are all important elements in providing for due administrative process, legal certainty, and a general protection for the public's rights and interests. And eventually such provisions, if fully and equally implemented, may contribute toward building the rule of law.

The reform of laws relating to public administration undertaken by the government of Vietnam under *doi moi* indicate a relatively stronger emphasis on (technical) legality and on reactive measures (complaints, litigation, rewards and punishments) than on proactive measures to promote general principles of good public administration that are recognized by many states, principles such as equality, proportionality, and qualitative legality. In the future, Vietnam can and should address issues of equality, proportionality, and qualitative legality more closely in its reforms of administrative law, through the drafting of a comprehensive administrative procedures law to govern the procedures that administrative bodies must follow. This would usefully cover the making of administrative acts, as well as their implementation, supervision, and monitoring of compliance with administrative law (both within institutions and from outside). Transparency could well be substantially increased through provisions of access to information on administrative acts by parties and interested third parties, such as journalists. Such law reforms should be complemented by training of civil servants in administrative law and its basic principles, and by making available to the public information on the procedures and principles to be observed by administrative bodies and on remedies to resolve irregularities.

The persisting emphasis on legality found in policy decisions and legislation promulgated as part of the public administration reforms focuses on technical rather than substantive legality. This reflects the continued instrumentalization of the Vietnamese legal reform process. Moving from instrumentalization to a more directed focus on rule of law issues will require substantial additional focus on substantive legality, equality, and proportionality, and the independence of institutional bodies to correct administrative errors.

References

Asian Development Bank. 2003. Fostering a more modern, accountable public administration in Vietnam. Hanoi: Asian Development Bank.

Bartholomew, Ann, et al. 2005. Vietnam's experiment with block grant budgeting. World Bank Group Research Reports, www.worldbank.org, accessed January 18, 2006.

Bergling, Per, Erik Haggqvist, Erik Persson, Le Thanh Long, Dang Thanh Son, Tran Dong Tung. 1998. *An introduction to the Vietnamese legal system.* Hanoi: Ministry of Justice.

Buhmann, Karin. 2001. *Implementing human rights through administrative law reforms: The potential in China and Vietnam.* Copenhagen: Djoef Publishing.

Council of Europe. 1996. The administration and you: Principles of administrative law concerning the relations between administrative authorities and private persons. Strasbourg: Council of Europe.

Dang Phong and Melanie Beresford. 1998. *Authority relations and economic decision making in Vietnam: An historical perspective.* Copenhagen: Nordic Institute of Asian Studies.

Dinh Duy Hoa, Thang Van Phuc, Nguyen Min Lien and Hoang The Lien. 2000. *Review of Public Administration Reform. Overall report.* Hanoi: Government Steering Committee for Public Administration Reform (with the support of the United Nations Development Programme).

Hoang The Lien, Uong Chu Luu and Vu Dinh Thuan. 2000. *Review of the public administration reform in the field of institutional reform*. Hanoi: Government Steering Committee for Public Administration Reform.

Law No. 09/1998/QH10 of December 2, 1998 on the Rights of Citizens to Lodge Complaints and Denunciations, amended in 2004 (Law No. 26/2004/QH11) and 2005 (Law No. 58/2005/QH11).

Liisberg, Jonas B. 1999. *Kinas retssystem og retsreformer: En introduktion*. Copenhagen: Jurist-og Okonomforbundets Forlag.

Ministry of Home Affairs. 2006. Public Administration Reform. Online at the Ministry of Home Affairs of the Government of Vietnam. Online at www.caicachhanhchinh.gov.vn/English/MasterProgramme, accessed January 18, 2006.

Nguyen Van Quang. 2005. The organisation and operation of Vietnam's administrative courts (unpublished paper).

Ordinance on the Procedures for the Settlement of Administrative Cases, 1996, amended in 1999 (Official Gazette No. 5 1999 (08-02-1999))

Ordinance on Handling of Administrative Violations. No. 44/202/PL-UBTV. July 2, 2002.

Painter, Martin. 2003. Public Administration Reform in Vietnam. In Anthony Cheung and Ian Scott, eds., *Governance and public sector reform in Asia*. London: Routledge, 208–26.

Peerenboom, Randall. 1999. Ruling the country in accordance with law: Reflections on the rule and role of law in contemporary China. *Cultural Dynamics* 11(3): 315–51.

Peerenboom, Randall. 2002. *China's long march toward rule of law*. Cambridge: Cambridge University Press.

Rose, Carol V. 1998. The "new" law and development movement in the post-cold war era: A Vietnam case study. *Law and Society Review* 32: 93–140.

Vietnam Law and Legal Forum. 2005. *In the pipeline: Draft amendments to the Ordinance on Settlement of Administrative Cases*. September 8, 2005.

World Bank. 2004. *Partnership note*, June 2004.

NOTES ON CONTRIBUTORS

Editors

Stéphanie Balme is a tenured research fellow at Sciences Po and CERI, its Center of International Studies and Research, as well as honorary research associate in the Department of Government and Public Administration of the Chinese University of Hong Kong, where she lives. Since 2003 she has co-headed the CERI Research Group on Contemporary Vietnam with one of its founding members, Christopher Goscha. Dr. Balme's research and teaching interests include sociology of law and political sociology, constitutionalism and rule of law developments applied to Asian socialism. She consults or is involved in legal cooperation projects with national and international organizations.

Mark Sidel is Professor of Law and International Affairs at the University of Iowa and Visiting Professor of Law at Harvard Law School (2005–6). He re-established and directed the Ford Foundation's programs in Vietnam in the early and mid-1990s and has published extensively on Vietnamese law. Sidel has taught and lectured on Vietnamese legal reform at Harvard, Iowa, Melbourne, the School of Oriental and African Studies (London) and Sciences Po, and has consulted on legal reform in Vietnam with the United Nations Development Programme, Oxfam, the World Bank and numerous other organizations.

Contributors

Ramses Amer is Associate Professor and Senior Lecturer in the Department of Political Science, Umeå University, Sweden. His PhD is from Uppsala University in peace and conflict research. Dr. Amer's major areas of research are security issues and conflict resolution in Southeast Asia and Pacific Asia, and the role of the United Nations in the international system. Amer has published *The Sino-Vietnamese Approach to Managing Boundary Disputes* (International Boundaries Research Unit, University of Durham, 2002), and *Vietnamese Foreign Policy in Transition* (Institute for Southeast Asian Studies and St. Martin's Press, 1999) (coedited with Carl Thayer), as well as numerous articles in international journals and other reports.

Karin Buhmann holds a PhD in law from the Institute of Law in the Department of Social Sciences, at Aarhus University (Denmark) and a law degree from the Institute of Legal Science (now Faculty of Law) in the University of Copenhagen. She is an Associate Professor at the Department of Social Affairs, Roskilde University (Denmark). Dr. Buhmann previously worked for the Danish Ministry of Foreign Affairs and Danida (Danish International Development Agency) as a consultant on development cooperation supporting legal and governance reform. Her research interests include governance and legal reform, as well as normative and legal aspects of corporate social responsibility.

Hien Do is a PhD candidate at Sciences Po and its Center of International Studies and Research as well as an active member of the Research Group on Contemporary Vietnam at CERI. She holds MA degrees from the Sorbonne University in political science and in international relations as well as an MA (in translation and interpreting) from the National University of Hanoi. Ms. Do has also served in the chancellery of the French Embassy in Vietnam (1993–6). Her research focuses on Vietnam's process of regional and international integration as well as interdependence within regional organizations.

John Gillespie holds a PhD from the Australian National University. He is a Professor of Law at the Department of Commercial Law and Taxation at Monash University in Melbourne. Professor Gillespie has taught and conducted research on Southeast Asian law and published extensively about legal reforms in the region. He has consulted on law reform projects in Vietnam, Laos, and Indonesia for the World Bank, the United Nations Development Programme, Asian Development Bank, and bilateral donor agencies. His research interests include rule of law and regulatory reforms, law reform through legal transplantation, the nexus between law and development, and human rights in Southeast Asia.

Leslie Holmes has been Professor of Political Science at the University of Melbourne since 1988. He studied at the Universities of Hull, Essex,

Berlin (Free) and Leningrad, and has been a Senior Associate Member of St. Antony's College Oxford on three occasions. His empirical research focuses on corruption and organized crime, while his principal theoretical interest is legitimacy. He has authored or coauthored six books—the most recent being *Rotten States?: Corruption, Post-Communism and Neoliberalism* (Duke University Press, 2006)—and edited or coedited a further six. He was President of the International Council for Central and East European Studies (ICCEES) 2000–5, and is currently President of the Australasian Association for Communist and Post-Communist Studies.

David Koh holds a PhD in Political Science from the Australian National University. He is Fellow and Coordinator, Regional Political and Strategic Studies, at the Institute of Southeast East Asian Studies in Singapore, and has specialized on Vietnam for more than 10 years. His research interests include local administration, state–society relations, and political leadership. He is the author of *Wards of Hanoi* (Institute of Southeast Asian Studies, 2006).

Vladimir Mazyrin is Associate Professor and Senior Lecturer in the Department of Political Science, Institute of Asian and African Studies at Moscow State University. He holds a PhD in history and a degree in international studies from the Russian Academy of Science. Professor Mazyrin previously worked for the Ministry of Foreign Trade and Ministry of Foreign Affairs of the USSR in Hanoi. His primary areas of research are public policy and social development in Vietnam and economic cooperation in Southeast Asia. Dr. Mazyrin's recent publications in English on Vietnamese deal with migrants in Russia, ASEAN enlargement, and other areas.

Penelope (Pip) Nicholson is a Senior Lecturer and Director of Teaching at the University of Melbourne Law School and Associate Director (Vietnam) at the Asian Law Centre. Her research interests are Vietnamese law, comparative law, and legal reform in Asia. Her current research explores the criminal and economic jurisdictions of the Vietnamese court system; local Vietnamese conciliation practices; and the relationship of comparative legal studies to empirical research on the diverse legal systems within Asia. Dr. Nicholson has coedited *Asian Socialism and Legal Change* (Asia Pacific Press, 2005) (with John Gillespie) and has published articles on Vietnamese judicial corruption and appointment practices. She has consulted on legal reform in Vietnam with the Asian Development Bank, AusAID, and Danida (the Danish International Development Agency).

Eero Palmujoki teaches in the Department of Political Science and International Relations at the University of Tampere (Finland). He holds the D.Soc.Sc. in international relations from Tampere. Dr. Palmujoki's research focuses on international relations, political language, and doctrinal change in Vietnam. He has published *Vietnam and the World: Marxist-Leninist Doctrine and the Changes in International Relations* 1975–93 (Macmillan, 1997); *Regionalism and Globalism in Southeast Asia* (Palgrave, 2001); *Sustainable Forest Management through Multilateral Environmental Agreements and Market-Based Mechanisms* (Helsinki, 2002, with Pekka Virtanen), and other articles and reports.

Nguyen Hung Quang is Managing Partner at N.H. Quang and Associates in Hanoi. He is a graduate of Hanoi Law University and a member of the Vietnam Lawyers Association and the Hanoi Bar Association. Quang's research interests include legal advocacy and commercial, civil, tax, and labor law. He has coauthored articles on the politics of appointment and promotion in the Vietnamese judiciary and on the reforms in the Vietnamese bar, and a number of reports for Vietnamese legal development projects.

Matthieu Salomon is a PhD candidate at Sciences Po. A member of the Research Group on Contemporary Vietnam (CERI), for which he has organized symposia, Salomon holds a BA and MA in political science from Sciences Po and a BA from the Sorbonne University in history and political science. His PhD dissertation focuses on the reforms of Vietnam's National Assembly under *doi moi*. Salomon has taught at the Institute for International Relations in Hanoi, where he lived for three years, and has published on Vietnamese contemporary politics.

Nguyen Hong Thao holds the PhD in Law from the University of Paris I (Panthéon-Sorbonne) and is Lecturer in the Faculty of Law at Hanoi National University. His research focuses on public international law, law of the sea, international organizations, and environmental law. Dr. Thao has published *Le Vietnam et ses différends maritimes dans la mer de Bien Dong (Mer de Chine méridionale)* (Paris: Pédone, 2004); and *Le Vietnam face aux problèmes de l'extension maritime dans la mer de Chine méridionale* (Villeneuve d'Ascq: Septentrion Presses Universitaires, 1997), as well as articles on South China Sea disputes and other maritime and international law issues.

Carlyle A. Thayer is Professor of Politics in the School of Humanities and Social Sciences, The University of New South Wales at the Australian Defence Force Academy. He holds a PhD in international relations from the Australian National University. He has published extensively on Vietnamese domestic and foreign politics and the Vietnam People's Army. In 2005, Professor Thayer served as the C.V. Starr Distinguished Visiting Professor at the School of Advanced International Studies, Johns Hopkins University (Washington) where he taught a graduate course on *Vietnam in Transition*. He is currently researching Vietnam's defense diplomacy.

Nguyen Vu Tung conducts research and teaches on Vietnamese foreign policy in the Department of World Politics and Vietnamese Diplomacy at the Institute of International Relations in Hanoi. He received his PhD (political science) at Columbia University in 2003. His publications include articles on the theoretical frameworks for Vietnam–ASEAN cooperation after the Cold War, on Vietnam–ASEAN relations in the 1970s, and he has coedited 77 *Conversations between Chinese and Foreign Leaders on the Wars in Indochina* (Cold War International History Project, Woodrow Wilson Center for Scholars, 1997).

INDEX

STÉPHANIE BALME is tenured Research Fellow at Sciences Po
(Paris Institute of Political Studies)–CERI (Center of International
Studies and Research) and, since 2003, Honorary Research Associate in
the Department of Government and Public Administration
of the Chinese University of Hong Kong, representing Sciences Po.
Her books include *Entre soi: L'élite du pouvoir dans la Chine contemporaine*
(*Between Norms and Guanxi: The Power Elite in Contemporary China*);
La Chine—Idées Reçues (*Preconceived Ideas on China*);
and the forthcoming *Constitutionalism and Judicial Power in China*
(co-edited with Michael Dowdle).

MARK SIDEL is Professor of Law and University Faculty Scholar at the
University of Iowa, and Visiting Professor of Law at Harvard Law School (2005–06).
His books include *More Secure, Less Free?: Antiterrorism Policy and Civil Liberties
after September 11*; *Philanthropy and Law in South Asia*;
and forthcoming books on law and society in Vietnam,
and on human trafficking from Asia.

LaVergne, TN USA
30 April 2010
181125LV00001B/38/A